ORBIS PICTUS

The Prints of Oskar Kokoschka 1906-1976

Selected from the collection of Reinhold, Count Bethusy-Huc

with essays by

Jaroslaw Leshko

E. H. Gombrich

Reinhold, Count Bethusy-Huc

To Brad, with fondest best regards Jerry

SANTA BARBARA MUSEUM OF ART, 1987

Front cover: *Rider and Sailing Ship,* (Cat. 4), reproduced actual size
Back cover: *Kouros* I (Cat. 135)

Participating Institutions
Santa Barbara Museum of Art, Santa Barbara, California
The Nelson-Atkins Museum of Art, Kansas City, Missouri
Smith College Museum of Art, Northampton, Massachusetts

Edited by Deanne Violich
Designed by Nancy Zaslavsky, Ultragraphics, Venice, California

Printed in an edition of 3,000

Production art by ML Peacor
Typography by Mondo Typo, Santa Monica, California, in Berthold Weiss-Antiqua and Fanfare
Lithography by Typecraft, Inc., Pasadena, California

Photographs of works in exhibition by Thomas P. Vinetz
Additional photographs by Wayne McCall
Photo Credits: pp. 7, 8, 12, 13, 14, 15, 17, 50, 60 courtesy Reinhold, Count Bethusy-Huc;
p. 11-Olda Kokoschka, p. 64-Horst Tappe; p. 67-Gilbert Lloyd

Library of Congress Cataloging-in-Publication Data

Kokoschka, Oskar, 1886-1980
Orbis pictus, the prints of Oskar Kokoschka, 1906-1976.

Exhibition catalog.
1. Kokoschka, Oskar, 1886-1980—Exhibitions.
2. Prints, Austrian—Exhibitions. 3. Prints—20th century—Austria—Exhibitions. 4. Expressionism (Art)—Austria—Exhibitions. 5. Bethusy-Huc, Reinhold, Graf.—Art collections—Exhibitions.
6. Art—Private collections—Austria—Vienna—Exhibitions. I. Leshko, Jaroslaw, 1939-
II. Gombrich, E. H. (Ernst Hans), 1909- . III. Bethusy-Huc, Reinhold, Graf. IV. Santa Barbara Museum of Art. V. Title.
NE646.K6A4 1987 769.92'4 87-9853
ISBN 0-89951-067-1

Contents

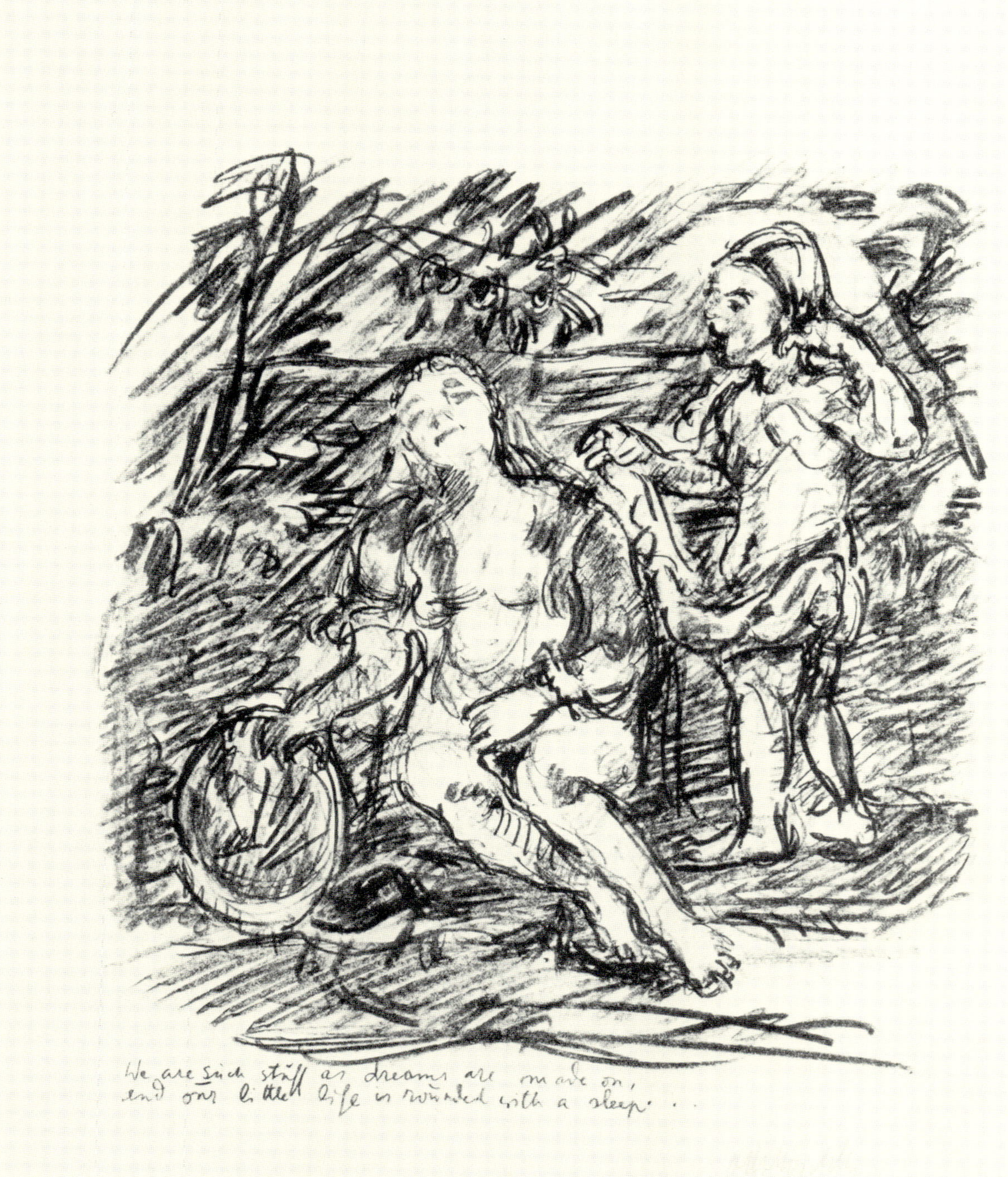

Cat. 32 *The Dream (Shakespeare Vision)*, 1916–1917

Foreword

Richard V. West
Director

This exhibition had its genesis some years ago in a letter from Count Bethusy-Huc inquiring about Kokoschka works in American collections. From the exchange of letters which followed grew the idea of celebrating, in a modest way, the 1986 centennial of Kokoschka's birth. Count Bethusy-Huc generously offered to lend his collection for such a celebration, setting into motion the planning of this exhibition. As we progressed, the "modest celebration" soon evolved into a major exhibition of Kokoschka's prints, covering the entire span of his career. The hoped-for significance of the exhibition became a reality when Dr. Jaroslaw Leshko agreed to write a major essay on Kokoschka's prints and Sir Ernst Gombrich graciously allowed the translation and publication of a commemorative address never previously available in English. Count Bethusy-Huc's homage to Greece is a fitting companion to these two essays.

For me, and I daresay for most art lovers, Kokoschka's contribution to art in the twentieth century is recognized primarily through the paintings, drawings, prints, and stage pieces created in Vienna between 1907–1914. Yet, these works comprise only a small portion of the artist's total *oeuvre.* The opportunity I had to go through Count Bethusy-Huc's encyclopedic collection at the Victoria and Albert Museum was a real revelation. In his later works, the passion of Kokoschka's early years is distilled into a visionary humanism. The artist never lost his toughness and tenacity, but found in Greek myth, Biblical parable, Shakespearean tragedy and texts of his own devising a source for visual images that expressed his concern for humanity in the face of political and technological totalitarianism.

When this exhibition was first conceived, it was thought that it would be one of many marking the artist's centennial. Certainly, the major retrospective mounted by the Tate Gallery, London, and seen in Zürich and New York has introduced thousands to Kokoschka's life work. Sadly, no other comprehensive exhibition has been organized in the United States, to my knowledge. Thus, we hope that this exhibition, seen on the West Coast in Santa Barbara, in the Midwest at the Nelson-Atkins Museum of Art, and on the East Coast at Smith College Museum of Art, will allow thousands more to learn about Kokoschka, as well as make a contribution to art historical scholarship.

The fact that this exhibition was organized in Santa Barbara should not be considered an aberration. The museum possesses an important collection of works by the early modernists, ranging from Kandinsky and Jawlensky to Picasso and Dali. The second director of the museum, Ala Story, organized one of the first major Kokoschka exhibitions in the United States in 1954, establishing a tradition here of significant exhibitions devoted to twentieth-century artists of international reputation. It is to her memory that this exhibition is dedicated.

The exhibition could not have been mounted without the help of many people. I am extremely grateful for the gracious cooperation of members of the staff of the Victoria and Albert Museum, including the former Keeper of the Department of

Designs, Prints and Drawings, Michael Kauffmann, and his successor, John Murdoch; Deputy Keeper Susan Lambert; and Conservator Pauline Webber. The Victoria and Albert Museum and Mr. and Mrs. Andrew Macnab generously consented to lend works formerly in the Bethusy-Huc collection. I am indebted to the editing skills of Deanne Violich, who was undaunted by the size and scope of this project. Finally, I extend my appreciation to current and former members of the Santa Barbara Museum of Art staff, especially Registrar Elaine Dietsch, Curator of Exhibitions Merrily Peebles, Museum Designer Terry Atkinson and my executive secretary, Elizabeth Bradley, all who kept this project on track; and to Gunda Müller-Palm, who translated E. H. Gombrich's essay from the German.

Commemorative Address for Oskar Kokoschka

E. H. Gombrich

To see I was born, to look I was called.

The works of the watchman on the tower from Goethe's *Faust* would form a fitting epitaph for Oskar Kokoschka, who departed from us on February 22 of this year at almost 94 years of age. The riches of the oeuvre he left us testify to his vocation. To this indomitable earthy giant every fresh encounter with the visible world was a new adventure. It was his profound conviction that each visual experience was irretrievably unique because every moment changes both the object we see and our own perception. It was precisely this insight that gave him the courage to dare, the courage to resist the pressures of ingrained visual habits and the even more seductive pressures of modish trends.

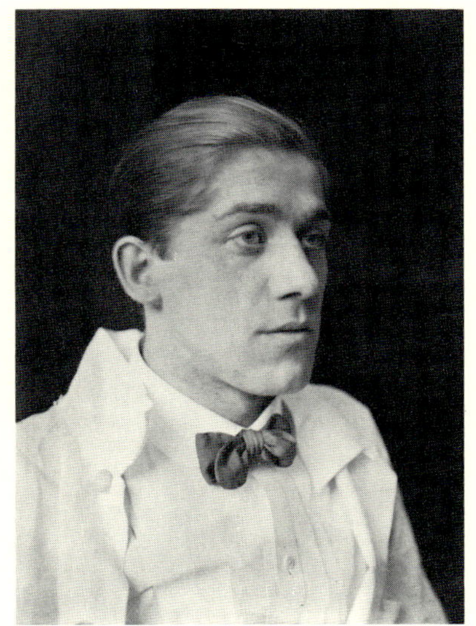

Oskar Kokoschka as a young man

Decried as a crazy rebel at the beginning of the century, outlawed as a degenerate in 1933, finally abused by the avant garde as a reactionary, this "loner" never allowed himself to be deflected from his pursuit. He remained true to himself in all the vicissitudes of his life, however restless the times, the main stations of which—Vienna, Berlin, Dresden, Paris, Prague, London, and finally Villeneuve by the lake of Geneva—he has himself described to us. His searching portraits, his visionary cityscapes, his unconventional symbolic compositions, his delicate flower paintings, his sensitive travel sketches, his deeply felt illustrations of old and new texts, no less than his poems, plays, stories, speeches, comments and manifestos are all of a piece.

Ogni pittore dipinge se stesso—"every painter paints himself"—was said by the old Florentines. Again and again in Kokoschka's art we find spontaneous self-projection surprisingly fused with a sure eye for reality. His work and his mind always remained open to the wild forces of the dream without ever letting them take over.

Whoever had the good fortune of meeting Kokoschka in person knows that this gift made him irresistible. He himself was certainly aware of his power over people. He knew that he could perform magic and weave spells, whether he let himself be carried along by his imagination or steadily fixed his eyes upon persons and things. Widely educated but never artificial, he spoke with equal involvement about painting and music, literature and history.

Born in 1886 in Pöchlarn on the Danube and raised in Vienna, he himself has emphasized how far his roots reached down into the tradition of the Danube monarchy—what he describes as a still idyllic Austria in which life had not yet been wholly subjected to factory routine, not citified, industrialized, mechanized. In Vienna he learned from his older friend and comrade-in-arms, Adolf Loos, to value the unselfconscious traditions of genuine craftsmen more highly than the fashionable arts and crafts movement. In Vienna, also, Karl Kraus convinced him of the dangers to the life of language from the thoughtless cliches of journalism. Karl Kraus spoke of "the end of the world through black magic"—referring to printer's ink. What might he have said of the glittering magic of the television screen?

Kokoschka always took this threat to western culture from the machine and from the masses very seriously. I can still hear him growling, "This is the most stupid time that ever was." This was during Kokoschka's visit to London at the age of 84. When I asked him, "Why do you think so?" he replied convincingly, "It just all happened much too quickly." Man, life, could not keep up with technical developments; and while the overburdened intellect sought refuge in formulas, the life of the senses wasted away. This moral and spiritual impoverishment was for him the terrible consequence of what he called functional thinking, the strangling of the imagination and with it of human compassion.

Whoever is familiar with Kokoschka's work knows the great share he accorded to compassion, passion and suffering in all his creations. But the appeal by utopian visionaries to collective passions conflicted with his sense of personal responsibility. "It is up to the self," so he wrote in 1950, "to make a free choice between reason and madness, humanity and brutality, love or hate, between the organic growth of life and the chaos that dazzles the intellect." It was because he did not allow his intellect to be dazzled by chaos that he also distanced himself from the cult of the unconscious in art. What primitive and abstract art lacked, in his opinion, was what mattered most to him—the personal visual experience.

In pointed contrast to these movements, he called the summer courses which he initiated at the castle of Salzburg in 1953, "School of Seeing." Whoever wanted to participate had to leave all academic ballast at home. Instead of working from a posed model, the student had to observe and capture the figure in motion so that he should not lapse into formulas. Kokoschka also forbade any corrections and therefore insisted on the use of watercolor, which excludes over-painting, let alone erasure. Not that he ever claimed that this practice would immediately make a master. On the contrary, like Ruskin, who urged his Oxford students to copy nature faithfully so that they should learn how hard it is to paint, Kokoschka wanted to teach his students to be humble, humble in front of appearances and humble in front of the miracles wrought by art.

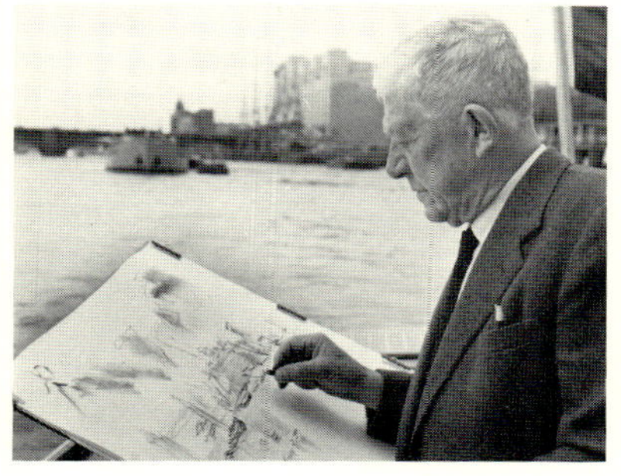

Kokoschka drawing on the River Thames, 1967

There is an unforgettable letter by Kokoschka from the year 1920 in which, at the age of 34, he first candidly describes to the anxious father of a budding student the external and the mental dangers of an artistic career, but closes all the same with the words: "Yet I must not close the door to the person who believes that he alone out of many thousands would find this way to what enlightened spirits call divine; indeed as a real teacher, I even want to encourage him to stake a life so that the vision of the divine should not remain without a priest, nor life without the greatness of classical antiquity. From my heart I welcome the apprentice who comes full of reverence."

Kokoschka's grateful reverence before the Greek heritage stems from his insight that it was the Greeks who first furnished the artist with the means of re-creating in their work the breath of life in space and in light. For neither light nor movement can be immediately transposed into an image. Those luminous color harmonies which arouse the impression of shining radiance had first to be invented and developed. The masters of the palette, the early Netherlanders, Altdorfer, Titian, Tintoretto, the later Rembrandt, but also Maulbertsch and Romako could move him to tears.

The unique element of Kokoschka's art may be precisely in this tension between the impulsive gesture (which, regardless of the pleasing line, struggles to express the inner and out vision) and his tireless effort to conquer the luminous world of appearances which he so ardently loved.

In *Antik and Modern* Goethe wrote, "Let everyone be a Greek after his own manner, but let him be a Greek." I think Oskar Kokoschka would not have been displeased to hear me say that in his own way he was a Greek.

(Delivered at the Session of the Order *Pour le Mérite,* June 3, 1980)

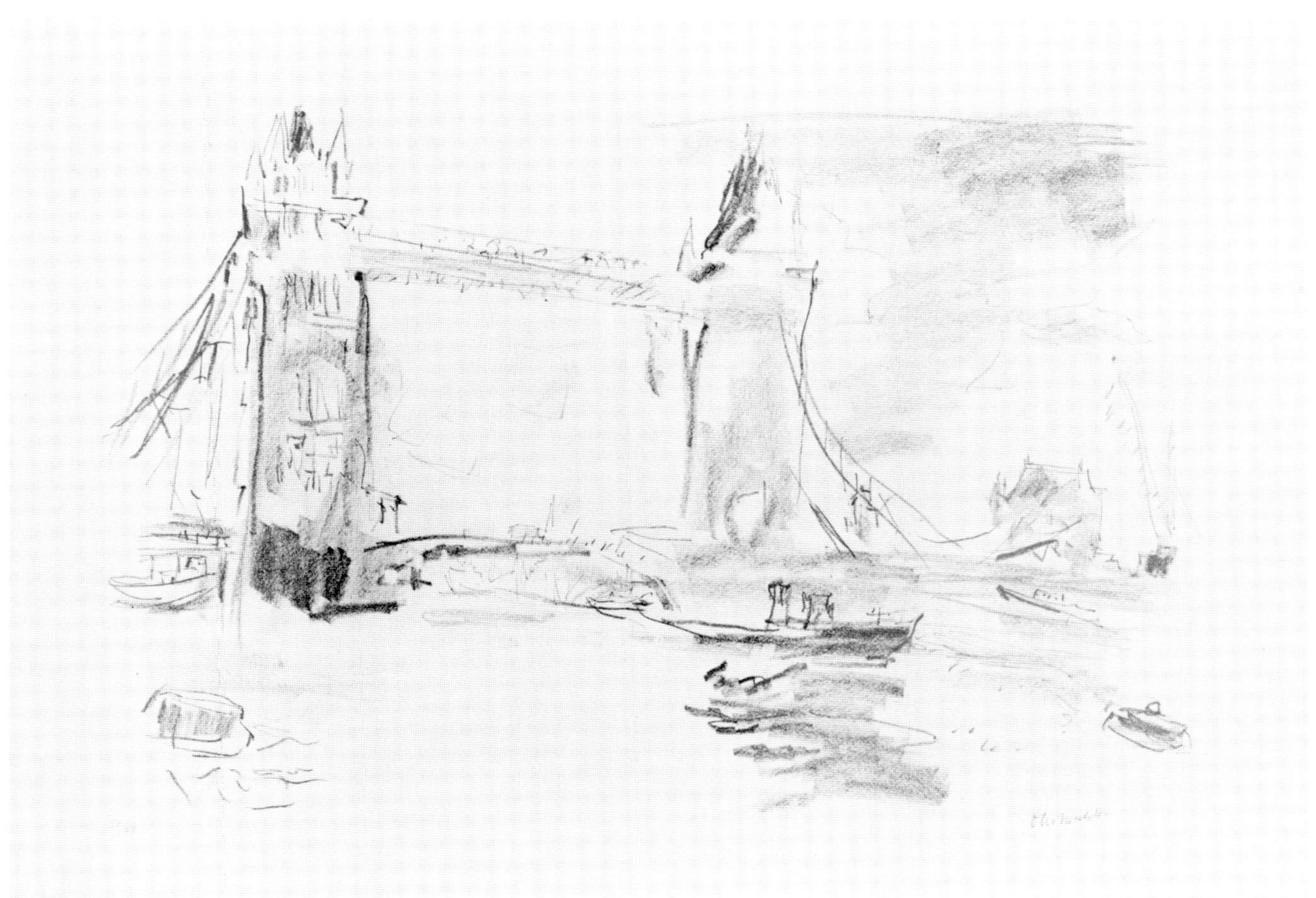

Cat. 113 *Tower Bridge* II, 1967

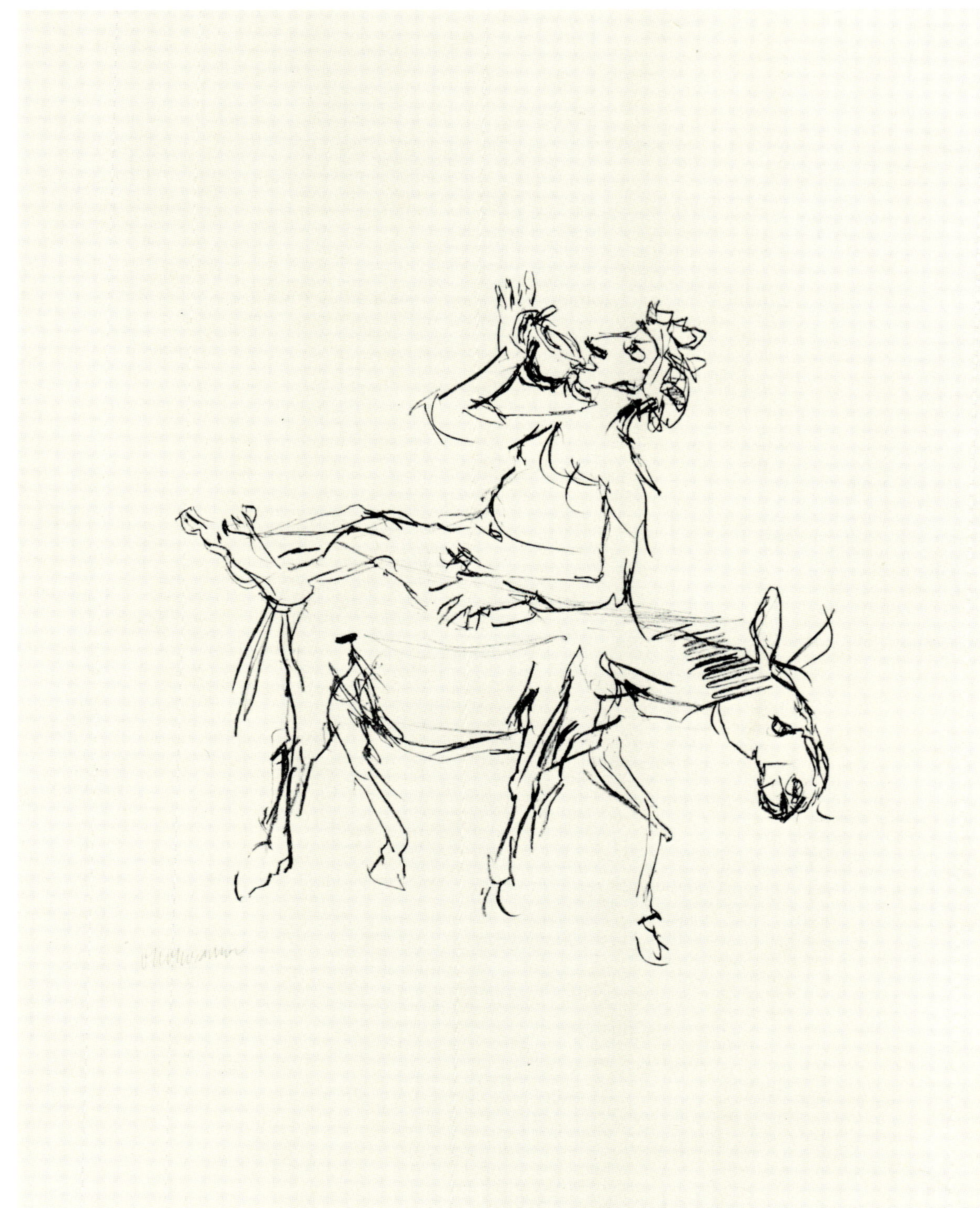

Cat. 73 *Dionysos Riding an Ass*, 1964

My Greek Journeys, 1976–86*

Reinhold, Count Bethusy-Huc

"Love consists in this, that two solitudes protect and touch, and greet each other."
Rainer Maria Rilke

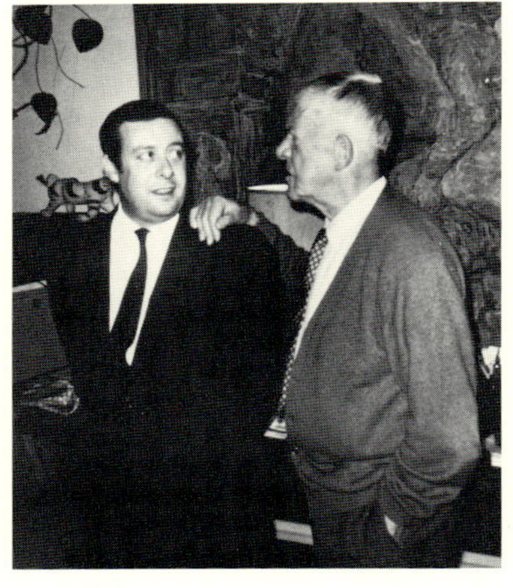

Oskar Kokoschka and Reinhold, Count Bethusy-Huc in the artist's library, Villeneuve, 1970.

It is not my intention to interpret Oskar Kokoschka's work and its connections with Greece, but I may be allowed to illustrate why my impressions of Hellas—the country, its people and its tradition—are for me often so closely linked to images Kokoschka has created and which I was privileged to collect over the years. It is my wish to share this experience with other people who may not have had the opportunity to travel so extensively to the Greek islands as I have done since 1968 and to whom some of the images drawn by Kokoschka are not familiar. For me each visit to Greece is a pilgrimage; and I come to these Mediterranean shores with humility, prepared to listen, to open my eyes but also to forget at least for a moment in life the struggle for existence, all trivialities and mediocrities of everyday life.

It was in the spring of 1976 that I returned to Crete, the western half of the island and its northern shores, to Kastelli Kissamu to revisit Polyrrinia to enjoy the superb view over the bay of Kissamu with the peninsula of Gramvusa on the left and that of Rodopu on the right.

It was my fervent wish to return first to Gramvusa and to stay overnight in the bay of Tigani. This place is so remote and totally uninhabited that it can only be reached by foot in about 6 hours, if you are familiar with goat paths, or by boat, if the sea allows. It took me days before superstitious fishermen were prepared to take me along. Because of the rough sea they had to drop me off on the eastern shore of the peninsula in Agnion which meant I had to climb over the top to reach Tigani on the western side. When I reached the top and looked back, I could see my *kaiki* returning to Kastelli and suddenly realized that I was alone, totally alone; but looking towards the setting sun, I could see Tigani in all its splendor. With a stroke of good luck I found the goat path down to the bay. Night set in quickly with a full moon and a sky full of stars. It got colder as the hours passed and the winds increased. I was totally unequipped for this excursion and felt utterly exposed. I watched with apprehension wild donkeys roaming and listened to the melancholic calls of my beloved *gionis* and other nightbirds. I could not go to sleep all night because of the cold and exhilaration. When at last the sun rose and I got warm again, I was able to experience what I had hoped for—to be alone with nature. Naked, I strolled all over the spacious archipelago covered with pink and honey-colored dunes. The seagulls and sandpipers did not mind my company, and I watched the cormorants on the nearby rocks catching fish. I swam amongst swarms of fish and watched the playful leaps of dolphins. I was not afraid of snakes. I discovered beautiful flowers and admired the delicate blossoms of capers. A delicious breeze from the gigantic mountains surrounding me kept me company during the midday sunshine. I surrendered again and again to the caressing waves of the sea

*The first part of "My Greek Journeys, 1968–1975" was published in the catalogue of my exhibition of prints by Oskar Kokoschka, "Homage to Hellas," in the National Pinacothek and Alexander Soutzos Museum in Athens in 1976.

to find myself afterwards falling asleep on the beach. When I awoke again, I thought of Gauguin's "Whence do we come? What are we? Whither are we going?" In the late afternoon I discovered a tiny deserted chapel which gave me shelter for the next night. I sat a long time in the doorway watching the night fall. I thought of people who were dear to me and had gone. I thought of images I had collected and which suddenly had a much deeper meaning to me. I began to realize that they became part of me and that nobody could deprive me of them for as long as I breathe. I felt so alive, so happy and so grateful. I know how much I owe to Oskar Kokoschka, who opened my eyes and made me strong to face this life which is so precious, so unique and worth living.

After one more day I had to leave this earthly paradise because of lack of food and water. Before I reached the village of Kalyviani after many hours of walking in the blazing sun, I met an old goatherd with his flock. He was obviously surprised to see me; I watched him picking some herbs and wildflowers which he handed to me as an offering. What an encounter! We sat and had a smoke together, surrounded by the gentle sound of the bells of his goats. Before we parted, he told me where to find water. Hours later I found myself sipping delicious cold water in the company of bees and butterflies. Kokoschka once said to me, "Butterflies are love letters from the good Lord." I was blissfully happy.

After a few days of rest I made excursions to Elaphonissi and the monastery of Chrysoskalitissis on the southern coast and then returned to Rethymnon. I walked through the Samaria gorge and revisited Preveli Monastery. A night up in Asomatos as well as the unspoilt beaches of Plakias are particularly memorable to me. I paid my homage to Arkadiu Monastery and spent a few days up in Amarion before I set out again to discover the uninhabited peninsula of Rodopu.

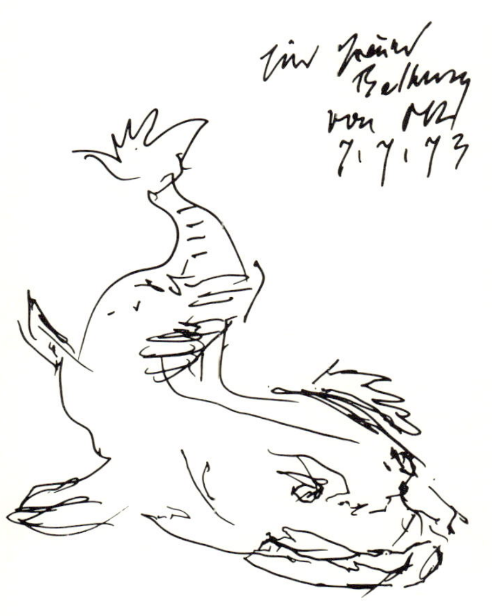

Dolphin, 1973, pen and ink

It was a long walk before I reached the ancient Diktynnaeon. Following goat paths and the gentle directions of goatherds, I saw pheasants and partridges, hares and falcons and was no longer frightened by frequent encounters with snakes because I had my Cretan *magoura* and was told how to use it. The approach to the ancient site from the top of the mountains was overwhelming—a delightful white beach flanked on either side by high rocks. The light, the colors, the calm sea and the stillness of it all were breathtaking—and not a soul in sight. What bliss to be alone. I could not get down the precipitous path to the sea fast enough after all those hours of walking in the sun with no water to drink. Before reaching the beach, I noticed a huge turtle and many large lizards in poisonous green and sky blue colors. The bay was mine. Lying on the white beach with an abundance of pretty colored shells around me, I watched some flying fish.

The stillness of the place was almost disconcerting. It was the hour of "Pan" and I fell asleep. I was awakened by the fearful screaming of a goat followed by her baby. They were running along the edge of rocks way above the sea. I could not understand their anxiety until I noticed an eagle hovering over them. There were no trees or shrubs for shelter, and I had to witness this fearful struggle for survival. Losing sight of the goats and the eagle, I hoped for the best. After a while the mother goat returned desperately looking for its baby. In vain. The eagle had disappeared. I was sad to have to return that night to Kastelli, but my friends were getting worried about my excursions to "another world."

E. H. Gombrich wrote in his introduction to the last exhibition of my Kokoschka prints, "Here empathy was and remains his principal tool, the capacity to explore his own response as a key to the feelings and reactions of his fellow humans."[1] May I be allowed to add to this comment that Kokoschka's empathy extended also to his drawings of animals and landscapes. Kokoschka's "power of projecting his personality into the objects of contemplation" is always present to me. His work becomes dearer to me every year.

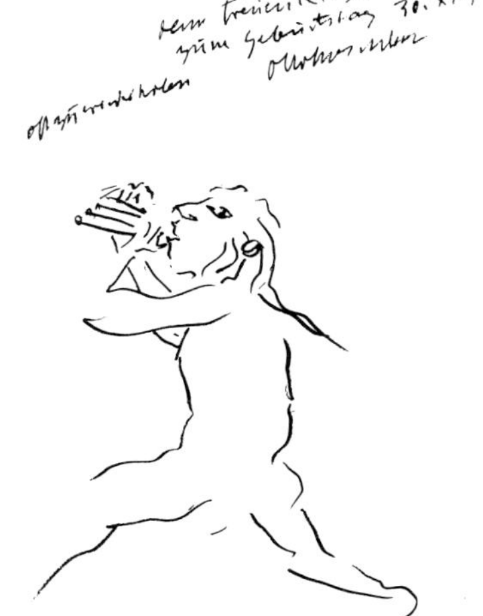

Dancing Figure Playing the Pipes, 1970, pencil

My odyssey continued in 1981 and 1982. I visited Rhodes and Symi and wandered all over Karpathos. Most memorable excursions to Delos and the village of Perdika on Egina followed.

In 1983 I returned to Samothrace, determined to see more of this Greek island I love most. There I learned why fishermen rarely take other people in their *kaiki*. Quite early one morning in Loutra while drinking my cup of Greek coffee, I noticed a *kaiki* arriving. I was told that Kiriakos and his brother were bringing fish to my host. Soon they were preparing fish soup for their breakfast, and I was invited to join them. My host knew of my fervent desire to find a boat to enable me to view a part of the island between Akrotiri Kipos and Pahia Amos which you can explore only from the sea. Kiriakos and his brother granted me this privilege, and so we left in brilliant sunshine and a calm sea. How I enjoyed the view of Mount Fengari from the sea. Suddenly we came across a shoal of fish—thousands of them. Kiriakos and his brother made the most of the opportunity. The deck was soon full of leaping little fish, and it was my task to gather them. I fail to find the words to describe the uniqueness of the experience. My friends were happy. We soon reached the point where the mountains literally fall into the sea—the scenery is dramatic and of exquisite beauty all the way to Amos. There we dropped anchor; and while my friends had their sleep, I swam in the bay of Amos with its white beaches and roaming black goats.

Quite unexpectedly, Kiriakos called me to return to the boat at once; I could not understand the reason for it. Back on the *kaiki* they pointed to the rapidly forming clouds over Mount Fengari. They knew what was coming, I did not. Falling winds, thunder and lightning came over us in no time; we were miles away from the only port on the island. I watched the growing concern on my companions' faces. The change from heaven to hell happened within minutes, it lasted for many hours. I did not realize until it was all over how close we were to death. It would take too long to describe here in detail what we went through. The next day I recovered from my trip lying on the roof of the cottage of my friends, Petros and Pellagia. I enjoyed the view of Mount Fengari on one side and the peaceful sea on the other. Watching *kaikis* going by, I now looked at them in a different way, reliving my experience with brave Kiriakos and his brother, holding in my hand a little shell they gave me when we parted that night; and I began to understand the meaning of the nearby sanctuary of Samothrace. I feel now that I belong to this island and the company of such people.

I returned to Samothrace again in the summer of 1984 to stay with my friends, Petros and Pellagia, in Paleopoli. I wanted to revisit at leisure the places which mean so much to me like remote Xiropotamos, the delightful mountain stream with its inviting pools of delicious cool water. I climbed this gorge bordered with pink, white and dark red oleander bushes, wild chestnut, plane and walnut trees. The scenery is animated by rare birds, magnificent butterflies, lizards and many snakes. The climb is long and strenuous, full of surprises and most evocative. Finally I rested near a deep pool, the coloring of which only Adalbert Stifter could describe. On its edge many pretty green frogs dove to the bottom. I tried to hold still, and they came back to the surface one by one to continue their sunbathing. Gently I swam closer to them and discovered another world. Afterwards on one of those big warm stones I sunbathed, looking into a beautiful sky and at the mountains surrounding me. The occasional breeze caressed my naked body while I watched dragonflies drinking from the drops of water on me. Thank God for places like that. At night in my little room with shadows reflecting on a wooden ceiling from the kerosene lamp, I looked at Kokoschka's "Kouros," a gift of friends from Salonika to Petros and Pellagia. What a coincidence! And there was my gift to them from the previous year, the "Pegasus." I dreamt of my jolly green companions in Xiropotamos.

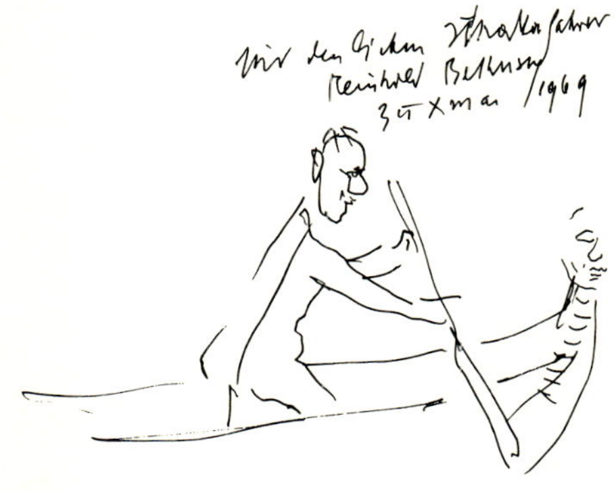

Oskar Kokoschka Rowing to Ithaca, 1969, pencil

At the end of my stay, late one afternoon on the western shore of Samothrace, not far from Agios Dimitrios, I was recovering from a long and strenuous walk in the mountains. The sea was calm and inviting. While swimming along the shore looking over the endless golden wheatfields at the foot of my beloved Mount Fengari, I noticed somebody else swimming nearby in the bay. We greeted each other. Later we sat together on the pebble beach and exchanged our impressions of the island; he was due to leave the next day. He spoke of "the sweetness of the evening sun," and I enjoyed his congenial company. I was reminded of Goethe's "Wahlverwandschaften." We spent the evening together in a taverna in Kamariotissa, and I was sorry to see him leave the island the following day. I know now that the encounter was not chance. We became friends. We have met again since then. From his home in Kalamata we have made excursions to Mani and two remote villages in the Taigetos Mountains, Methoni and Koroni. In December we spent some days together in Istanbul as I wanted to show him—in exchange for all his hospitality in the summer—the views Kokoschka painted of this beautiful city. He shares with me an admiration for Kokoschka.

My Greek journey would by no means be complete without paying homage to my dear friend, Pandelis Prevelakis. It was in Rethymnon that I found a copy of his novel, *The Angel in the Well*. I read it again and again during my stay on his island, and it became my fervent wish to meet the man who had created so powerful and noble a work of art. When I wrote to him, he invited me to visit him in Ekali. I was aware of the privilege I enjoyed. Every year when I returned to Greece, I was allowed to visit him, and we shared our admiration for Oskar Kokoschka. It was Mr. Prevelakis's wish to write to Kokoschka, which he did on the 28th of October 1979:

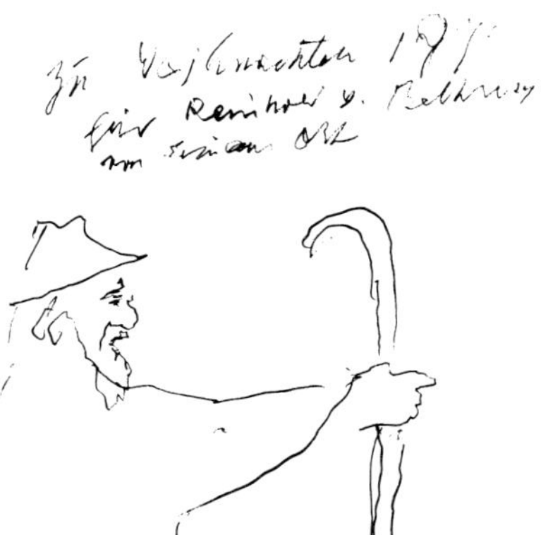

Shepherd with a Magoura, 1975, pencil

Dear Mr. Kokoschka,

I have admired your art for many years, and I have often commented on and praised it to my students at the Athens Academy of Fine Arts. Your work is great not only because of its inner perfection, but also since it is in harmony with our time.

I am taking advantage of my meeting with our mutual friend, Mr. Reinhold Bethusy-Huc, to send you these greetings. He has shown me your drawings from ancient Greek sculpture and your illustrations of Homer's *Odyssey.* I admired your power in interpreting the ancient world while remaining true to yourself.

All events that befall us are symbols of another reality. It is not fortuitous that in the twilight of my life I am given the opportunity of expressing to you my admiration through our mutual friend.

Pandelis Prevelakis

I forwarded this letter together with a copy of Mr. Prevelakis's novel, *The Angel in the Well,* to Kokoschka. He replied and sent Mr. Prevelakis a copy of his *Odyssey.* Soon afterward Oskar Kokoschka died.

In the years to follow I was privileged to visit Pandelis Prevelakis in his home in Ekali each time I came to Greece. I read all his books and essays available in translation. His letters and dedications to me are precious to me, and I wish to quote one which he wrote into a copy of his book, *Nikos Kazantzakis and his Odyssey—a Study of the Poet and the Poem:* "To my friend, who has the wings of the Nike of Samothrace on his shoulders, Pandelis Prevelakis, 1983."

Now it is almost one year since the author died, and I deeply mourn his passing. He will accompany me like Oskar Kokoschka to the end of my path. I am full of gratitude to both of them for what they have given me and continue giving me through their work.

Finally I wish to thank the Director of the Victoria and Albert Museum in London, Dr. Roy Strong; the Keeper of the Department of Prints and Drawings, Mr. J. Murdoch; the Deputy Keeper, Ms. Susan Lambert; and all their colleagues for their kind assistance in sending my prints by Oskar Kokoschka for another tour to the United States of America.[2] I am equally grateful to Richard Vincent West, Director of the Santa Barbara Museum of Art, for his continued and increasing enthusiasm to show my prints by Oskar Kokoschka again in America. I am grateful to my dear friends, Kiki and Andrew Macnab, for their generosity of heart, patience and understanding for my Odyssean wanderings. I wish to thank Madame Dr. Eleni Kontiadi for her friendship all these years and Sir Ernst Gombrich for his contribution to this catalogue. For his essay on Oskar Kokoschka I wish to thank my dear friend, Dr. Jaroslaw Leshko, from the bottom of my heart. I will always be grateful to Hermine and Erich Kreuzer for their affection, care and friendship for nearly two decades.

Maroussi, Christmas 1986

NOTES

1. "Kokoschka—Prints and Drawings," exhibition catalogue of the Victoria and Albert Museum, London, 1971, page 6, introduction by E. H. Gombrich.
2. My exhibition, "Homage to Kokoschka" in the Victoria and Albert Museum in 1976 was circulated by the International Exhibitions Foundation in Washington, D.C., during 1978 to 1980 to the following museums: The Phillips Collection in Washington, D.C., Florida International University in Miami, University Art Museum in Austin, Edwin A. Ulrich Museum of Art in Wichita, University Gallery in Minneapolis, Musee d'art Contemporain in Montreal, Los Angeles County Museum of Art, Helen Foresman Spencer Museum of Art in Lawrence, The Arkansas Arts Center in Little Rock and finally to the Stedelijk Museum in Amsterdam. The catalogue from the Victoria and Albert Museum with the introduction by E. H. Gombrich and essays by E. Hoffman, F. Novotny, H. Bollinger, J. Tomes, B. Baer and me accompanied the exhibition.

Kokoschka's Graphic Works: Themes and Variations

Jaroslaw Leshko

During Kokoschka's long, productive life, his graphic works remained a critical outlet for his creative energies. They were, throughout his career, a vital thread in a fabric of imagery without which the whole of his work would be profoundly diminished. The uniqueness of Kokoschka's graphic oeuvre lies in the near constant association with other aspects of his creative process.

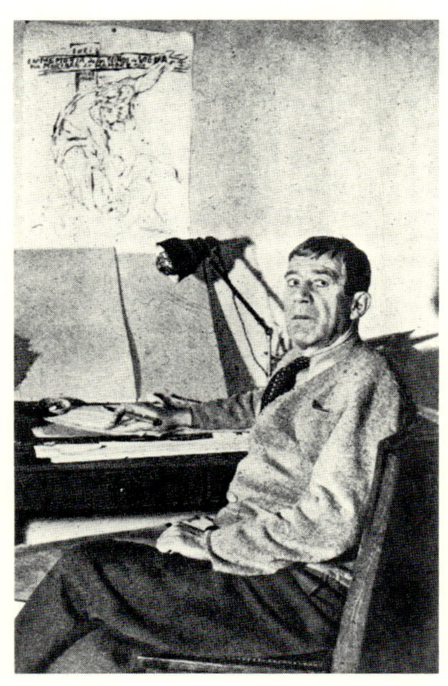

Oskar Kokoschka in his studio, London, 1945

If there is a key to understanding Kokoschka's art, it is in the principle of interrelatedness of his vision in which his prints and drawings, writings and paintings coalesce into a larger whole. Each of the parts carries an important element of the whole, each has an identity, often a completeness of its own, yet each is nurtured by the other and is understood most completely only in the context of his total output.

In an attempt to define the nature of Kokoschka's expressionism and understand its roots and evolution during the first, formative, years of his career, our attention must, of necessity, focus first on his graphic and literary works. Kokoschka's development as a painter at this time is a separate, and slightly later, part of his artistic growth, which has its own quite distinct evolution.

The reason for this condition is a result of circumstances and decisions made early in Kokoschka's artistic career which is inexorably linked to Vienna at the turn of the century.

He was born on March 1, 1886, in the small town of Pöchlarn outside Vienna, and soon thereafter the family moved to the Austrian capital. Kokoschka's parents would, in very different ways, exert an important influence on their son. His mother, a woman of immense native intelligence, would have the more profound impact on him. She was, according to Kokoschka, a woman of great intuitive powers, possessing "second sight"—an ability to peer into the future which the artist believed he inherited from her and which would play a major role in his own perception of his artistic talent. His father, a jeweler from a distinguished family of Prague jewelers, met with diminishing success in business as a result of processes of industrialization and mass production, placing the family often into resultant difficulties. Kokoschka would, therefore, develop in life a strong sense of financial responsibility toward his family. Yet Kokoschka respected his father's integrity and his commitment to high principles of craftsmanship.

It was also his father who gave the young boy a book which would have a formative influence on the latter's life—Jan Amos Comenius's *Orbis pictus,* an illustrated volume of teachings for the young by the Czech seventeenth-century humanist, pedagogue and bishop of the Moravian Brethren. Kokoschka writes:

> My first book has influenced my entire life: it was the *Orbis pictus* . . . In this book he set out in pictures, for the young, everything he knew to exist. You could read the explanation of each picture in four languages. I kept to the pictures at first, for this was the real world that lay in wait for me. Comenius was a humanist, and from the *Orbis pictus* I learned not only what the world is,

but how it should be in order to become fit for human beings to live in.[1]

The depth of the artist's involvement with Comenius's teachings manifests itself at different stages in a long career with a force and explicitness which make us that much more aware of the sustaining and nurturing impact of this early influence.

For example, in his portrait of Thomas G. Masaryk, painted in Prague in 1935, Kokoschka places to the left of the President of Czechoslovakia the image of Comenius holding up his *Orbis pictus* like Moses displaying the tablets. This unusual inclusion, making of the work a symbolic double portrait, was a result of deep mutual respect for the humanist shared by the artist and Masaryk.

And as late as 1972, Kokoschka completed his fifth and final play, *Comenius*—a work he had started many decades earlier—as an homage to the life and spirit of an individual who embodied most closely the artist's own world view. It is therefore most apt that the present exhibition, which explores Kokoschka's own picture of the world, incorporates in its title a reference to this central, lifelong influence.

His early development had to be achieved in a cultural milieu generally hostile to innovation . . .

Kokoschka won a scholarship to Vienna's Kuntsgewerbeschule (School of Arts and Crafts) and began his studies there in October of 1904. His early development had to be achieved in a cultural milieu generally hostile to innovation and in the artistic environment of a school bound to the aesthetic principles of Jugendstil. He exhibited from the outset an impatience toward the school's teaching curriculum, specifically the traditional approach to figure study from a static, posed model.

Kokoschka's alternative was to introduce into the curriculum what he referred to as "five-minute sketches"—a quick capturing on paper of a model who was constantly in motion. Often these models were not professionals but children of circus performers and themselves acrobats—angular, supple, graceful figures whose constantly changing movements challenged and stimulated the young artist in the way that conventionally posed models never could. This approach to drawing, akin to Rodin's quick sketches of models in constant motion, produced a body of drawings of incomparable originality, sensitivity and strength. For Vienna at the outset of the new century, the above approach was a startling innovation—it would be one of many that Kokoschka would impose on this tradition-bound city over the next five years.

Kokoschka's actions should not be regarded, however, as an act of open rebellion toward his teachers at the Kunstgewerbeschule, among whom were Berthold Löffler and Carl Otto Czeschka. In fact, Kokoschka's relationship with both, particularly with the latter, was always warm and respectful. In his pedagogical approach Czeschka was quite receptive to new ideas, and he gladly welcomed Kokoschka's innovative approach to figure studies.

It was also largely through Czeschka's intervention that Kokoschka became involved with the Wiener Werkstätte, an institution closely connected with the Kunstgewerbeschule and inspired by the English Arts and Crafts movement. Kokoschka's work for the Wiener Werkstätte included book illustrations, fan decorations, postcards and other projects associated with the arts and crafts curriculum. The outstanding omission in Kokoschka's early training was oil painting.

1908 Kunstschau; The Dreaming Youths

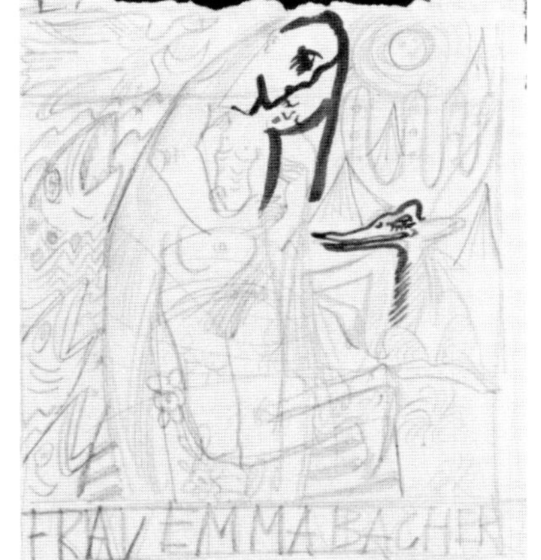

Cat. 176 *Madonna*, c1906

Kokoschka's first public manifestation of his talent was at the famous Kunstschau of 1908. The exhibition, exploring the best and most innovative strain of art and crafts produced in Vienna at this time, was the creation of Gustav Klimt, whose brilliant, sumptuously decorated golden paintings—icons of the Art Nouveau movement—were its culmination.

Among Kokoschka's contributions to the exhibition were three large tempera panels—designs for tapestry—entitled *The Dream Bearers*, which were purchased by the Wiener Werkstätte and have been subsequently lost.

Kokoschka and other writers, attempting to conjure up how these lost works must have looked, compared them to the artist's book, *Die Traumenden Knaben (The Dreaming Youths)*, written and illustrated by him in 1907 and published by the Wiener Werkstätte in 1908. This book is the earliest and most complete statement of Kokoschka's early artistic intent. Stylistically, *The Dreaming Youths* reflects most closely the Jugendstil aesthetic; while its illustrations may be seen as a high point of this style, they do not break any new aesthetic ground.

If we grant the general similarity of the above works with the prevailing style, then the response in the press to the exhibition is surprising in its singling out of Kokoschka for either praise or vilification. An example is the comment of the eminent art historian Richard Muther:

> The *enfant terrible* here is Kokoschka. Since precocious success has already damaged many a young man it is pedagogically correct to apply the brakes. Therefore, Herr Kokoschka, your tapestry designs are dreadful: *Octoberfest* fun-fair, raw Indian art, ethnographic museum, Gauguin gone mad—for all I know. And yet I can't help myself: I have not experienced a more interesting debut in years . . . I must remember the name Kokoschka. For anyone who acts so much like a cannibal at the age of twenty-two might possibly be a very original, serious artist by the time he is thirty.[2]

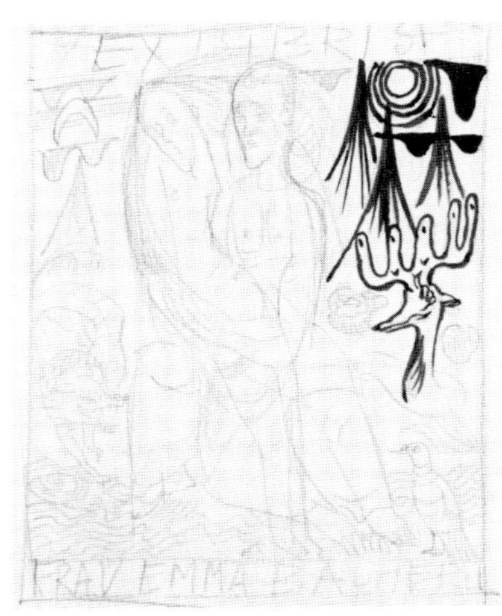

Cat. 177 *Lovers*, c1906

In light of such comments, it is likely that the three panels possessed qualities which must have distinguished them from the majority of contributions in the exhibition. They were probably rendered with a vigor, even roughness, which suggested more stylistic freedom and experimentation then are evidenced in the artist's illustrations of *The Dreaming Youths*, the execution of which were under the auspices and thus at least implicitly, under the control of the Wiener Werkstätte, and were destined, ultimately, for a different audience.

There is certainly enough evidence in Kokoschka's early oeuvre to warrant such a conclusion.[3] We have, for example, already referred to the stylistic strength and freshness of many of his "five-minute sketches."

Included in the present exhibition are two early drawings, *Madonna* (Cat. 176) and *Lovers* (Cat. 177),[4] usually dated 1906, which are brilliant examples of the degree of freedom and experimentation that Kokoschka was capable of at this time. In the two drawings, Ex Libris designs for Frau Emma Bacher, Kokoschka introduces many of the characters of his early Wiener Werkstätte fantasy illustrations—reindeer, birds, fish, mountains, trees, bodies of water, among others, and these serve as a backdrop for the human protagonists. In the *Madonna* drawing, the artist depicts a nude woman holding a child, also nude. In representing the age-old motif in this unusual, dramatic fashion, Kokoschka evokes imagery of such artists as Gauguin and Munch and also establishes a prototype in his own art in which religious themes are, at times, represented in a unique, even startling manner, as in his *Annunciation* and *Visitation* paintings of 1911.

While it is valid to date the explosive development of Kokoschka's expressionism to 1909, when both his pictorial and dramatic works acquire a new intensity, it is important as well to see in such early works as *Madonna,* elements which distinctly enunciate an expressionist predisposition in his art. In formal terms, the expressive possibility of line in this work already surpasses the even, sustained line which dominates his Wiener Werkstätte illustrations of 1907–1908. The line in this drawing moves over the paper with urgency and force, searching out expressive accents as in the dark outlining with black ink of the female's face and part of the child—unifying and dramatizing them within the setting which is more threatening than lyrical. Fish with gaping mouths dominate the left part of the work and a reindeer, whose leering face is also accented with black ink, is shown on the right. Above the fish is the moon and on the right above the reindeer's antlers is the sun, symbols which pair off to establish the man-woman equation.

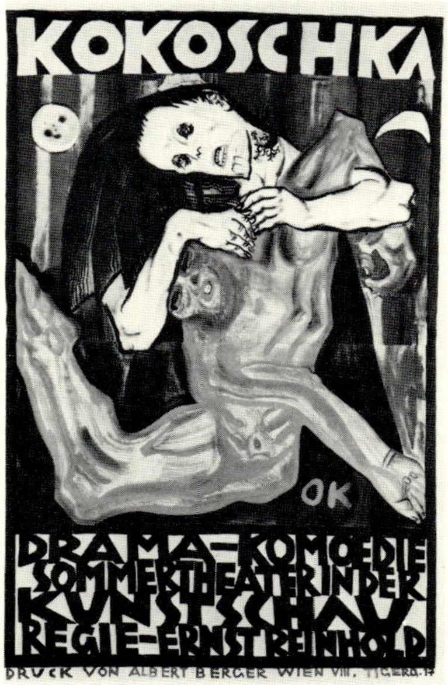

A few years later, in 1909, Kokoschka would distill elements of this drawing and transform them into one of the most powerful images of early expressionism—his poster, *Pietà* (Figure 1) for the performance of his play, *Mörder, Hoffnung der Frauen (Murderer, Hope of Women).*

Fig. 1 *Pietà,* 1909 (WW 31)

The other Ex Libris drawing for Frau Emma Bacher, *Lovers,* focuses even more explicitly on the man-woman theme, for the protagonists are young lovers. Furthermore, it is here that the autobiographical nature of much of Kokoschka's imagery of his early years becomes evident since the male figure in the drawing is clearly a self-portrait. He is seated, legs apart, with the woman on his lap. Both are shown semi-nude, with drapery covering the lower portions of their bodies. While the surrounding landscape is filled with creatures similar to those in the *Madonna* drawing, they are not as prominent an element here and the focus is more on the figures. Kokoschka uses once again the male-female symbols of the sun and moon—here even more prominently than in the other drawing. The man, Kokoschka, with an anxious, almost pained, expression on his face, embraces the woman as she turns away from him. Her hair, stressed here by the artist, entwines itself around his head as if to ensnare him. In the expressive use of hair, Kokoschka alludes to one of the most prevalent motifs of Art Nouveau imagery, where it often carries with it a sexually suggestive reference. The most powerful manifestation of this motif, and, for Kokoschka, the most influential, is the expressive works of Edvard Munch.

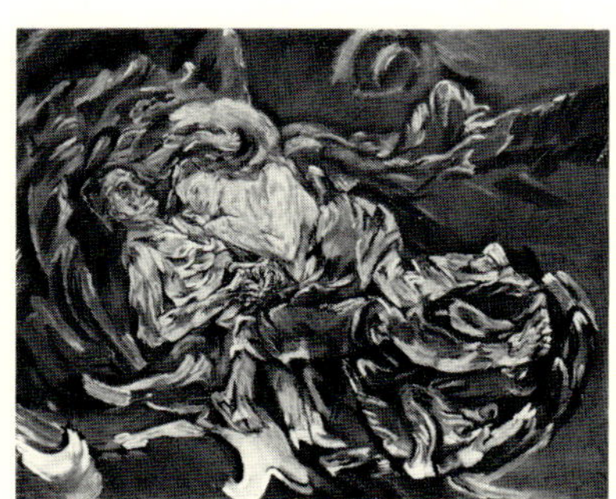

Fig. 2 *The Tempest*, 1913–14

In the most important aspects of this drawing, such as the anxious, unresolved liaison of man and woman within a landscape that is both beautiful and threatening, and also in its autobiographical nature, Kokoschka has already put in place elements which he will address often in his early career and most completely, as will be shown, in his masterpiece, *The Tempest* of 1914 (Figure 2).

It has already been observed that Kokoschka's most complete and important early statement in the graphic medium is his illustrated book, *The Dreaming Youths*, a series of two black-and-white and eight color lithographs. In their rich coloring—mostly red, green, yellow and blue, in their stylized interpretation of landscape and in the outlining of mainly unmodeled forms, Kokoschka's illustrations have been compared to such prototypes as medieval miniatures, popular peasant art, and Chinese scrolls. Among more specific prototypes for Kokoschka's illustrations, Wilhelm Laage's illustrations for his *Fairy Tale* have been suggested.[5]

In his interest in such disparate traditions, the artist shares an attitude with other Viennese artists. For example, Kokoschka's teachers, Löffler and Czeschka, were producing works evocative of similar sources and stylistically similar to his, works from which he obviously drew inspiration. Czeschka's illustrations from *Die Nibelungen* of 1908 are an example of the uniformly high quality of work produced at that time. It has often been pointed out, for example, that Kokoschka's poster for the 1908 Kunstschau is very similar in design to one produced by a fellow artist—a highly talented Croatian, Rudolf Kalvach.

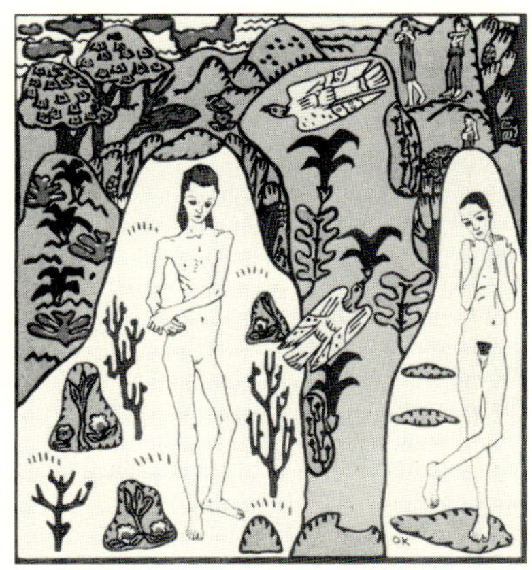

Fig. 3 *The Girl Li and I*, 1908 (WW 29)

Yet Kokoschka also exhibits in these works a need to go beyond the confines of an arts and crafts aesthetic. This is evident in his assimilation in these illustrations of influences from contemporary artists whose works transcend the narrow confines of the above aesthetic. In Kokoschka's "The Girl Li and I" (Figure 3), for example, the influence of Ferdinand Hodler's *Spring* of 1901 has often been mentioned. In Vienna the reputation of the Swiss-born Hodler was immense dating from the winter of 1903–1904, when there was a major retrospective of his art staged by the Secession in Joseph Maria Olbrich's newly constructed building for the organization. An even more compelling parallel exists with the works of the Belgian sculptor, Georges Minne. His Gothic youths—elongated, self-hugging, introspective—approximate closely Kokoschka's self-image in the above illustration. Kokoschka was deeply moved by Minne's works, which he could have seen in Vienna as early as 1906, when the sculptor had a major exhibition at the influential Miethke Gallery. Often during his long career Kokoschka has remarked about the profound influence on him of Minne's bony adolescents, which approximated the youths that he frequently drew at this time.

Another important factor that distinguished Kokoschka's work from that of his colleagues, beyond the differences which separate one talent from another, was the personal, autobiographical meaning with which he imbued many of the scenes. For example, it is in the illustrations for *The Dreaming Youths* that Kokoschka's special relationship with Gustav Klimt is best reflected.

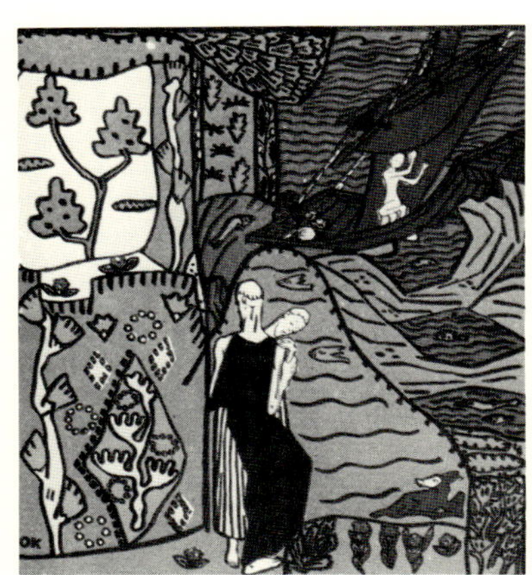

Fig. 4 *The Sailing Ship*, 1908 (WW 23)

In one of the illustrations, "The Sailing Ship" (Figure 4), Kokoschka depicts two robed men locked in a kind of embrace in the middle foreground of the composition. They are surrounded by a stylized, richly colored landscape—flowers, trees, and a body of water in which there are red fish and a sailboat with a man in it. The bearded monk-like figure with his back to the viewer has been identified correctly as Klimt. He holds up with his right hand a similarly garbed, leaning, youthful figure with Kokoschka's facial features. Edith Hoffmann, in referring to this scene in her book on Kokoschka, describes the two protagonists as "... men who lean against each other in a half awkward, half sentimental way [not unlike St. John of some carved groups of the Middle Ages, who rests his head on Christ's shoulder]."[6] In establishing a teacher-disciple relationship between the two, Hoffmann unwittingly refers to the scene's most salient feature: Kokoschka represents himself as a disciple of Klimt, on whom he depends for support and inspiration. The scene is, therefore, an homage to the older artist, which reiterates in pictorial form Kokoschka's dedication of his book: "To Gustav Klimt in respectful admiration."

The meaning of the illustration, however, is more complex and reflects a fundamental artistic difference between the two men. The figures are surrounded by a landscape that is vertically divided into two distinctly different halves. The older artist turns his gaze to the left, the part of the landscape that is richly ornamented with stylized trees and flowers, not unlike many scenes of gardens and parks painted by Klimt. The younger artist, even while leaning on the older one for support, turns his attention to the right part of the landscape, which, in contrast to the left, is sparsely decorated. The body of water with red fish represents the uncertain, even threatening, future. The figure in the embarked boat suggests Kokoschka's awareness that his own artistic adventure will be significantly different from Klimt's. Even the still life of grapes and bananas in the boat is a likely allusion to Van Gogh and Gauguin, two artists who led painting in an importantly different direction from Klimt and who had a profound influence on Kokoschka.

The expression of admiration for and gratitude toward Klimt which Kokoschka establishes in the above scene and in the book's dedication is therefore effectively balanced by an assertion of the different direction of his own art. This condition demonstrates eloquently the role Klimt played as a pivotal figure in Viennese art and underscores a phenomenon especially evident in Vienna, namely, the attitude of respect of younger artists toward their predecessors and the willing aid offered to them by the older artists—a condition described as a "sympathetic relation between the two generations."[7]

The autobiographical nature of Kokoschka's imagery reaches a high point in "The Girl Li and I" (Figure 3). In it he depicts a nude adolescent boy and girl within a tapestry of a richly colored, stylized landscape environment filled with trees, flowers, birds and, in the distance, people. The two figures are represented frontally in self-absorbed gestures suggestive of the moment of sexual awareness of self and other. The white, biomorphic shapes that envelop them allude to their distinct sexual nature—the one around the girl is ample, filled with budding trees and flowers, representative of fertility; the boy is outlined by a narrow and sparse shape, stressing his male sexual role. Their self-hugging gestures and their placement within the outlined shapes separates one from another, yet they are also linked in sharing their nudity within the same landscape environment. In the center of the composition a large red shape, placed between and attached to the white mandorlas, unifies the two figures further. Within this brilliant red confine are flowers and two yellow birds flying in opposite directions toward the two protagonists—like messengers establishing an evocative early dialogue between them.

The youthful boy is Kokoschka and the girl is a fellow student at the Kunstgewerbeschule, Lilith Lang, with whom the artist had earlier been deeply in love. In the autobiographical nature of this scene, as well as the nudity of the figures and the sexual overtones of the illustration, there are significant parallels, just as *The Lovers* drawing with *The Tempest*.

The prominence of the column of red in this scene, and, indeed, the recurrence of red in all of the colored illustrations, may have specific reference to Lilith's most characteristic trait of wearing a brilliant red coat which, according to the artist, had a central impact on him:

"... this color sent me into ecstasies—like a melody—like Mozart ..."

> It was one of the most remarkable reds I had ever seen—this color sent me into ecstasies—like a melody—like Mozart ... That was my first experience of color, and perhaps it was that which brought my whole color sense into being. Before that I'd only made drawings.[8]

The Dreaming Youths addresses a number of other concerns critical for Kokoschka's development. Preeminent among these is the clarity with which the artist enunciates the symbiotic relationship between the illustrations and the written word. In designing the book, the artist posits the poem in a narrow border alongside the brilliantly colored illustrations so that they coexist on a single page. The images do not illustrate the text nor does the text describe the images, their relationship is one of creative interdependence.

It is in the language of the poem that we can attempt to understand the nature of Kokoschka's expressionism at this time. The theme of the poem, adolescent sexual awakening, generally corresponds with the illustrations of it, in that both evoke a mood of fairy tale, other world. Yet in the poem, Kokoschka breaks this surface quietude with an undercurrent of pulsating tension which erupts repeatedly. As he probes in these verses the nature of his own sexuality, Kokoschka focuses on a range of emotions, such as violence, longing, anxiety—all expressed with a vividness and directness that may certainly be referred to as incipient expressionism. The opening lines of the poem intensify the context in which we view the illustrations:

Little red fish, little fish red
I kill you with the three-bladed knife
I tear you in two with my fingers,
that there be an end to the silent
circling . . .

Throughout the poem, the young boy's deeply felt, confused responses to the opposite sex are often accompanied by explicit sexual metaphors, such as "like a tongue-moistened tree is my body."

In one part of the poem, he identifies himself as an adolescent in the throes of sexual self-awareness and self-consciousness:

not the events of childhood go through
me and not those of manhood
but boyhood
a hesitating yearning
the unfounded shame before that which grows . . .

In another part of the poem he assumes the identity of a werewolf:

. . . I am the circling werewolf . . .
. . . my unbridled body
my body enhanced with blood and pigment
crawls into your arbors
roams through your villages
crawls into your souls
festers in your bodies . . .

The forceful, brutal imagery in the above quotation foretells the direction in which Kokoschka's visual and literary expression will evolve.

1909 Kunstschau; Pietà; Murderer, Hope of Women

Among the most important events in Kokoschka's early development was the establishment of a relationship with Adolf Loos, the pioneering modernist architect.

Among the most important events in Kokoschka's early development was the establishment of a relationship with Adolf Loos, the pioneering modernist architect. They may have met in 1908, but it was in 1909 that the latter became an active participant in promoting Kokoschka's career. Loos, whose passionate disdain of ornament was brilliantly explicated in his essay, *Ornament and Crime* published in 1908, was among a handful of influential Viennese intellectuals who saw the danger of both the obfuscating historicism of the past as practiced on the Ringstrasse, and the insidiousness of the excesses of Art Nouveau decorative schemes. Loos's counterpart in the literary realm was Karl Kraus, who attacked with equal passion the corruption of the German language in his journal *Die Fackel (The Torch)*. They, along with such figures as Sigmund Freud and Arnold Schoenberg, stood at this moment in the vanguard leading Vienna into the reality of the twentieth century as the illusion of an old empire became progressively untenable. Kraus's relationship to Kokoschka would also be important for the artist, but nowhere near as significant as that of Loos, who became at this time

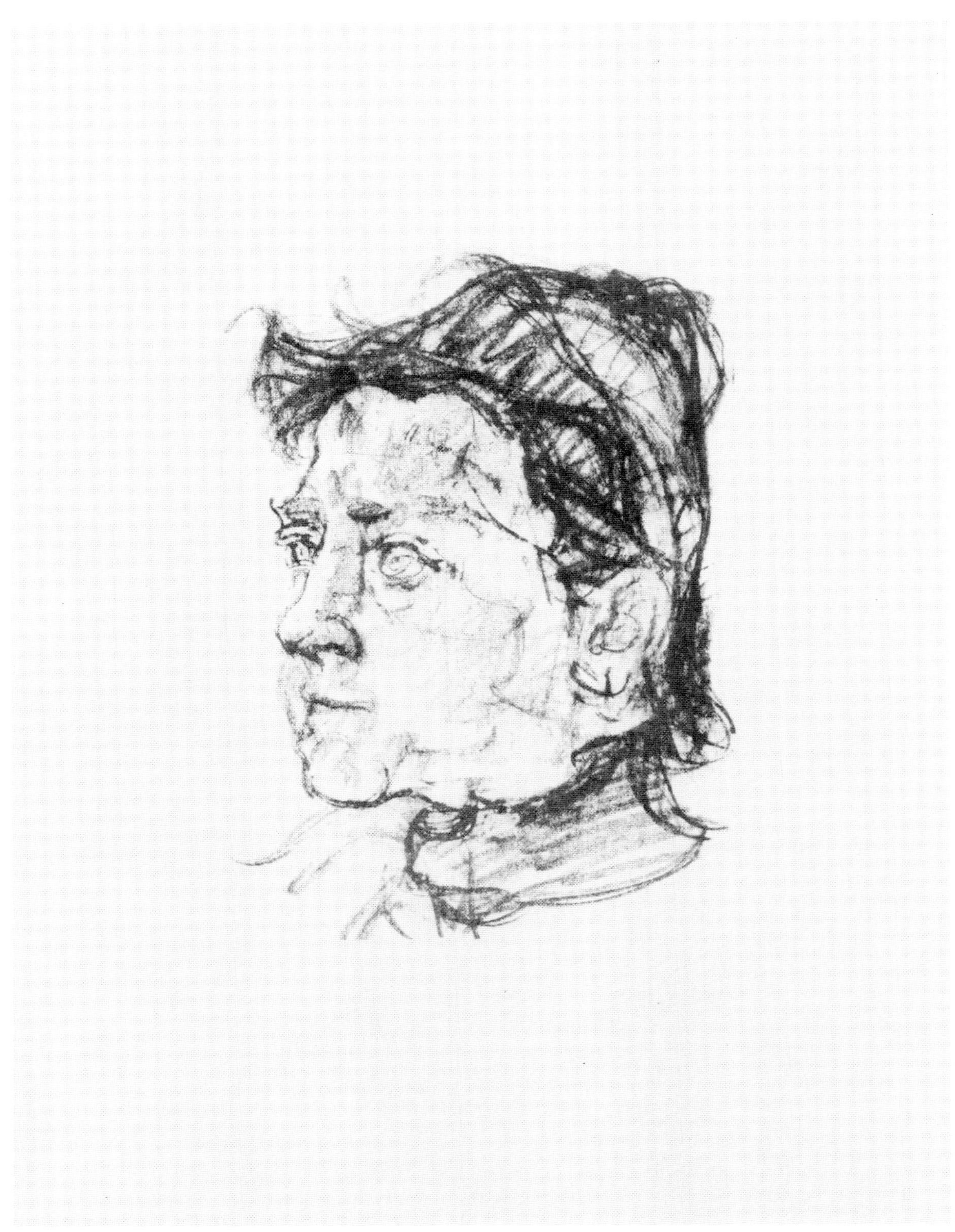

Cat. 33 *Romana Kokoschka,* 1917

Kokoschka's key source of support—financially, morally and otherwise.

As a result of the new alliance with Loos, who was perhaps Klimt's severest critic, Kokoschka's own position toward the older artist shifted. Klimt ceased being an influence on him at this time, and the latter's style irrevocably lunged in a new expressionist direction. This was most evident in the artist's contributions to the 1909 Kunstschau, which was an even more expansive production that its predecessor.

Whereas the 1908 show focused mainly on German and Austrian artists and on arts and crafts, the 1909 exhibition was international in scale with many of Europe's most important artists represented.

Kokoschka did not disappoint with his contributions, the most startling of which was a new drama, *Murderer, Hope of Women,* and the poster, *Pietà,* for its performance at the Summer Theater. The artist also exhibited an oil portrait of Ernst Reinhold, the lead performer in the drama. The work, known as *The Trance Player,* is considered among Kokoschka's earliest oil paintings. Despite its tentative manipulation of the oil medium, the work's historical significance lies in the fact that the artist introduces here a number of compositional features that mark the beginning of expressionist portraiture in Vienna, which he not only developed into a mature idiom but which also influenced Egon Schiele, among others.

... the artist introduces here a number of compositional features that mark the beginning of expressionist portraiture in Vienna ...

Kokoschka also contributed to the exhibition a work entitled *The Warrior,* a clay sculpture, possibly a self-portrait, of extraordinary expressiveness, freedom of execution and virtuosity in which the artist painted over parts of the head in brilliant colors that were as vigorously applied as the sculpture was modelled. Kokoschka's decision to paint the sculpture was undoubtedly the result of his avid interest at this time in masks from Oceania and Africa. The significance of this influence on the artist is pervasive, touching many important elements of his art, and must, of course, be seen in the larger context of European modernism.

During the latter half of the nineteenth century, museums throughout Europe acquired large ethnographical and ethnological collections, among the most prominent was Vienna's Naturhistorisches Museum. The availability of this new, exotic material provided a rich, stimulating source for artists in the early years of this century. Almost at precisely the same moment artists in various parts of Europe responded to this influence, which is especially evident in Paris in the works of Picasso and in Dresden in the works of *Die Brücke* artists.

From Kokoschka's vantage point, the biggest event of the 1909 Kunstschau was the performance on July 4, in the Summer Theater, of his new play, *Murderer, Hope of Women,* a brief one-act play in which two characters, identified only as MAN and WOMAN, confront each other in a dialogue of an elemental force, where an orgy of love, violence, and blood lust is explored. In comparison to the poem, *The Dreaming Youths,* in which Kokoschka brilliantly evokes images of dreamlands, the environment in the present work is brutally stark, unspecified by period and unencumbered by many props. Also in contrast to the poem is the play's language, which, in its simplicity and vividness, reinforces the violence of the action. The tenor of the whole drama is captured in the following passage toward the end of the play, where the woman addresses the man:

> WOMAN (more and more violent, crying out)
> I shall not let you live. You!
> You weaken me
> I shall kill you—you fetter me!
> I caught you—and you keep me captured!
> Let go of me—you embrace me as with iron
> chains—
> strangled—let go—help
> I lost the key—that kept you a prisoner.

The theme of Kokoschka's play, the tortuous conflict of the sexes, evolves from an established tradition of nineteenth-century art and literature. For example, the play has been convincingly compared to such earlier works as Büchner's *Woyczek* of 1836, to Heinrich von Kleist's *Penthesilia* of 1808[9] and also to Strindberg's plays.[10] Generally, it is the latter's "dream plays" that had the most profound effect on Expressionist drama. Works like *To Damascus* (1898–1904), *A Dream Play* (1902) and *The Ghost Sonata* (1907) were performed frequently in Germany and Austria and certainly also served as an important basis of Kokoschka's development as a dramatist.

In stripping away a recognizable ambience, in not defining the protagonists beyond their gender, in the negation of the traditional division of a play into separate acts, in the directness and simplicity of its language, and, above all, in the elemental brutality of its action Kokoschka enunciated in this play the beginnings of expressionist theater. The performance must have jolted the complacent Viennese society as they watched convulsive screams of anguish, lust and killing, all flashing in rapid succession like a nightmare before their eyes.

The intensity of the stage presentation was further enhanced by Kokoschka, who painted marks on the actors. He recalls:

"I wanted, in fact, to turn the figures inside out, to make the inner man visible."

> —the actors wore skin-tight, flesh-colored costumes, and I painted nerves and veins on them in vivid colors. I wanted, in fact, to turn the figures inside out, to make the inner man visible.[11]

Kokoschka, who had studied anatomy at the Kunstgewerbeschule and therefore knew the correct location of joints, muscles and nerves, was clearly also assimilating here the above mentioned influence of non-western art. He writes of his response to the latter:

> But seeing a Polynesian mask with its incised tattooing, I understood [it] at once, because I could feel my own facial nerves reacting to cold and hunger in the same way.[12]

In presenting the work to the public, Kokoschka transformed the spoken line into something convulsive, desperate and elemental; and in painting on the actors vigorous squiggles in vibrant colors, he attempted to reinforce visually the expressive intensity of the whole. In the process, he brilliantly and originally fused into a complete dramatic statement elements especially from symbolist and earlier nineteenth-century literary prototypes and from Oceanic and African art, to whose powerful images he responded strongly and intuitively at this time.

In *Pietà*, the poster for the play, Kokoschka again turns to these two traditions in evolving an image which is the most forceful visual representation in his oeuvre up to that time of the theme of torturous conflict of the sexes. In it, a pale, skeletal woman is linked in a death struggle with a contorted and distorted figure of a blood-red, possibly flayed, male. To the upper right and left of them, emanating from a dark-blue background, are their signs—sun for man and moon for woman. In the dramatic intensity of the image and its powerful impact on the viewer, the *Pietà* is comparable to such works as Francisco Goya's *Saturn Devouring His Children* of c.1820 and Edvard Munch's *The Cry* of 1889. It is, in fact, Edvard Munch's *Vampire* (Figure 5), done as a painting in 1893 and as a lithograph in 1895, which has convincingly been suggested as the source of Kokoschka's work. Especially emphasized is the placement of the figures—the woman hovering over the man, the expressive use of the woman's hair, and the positioning of the woman's right arm, as elements the two works share.[13]

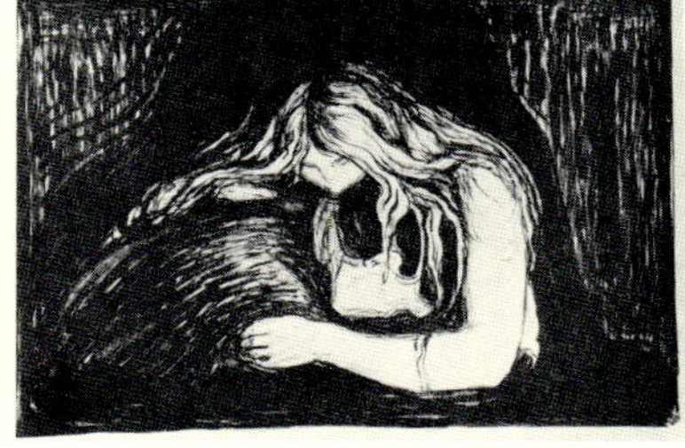

Fig. 5 Edvard Munch, *Vampire*, lithograph, 1895

The influence of non-western art in the *Pietà* may be seen most clearly in the male figure. The violently distorted features of his body culminate in an expressive head—whose squinting eyes, with surrounding hatch markings, and circular protruding mouth—bears a strong imprint of the above mentioned masks.

The relationship between Kokoschka's poster and Munch's works presents us with the first of many important parallels between the two artists, and Kokoschka turned to Munch's art during the early part of his career as a constant and major source of inspiration. The parallel also allows us to probe the difference in emphasis which separates him from Munch and other proto-expressionist and symbolist artists and writers from whose works he drew heavily at this time.

For example, Strindberg's plays are set in identifiable settings or environments, while Kokoschka's players in *Murderer, Hope of Women* act in an unspecified ambience, wrenched, as it were, out of any cultural or social context. In a similar way, in Munch's *Vampire*, the artist clearly identifies the woman as the classic femme fatale who is sucking blood out of the cowering, helpless male. Kokoschka's confrontation of the sexes in the *Pietà* poster and in the play is more ambivalent and unresolved. Despite the woman's upper position in the poster, Kokoschka represents them both as victims of the torturous struggle. The words that the woman utters in the play perhaps best exemplify that position: "I caught you—and you keep me captured." Also, to the extent that symbolist tendencies are linked to the Jugendstil aesthetic, Munch achieves expressiveness mainly by a brilliant manipulation of the curving line. Kokoschka in his poster employs violent, angular, disruptive contortions of the line to achieve the interlocking of the two forms.

Associated with the play, and similar in expressive intensity to the *Pietà* poster, is a series of four drawings that Kokoschka executed probably around the time that the play was performed, that is, in the summer of 1909. He reiterates in these drawings his need to give visual expression to his literary work. In the most dramatic and innovative of the four, the artist represents a man, again in a self-portrait, standing over and struggling with a recumbent woman (Figure 6). In his outstretched left hand he holds a knife, and with the forefinger of the other hand he reaches into the woman's mouth, while his right foot presses on her torso.

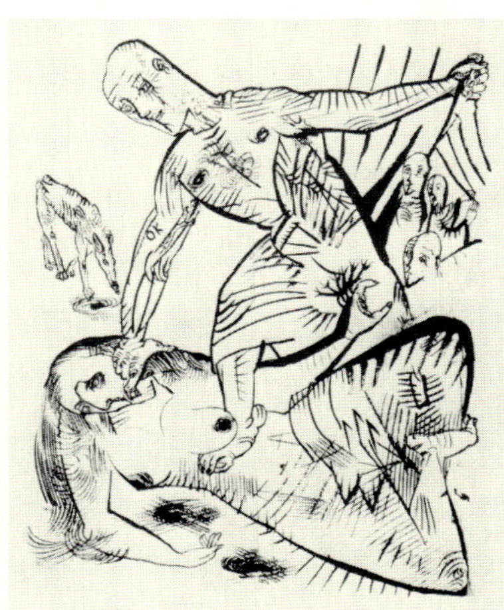

Fig. 6 Illustration to *Murderer, Hope of Women*, 1910

The bodies of the woman and especially the male are energized with squiggles and striations. According to Kokoschka, these are meant to represent the nerve ends and other anatomical parts, much like those he painted onto the actors. These expressive markings, also influenced by his visits to the Ethnographical Museum, introduce an important device into Kokoschka's pictorial vocabulary. When the drawing is compared with Kokoschka's illustrations of the poem, such as "The Girl Li and I," we see the degree to which the uninterrupted angular, Gothic line of the earlier work has been effectively shattered here. In the poem illustrations, the outlined, frail human form is caressed by a fairy-tale landscape that decorates the rest of the page. In the present drawing, the decoration has been transformed into violent squiggles and other marks that have been set within the contours of the figure. As such, they become the visible extension of the person's inner state.

Here Kokoschka also introduces an important innovation by depicting a face simultaneously in profile and frontally. This is evident in the features of the central male figure and is especially clear in the faces of the three men in the background. The purpose of the innovation in the illustration is to heighten the expressiveness of the image, and it is one of many devices Kokoschka employs. In using it, the artist illustrates the restlessness and inventiveness of his experimentation; he repeats the use of this device a few more times during 1909–1912 and then abandons it for a long period. This principle of simultaneous views of the face would be employed by artists such as Picasso, among others, and becomes one of the most recognized formal elements associated with modernism. For Kokoschka, however, the formal implications of this experiment were of little consequence. He states: ". . . I didn't conceive this device intellectually. I really saw those heads like that."[14]

The *Pietà* poster, the drawings associated with the drama and the play itself underscore the fact that it is in his graphic and literary works that Kokoschka first achieves a mature expressionist syntax.

The years between 1910 and 1912 were for Kokoschka ones of tumultuous events in his career. In February 1910 Kokoschka arrived in Berlin and for the first time became part of a society which willingly accepted new ideas and gave support to his unbridled talent. Two men especially, Herwarth Walden and Paul Cassirer, had a significant impact at this time on Kokoschka's career. The former was a brilliant, aggressive impresario, who in March of 1910 began publishing the periodical *Der Sturm*, which quickly became the most important avant-garde journal in Germany. Kokoschka joined

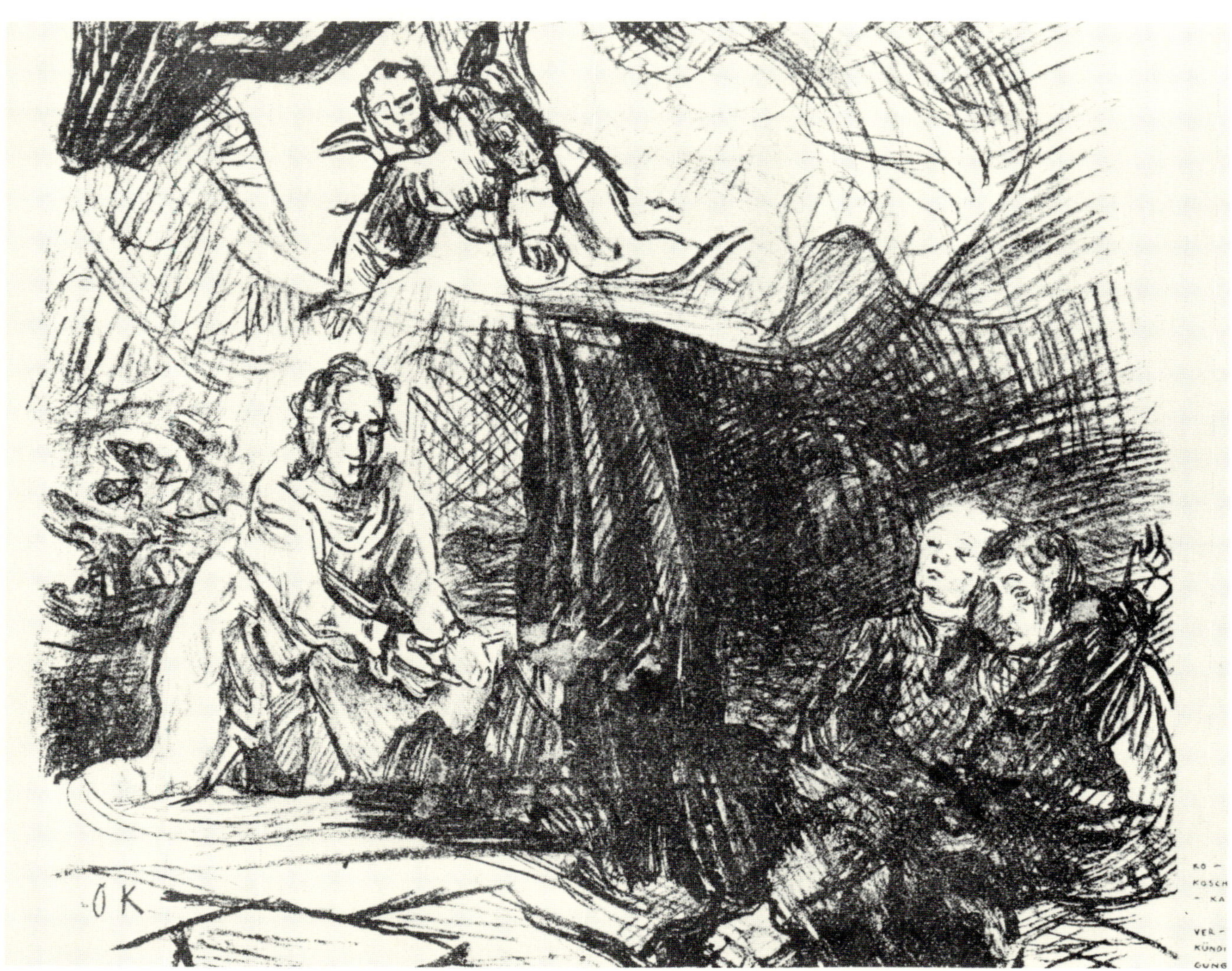

Cat. 27 *Christ on the Mount of Olives*, 1916

Walden in this venture from the very beginning and became, especially during 1910, the most frequent and important contributor to *Der Sturm.* A series of his writings appeared in its pages, and his drawings were a regular feature on the journal's front page. Through this vehicle the artist was able to hone further his graphic skills. *Der Sturm* also provided high visibility for Kokoschka's talent and, as such, enhanced his international reputation appreciably. Kokoschka willingly shared in all facets of the publication of the journal, even its distribution. Consequently, he became an intimate of the circle of intellectuals gathered around *Der Sturm,* many of whose portraits he drew and painted.

Kokoschka's early success culminated with the publication in 1913 of the first monograph on him, by Paul Stefan, entitled *Dramen und Bildern.* This was an important moment for the young artist, who had made his artistic debut only in 1908.

It is significant that at precisely the moment that Kokoschka's early achievements were being celebrated, his art from this period shows a marked departure from his earlier works. The most important change was a decided concentration in his work on formal problems. This new condition was unquestionably the result of his stay in Berlin during 1910–1911. Unlike the hermetic, festering intellectual life of Vienna, the German capital was a mecca for the avant-garde. At the nerve center of the tempo of intellectual activity of the city was, of course, Herwarth Walden, and his publication, *Der Sturm.* It is in large part through the publisher's efforts that many major artists and artistic movements in Europe would be introduced to the German public.

In 1910, the *Neue Secession* (New Secession) was formed and included in its first exhibition, among others, the members of *Die Brücke:* Ernst Ludwig Kirchner, Erich Heckel, Karl Schmidt-Rottluff and Max Pechstein. By 1911, the Munich artists, Wassily Kandinsky, Franz Marc and Alexey Jawlensky, also participated in the group's exhibition, as did Kokoschka himself.

This new, important contact with art which in many ways was more radical than his own made Kokoschka reconsider his artistic position. What he found in this art was something completely lacking in his own works—a serious concern with pictorial problems of structure and color. It is certainly in large part because of Kokoschka's exposure to the above artists, that he started to rethink his own aesthetic position, which he had never up to this time considered in formal terms. The result of this reevaluation was that, as mentioned, his works of 1911 began to show strong formal concerns.

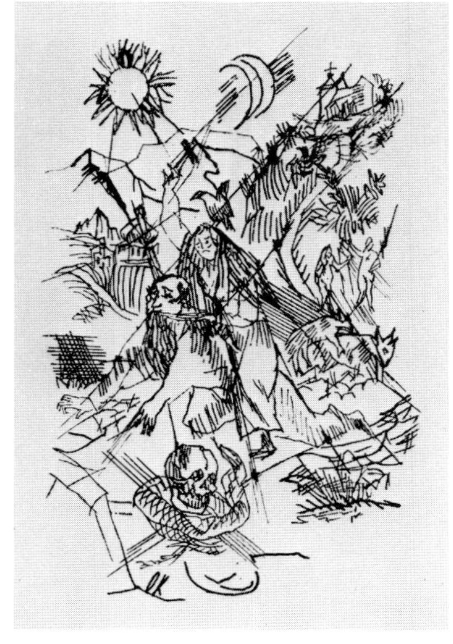

Fig. 7 Illustration to *Tubutsch,* 1911

The most evident example of this new focus can be seen in Kokoschka's illustrations for Albert Ehrenstein's *Tubutsch* (Figure 7) published in 1911. In these drawings, the artist redefines natural elements, such as figures and landscape, to respond to a delicate weblike superstructure of abstract lines which unify the composition but also impose an abstracting quality on the scene and stress the two-dimensional property of the work. Whereas the figures in Kokoschka's early expressionist works succumbed to a highly intuitive, almost emotional attack by the artist, in the above work they respond to an order which has been intellectually conceived.

Kokoschka also explores in his paintings of this period formal elements similar to those in the *Tubutsch* illustrations. This important shift in the artist's painting style is accompanied by the introduction of a new iconography. Some of Kokoschka's stylistically most advanced works from this period are small paintings with religious themes—*Knight, Death and Maiden, Flight into Egypt,* and *Crucifixion,* all done in 1911—and they share similar formal properties in varying degrees; the diamond faceting of the *Tubutsch* illustrations is here translated into paint. Kokoschka's tendency toward experimentation with the imagery and form of his art during the 1910–1912 period resulted in an oeuvre which was partly unresolved and, ultimately, unsatisfactory in the context of his innate tendency toward a more intuitive, expressive style.

Cycles: The Fettered Columbus, The Chinese Wall, Bach Cantata

In 1912, important events in Kokoschka's personal life produced a significant shift in his artistic development. In that year Kokoschka met Alma Mahler, the widow of the prominent Viennese composer and conductor, Gustav Mahler, who died in 1911. Already a leading light in Viennese society at the time of their meeting, she was much admired for her strength of personality, beauty and intelligence. In contrast, Kokoschka's talent and personality were still evolving. He had achieved a degree of notoriety and grudging acceptance of his work in Vienna and, more generously, in Berlin.

The affair, at times exhilarating, more often torturous and violent, lasted for nearly three years and left a profound impression on both participants.

. . . the redefinition of the man-woman theme in an intensely personal context.

The main immediate result of this liaison was to reintroduce a sense of focus into Kokoschka's art. This new direction was in part, iconographic—the redefinition of the man-woman theme in an intensely personal context. The most complete manifestation of this theme can be seen in a series of graphic cycles of 1913–1914, such as Karl Kraus's *Die Chinesische Mauer (The Chinese Wall), Der Gefesselte Kolumbus (The Fettered Columbus),* both of 1913, and *Bachkantate (Bach Cantata)* of 1914. In each of these the main protagonists are primarily Alma Mahler and Kokoschka himself. In the above cycles we also see a stylistic shift away from works like the drawings for *Murderer, Hope of Women* and illustrations for *Tubutsch* to a softer, more "painterly" technique. The artist addressed this point thoughtfully and completely in a 1966 interview:

> The difference in style comes from the technique I adopted in each series. I made preparatory drawings with a very fine pen for the *Murderer, The Hope of Women* illustrations, and the result was a sharp, incisive line. The contours of the figures consequently stand out against the white of the paper. In the later series I used lithographic chalks which permit a more painterly treatment of the theme. With this technique more depends on the contrasts between black and white and on the various intermediate tones which you can achieve when you work in chalk. It is possible to get the various tones between black and

> white even without using color. These "color values" are enormously important for me, of course, for they are vital to my conception of space, the advancing and becoming clearer, the gradual disappearing, turning to yellow, turning to white . . . It was for this reason that I took up lithography, because it permitted me to draw colorfully what *I* felt, without using color—just with black and tonal values.[15]

This observation emphasizes the artist's predisposition toward black-and-white lithography which is, in fact, the dominant, if not exclusive, form of expression throughout his career. Only rarely will Kokoschka introduce multiple colors in his prints—a process which he found technically too confining: "It would hamper my imagination and spontaneity."[16]

During the first years of the century, the print had become a significant form of expression for many avant-garde artists, especially the Germans. It is, therefore, worth reflecting on the different attitudes toward the medium of a group like *Die Brücke* in comparison with Kokoschka:

> As the members [of *Die Brücke*] became more interested in the [print] medium, their style developed beyond its origins in Jugendstil; they took up etching and lithography in addition to woodcut, and they devised for themselves a range of techniques and styles of unprecedented originality and remarkable ambition. Their works are . . .the center of any history of twentieth-century printmaking, and one of the turning points in the history of the medium.[17]

Such generous and essentially valid observations taken from the recent exhibition catalogue, *The Print in Germany 1880–1933,* cannot be made for Kokoschka's graphic oeuvre. It is fairer to say that Kokoschka's prints made more of a contribution to the development of expressionism in general than they did to the history of the print medium. In technique, Kokoschka's prints break no new ground and, as mentioned, are limited almost exclusively to lithographs. His choice of lithography is at least in part related to a lack of interest in the technical niceties of printmaking. For him, lithography was the most direct and unencumbering of the various possibilities that printmaking presented, and one which was closely aligned to drawing. Since at the core of Kokoschka's expressionism is impulse and spontaneity—a rush to put down things imagined—he searched out the most direct method of accomplishing this.

. . . at the core of Kokoschka's expressionism is impulse and spontaneity—a rush to put down things imagined . . .

In fact, the three above mentioned cycles are a result of different impulses. The eight lithographs of *The Chinese Wall* of 1913 illustrate a story by Karl Kraus written in 1910 in which the author portrays in vivid imagery the murder of a white woman in the Chinese quarter. Kraus uses this single event to probe the differences between eastern and western mores, and in the process exposes the latter's pervasive stultifying hypocrisy.

The Fettered Columbus of 1913, a series of twelve illustrations, is linked to Kokoschka's recent past and to his present liaison with Alma Mahler. Accompanying the scenes is a text nearly identical to that written by the artist in 1908–1909, entitled *Der Weisser Tiertöter (The White Animal Slayer).* There also exists a close link between the scenes and Kokoschka's play *Der Brennende Dorbusch (The Burning Bush),* written in 1911 and published in 1913. In the latter two works Kokoschka addresses the man-woman theme, and thus, in delving back to such imagery in the present illustrations, he emphasizes the renewed significance which this subject acquires for him in the context of the new relationship.

The culminating point of Kokoschka's early development as a graphic artist is *Bach Cantata* of 1914, a series of eleven lithographs, which was first published in 1916–1917. Universally accepted as Kokoschka's greatest achievement in the graphic medium, the illustrations, according to the artist's own testimony, are a response to the words rather than to the music of the *Cantata.* Here Kokoschka and his lover take the roles of Fear and Hope, the major characters in the *Cantata,* and alternate from scene to scene in their identification with one or the other.

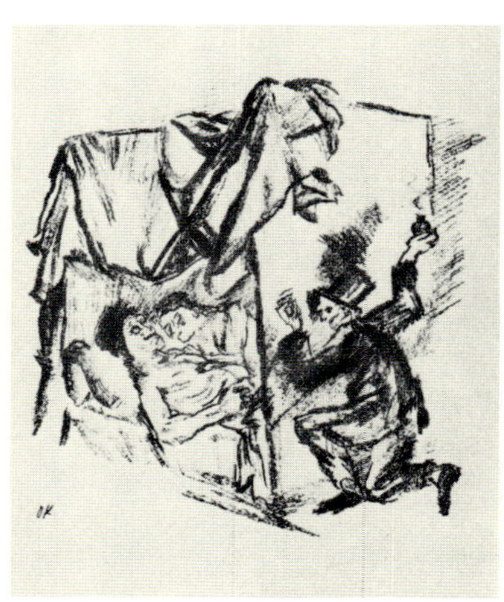

Fig. 8 *The Eavesdropper,* 1914 (WW 41)

The rich complexity of interaction among Kokoschka's graphic works, the writings which they accompany plus his paintings reaches a new level of cohesion in the above cycles and is further enhanced by the artist's conscious assimilation of sources which reflect his stylistic and iconographic concern.

For instance, the important scene in *The Chinese Wall,* "The Eavesdropper" (Figure 8), depicts Kokoschka and Alma Mahler, side by side in bed, seen naked from the waist up. Two tall partitions define the bed over which is a canopy of loosely flung draperies. Behind the partition at the foot of the bed is a kneeling figure of Death, dressed in black, top-hatted and visible to us but not to the lovers. It kneels on one knee and beckons with its left hand while in its right it holds what looks like a smoking bomb—the explosion of which will transport the two figures into the turbulent environment of *The Tempest,* (Figure 2) for which this scene serves as a major source.

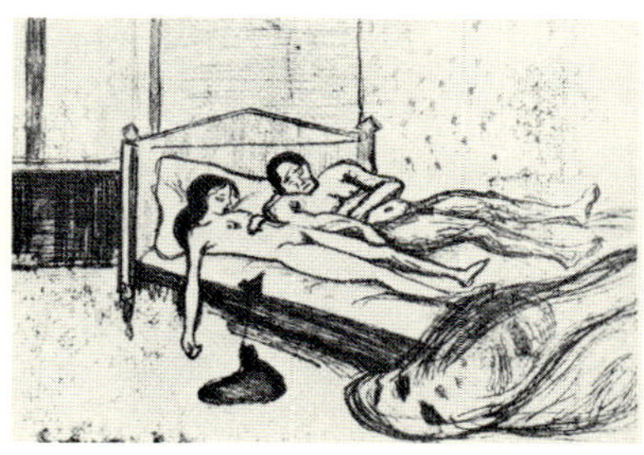

Fig. 9 Edvard Munch, *Dead Pair of Lovers,* etching, 1909

The passage in Kraus's story which comes closest to the above scene deals with the woman's murder in Chinatown as she searches for pleasure, is seduced by an opium-filled environment, "strangled by a yellow hand" and disposed of— "in this way she went from the blue canopy bed into a suitcase . . . and now the world smells of decay."[18] The tenor of Kokoschka's scene and Kraus's passage is reinforced by the likely source which inspired the artist, Munch's etching, *Todes Liebespaar (Dead Pair of Lovers)* of 1909 (Figure 9), in which a nude dead couple lie in bed, likely victims of a murder-suicide or double suicide. Munch's work, Kokoschka's scene which is based on it and the passage from Kraus all make explicit reference to violent death and, as such, introduce into our interpretation of Kokoschka's seminal painting the strong likelihood that in *The Tempest* the artist does not address the issue of the unification of the two lovers but dwells instead on the torturous, even violent, dissolution of that union.[19]

To enhance the exotic, haunting quality of Kraus's story, Kokoschka turns to yet another artist who shares with Munch a visual and psychological intensity—Francisco Goya. Elements of the latter's suite of etchings, *Los Caprichos (The Caprices)* of

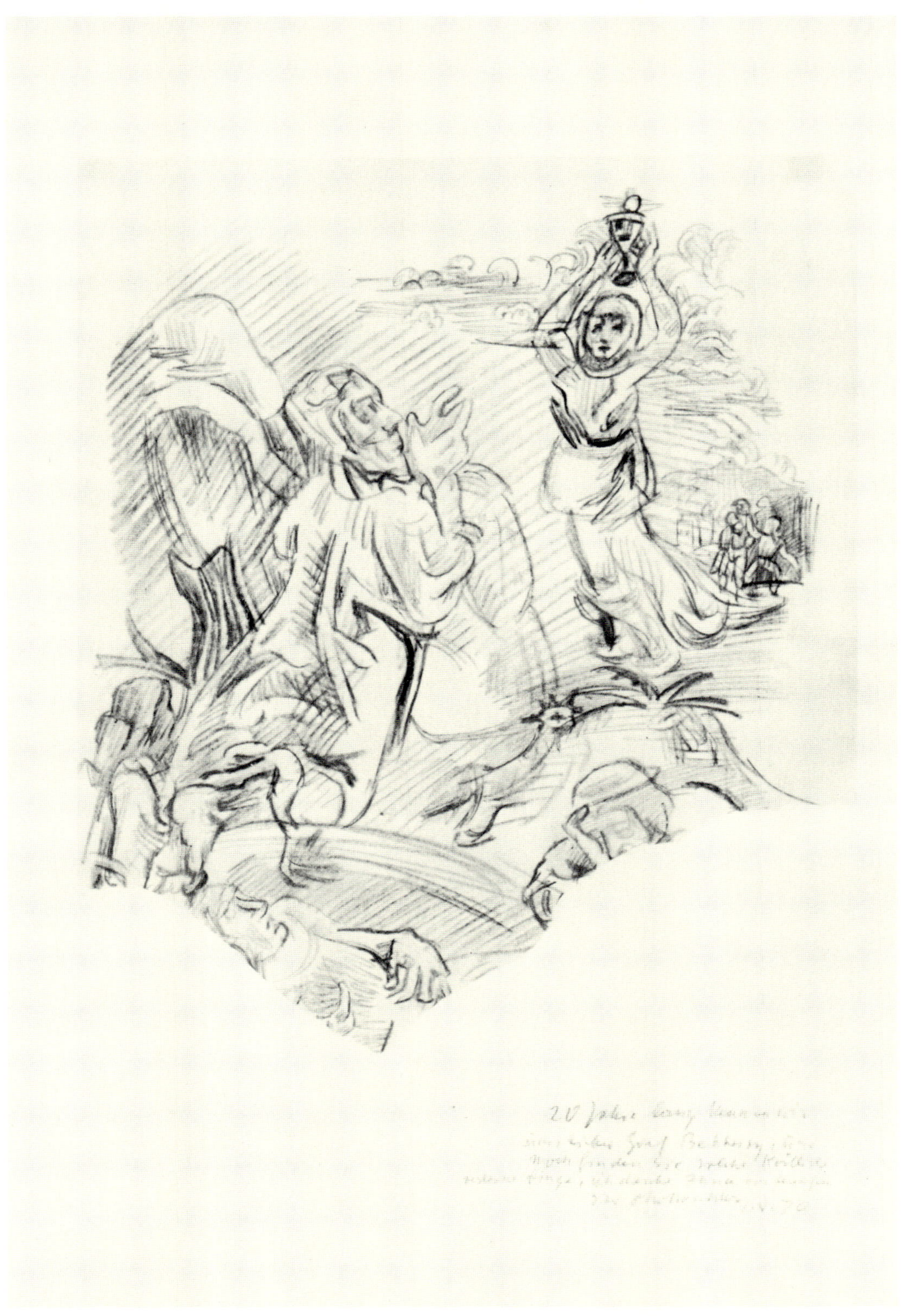

Cat. 180 *The Agony in the Garden*, 1916

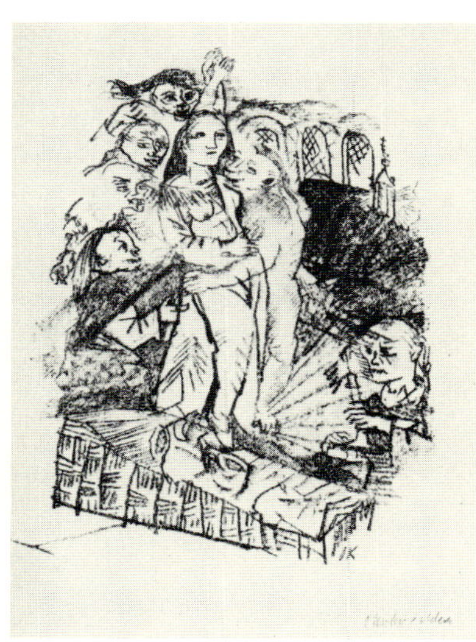

Fig. 10 *Woman Desired by Man*, 1914 (WW 40)

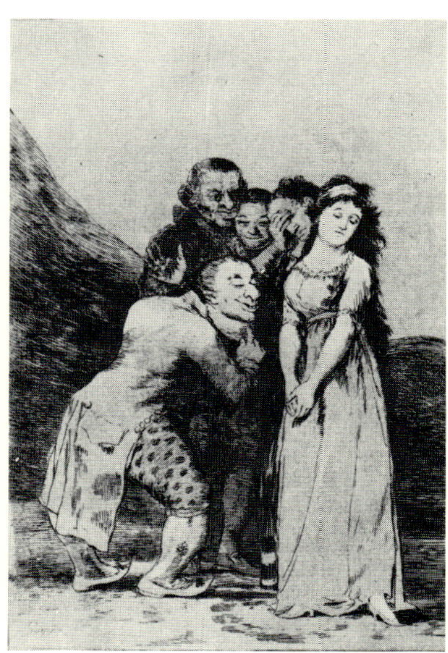

Fig. 11 Francesco Goya, *Qué Sacrificio!*, etching, 1799

1799, were assimilated by Kokoschka into certain of his scenes—the most direct example of which is the sixth scene of the cycle, "Woman Desired by Man" (Figure 10), with the fourteenth plate of *Los Caprichos*, "Qué Sacrificio" (What Sacrifice) (Figure 11). In both, a standing woman becomes an object of desire of a group of leering men that crowd around her. In another scene from *The Chinese Wall*, "The Intruders" (WW 42),* Kokoschka creates a pyramid of haunting, threatening grotesques which is derived from Goya's nightmarish painting, *The Sorcery that Failed* of 1798. In both borrowings Kokoschka not only repeats the general compositional elements of Goya's works but, more importantly, responds to Goya's unique and psychologically penetrating vision.

Alma Mahler's recollection of the inception of *The Fettered Columbus* cycle is almost anecdotal, relating to a film about Columbus that both had seen in Munich in 1912. Kokoschka places the work in a heroic, symbolic context:

> Columbus Bound is me again, of course, and in this sense the title is symbolic—bound by a woman whose features I have depicted on the title-page. My Columbus ventures out not to discover America but to recognize a woman who binds him in chains.[20]

The above assessment by the artist of *The Fettered Columbus* emphasizes the central role it plays in explicating his relationship at this time. The three scenes which exemplify this most fully explore the tense, unresolved sexual nature of the liaison.

In "Man and Woman in a Candle-Lit Room" (Figure 12), the couple are depicted in a room facing an open window beyond which is a crescent moon. She is seated on a bed and he stands behind her. His right hand reaches out as if to caress her while his left, raised to the face, seems to pull back, possibly shielding his anxious, frightened face from the light emanating from the candle and the moon. He is in a tense, suspended state placed in the shaded area of the dramatically lit room while she is bathed in light—calm, even smiling, as she gestures with her hands to both the candle and the moon, as if initiating him into her mysteries. The scene, charged with tension, revolves around the immortal and sensual nature of woman and man's ambivalent response to it.

In another scene, "The Apple of Eve" (Figure 13), the two are on either side of a table within a landscape with hills and trees in the distance. The ubiquitous symbol of woman, the crescent moon, hovers above. She, Alma-Eve, sits and with her outstretched right hand offers the apple to the kneeling supplicant. With his left hand he is about to take the fruit while with the right hand he touches his face near the eye in an anxious gesture similar to that in the previous scene. Here too, the artist shows himself in a tense, as yet unresolved, moment, although the inevitability of the outcome is all too clear. Considering the subject—a highly personal translation of the temptation story—the scene is curiously devoid of the dramatic tension of other scenes where the artist deploys a strong use of light and shade. There is a detail here which even further

*WW = Wingler/Welz. Kokoschka, Das druckgraphische Werk. Salzburg, Galerie Welz. Vol. I, 1975; Vol. II, 1981.

diffuses the confrontational nature of the event—on Eve's left shoulder is perched a small dog, possibly a Pekingese—which is not immediately evident, first, because of Kokoschka's loose, gestural mode of execution and, second, because it is such an unexpected element within this context. The scene seems to have a bit of wit and play-acting about it, as the two address each other with elaborate gestures. In perhaps the most successful of the illustrations, "The Meeting" (Figure 14), the two once again confront each other—here in a mountainous landscape. She is nude and facing us as well as him. He is seen from a three-quarter back view, his lower body draped. With his right hand he unfurls the drapery and exposes his nudity before her. Thus the dialogue between them revolves around their sexual nature and alludes again to the Adam-Eve context. Much as in the scene from *The Dreaming Youths*, "The Girl Li and I," where the two alternately share a predicament and yet are also separate, so in "The Meeting," there seems to exist both an attempt at union and also a curious distancing of the two. They are engaged in a tantalizing, dance-like ritual which echoes and intensifies the similar encounters of pairs strutting through eighteenth-century love scenes by artists like Watteau. The rationale for the temptation is here more explicitly addressed.

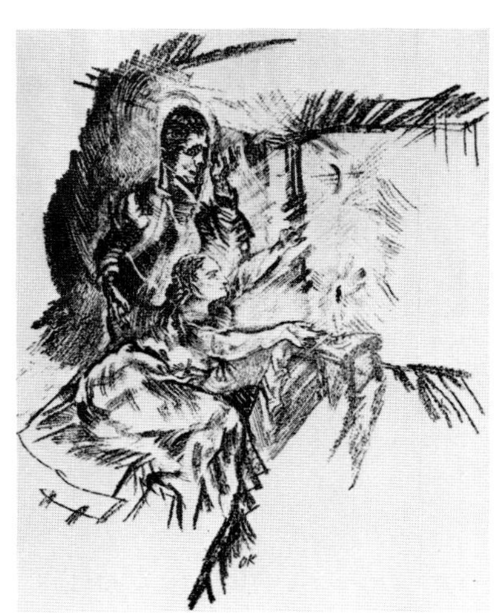

Fig. 12 *Man and Woman in a Candle-Lit Room*, 1914 (WW 47)

It is in this context that the general affinity between "The Meeting" and Albrecht Dürer's engraving of *Adam and Eve* (Figure 15) of 1504 not only aids our understanding of Kokoschka's scene but also demonstrates the artist's ability to absorb from a single source ideas which he will apply to other works.

The Dürer print would in fact have yet another important and specific impact on Kokoschka's imagery of those years—in the pivotal painting, *Still-life with Cat, Rabbit and Child* (Figure 16) of 1914. The two major protagonists, placed in the center of the composition, are the cat and rabbit, representing Kokoschka and Alma Mahler respectively. The unusual juxtaposition of these two animals in the painting is a highly symbolic one in the context of Kokoschka's personal, hermetic imagery, and may in part be explained by its correspondence to a detail in the Dürer print where, in the lower foreground, we see, among other animals, a dominant presence of a cat and rabbit in a similar relationship to one another as they are in the painting. Here the link to Dürer is made that much more explicit since the rabbit in the painting is based on his famous watercolor of a rabbit of 1502. The meaning of the *Still-life with Cat, Rabbit and Child* is a complex one and deals with some of the more desolate moments in Kokoschka's affair with Alma Mahler—the abortion of their child, an event which contributed critically to the ultimate dissolution of the relationship and which explains the prominent presence of the infant at the extreme left in the painting.[21]

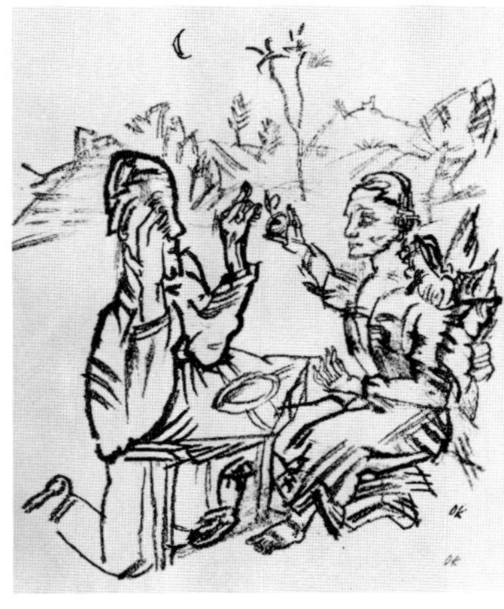

Fig. 13 *The Apple of Eve*, 1914 (WW 48)

Kokoschka's lifelong admiration of Dürer goes beyond the assimilation of certain sources from the German artist, as consistent and significant as this was. Nor was Kokoschka necessarily influenced by Dürer's extraordinary technical achievements in the print medium. He saw in Dürer primarily an artist who, like himself, was willing to investigate all aspects of experience—from probing portraiture to landscape—and who, as well, created an intensified, visionary image of the world in which the elevated and the terrifying often coexisted and helped to define the human condition.

And especially later in Kokoschka's career, when the Mediterranean world had a strong claim on his imagination, he began to appreciate even more fully Dürer's role as an artist who, in spanning the gap between northern art and that of the south, was able to create a more universal pictorial language.

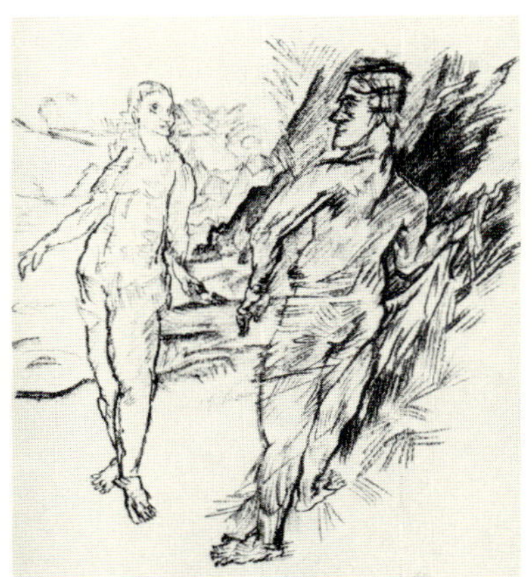

Fig. 14 *The Meeting*, 1914 (WW 51)

In all three cycles, then, Kokoschka deals with the man-woman equation and, as such, continues the development of themes begun in his earlier dramas and illustrations. Of the three, *The Chinese Wall* and *The Fettered Columbus* are closer to the earlier works, not only in a chronological sense, having been executed earlier, but thematically as well. The exotic, lugubrious context of Kraus's *The Chinese Wall* is replete with sexual themes which the artist eagerly explores in the context of his new relationship. *The Fettered Columbus*, as already stated, aligns itself explicitly with texts of Kokoschka's earlier works while the artist's protagonist in the illustrations is Alma Mahler. In both cycles, then, Kokoschka attempts to define his new liaison with Alma Mahler in the context of themes which he had already codified in his art.

In this important sense, *Bach Cantata* is different. In it, Kokoschka elevates the predicament of the protagonists from one which is mutually inflicted, as in the two earlier cycles, to one into which both of the participants are thrust and to which both must respond, by and large, together. It is a view of the Adam and Eve of Paradise Lost. As already mentioned, Fear and Hope, the two major characters of the *Cantata*, are, alternately, man and woman—thus Kokoschka and Alma Mahler. If we, for example, compare such scenes as "Woman Guides Man" (Figure 17), relating to the cantata text, "Oh weary road to life's last struggle," with "The Meeting" from *The Fettered Columbus*, we see in the former the image of man and woman after the fall, as the two striding, clothed figures remind us of numerous representations of the expulsion from Eden. "The Meeting" scene still clearly posits man and woman in paradise, much as they are in "The Girl Li and I" illustration from *The Dreaming Youths*.

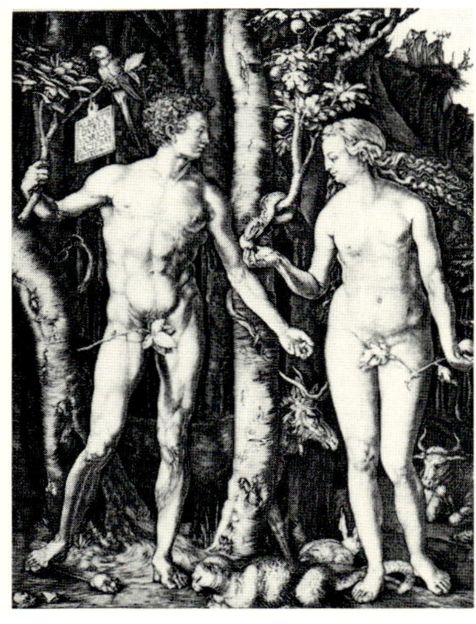

Fig. 15 Albrecht Dürer, *Adam and Eve*, engraving, 1504

Another scene from *Bach Cantata*, "Male and Female Nudes in a Landscape" (WW 63), refers to the words of the cantata: "My last resting place terrifies me." Here the two are shown resting, anxious, and pondering their fate, sharing in their predicament rather than orchestrating it. Their ultimate goal, the mountain in the background with the sun miraculously reflecting in front of rather than behind it, intensifies the couple's dilemma. Kokoschka spoke eloquently of this series and of the significance of the mountain in it:

> The central motive is the mountain, first seen from afar, swimming in light, luring the wanderers and again disappearing before their eyes, like a mere reflection changing into an arid conglomerate of rock and falling stone when the pilgrims reach their goal, a hole under its summit where man is to be buried.[22]

The dominant scene from the cycle is "The Man Raises his Head from the Grave on which the Woman is Seated" (Figure 18). Kokoschka's head, with his hands on either

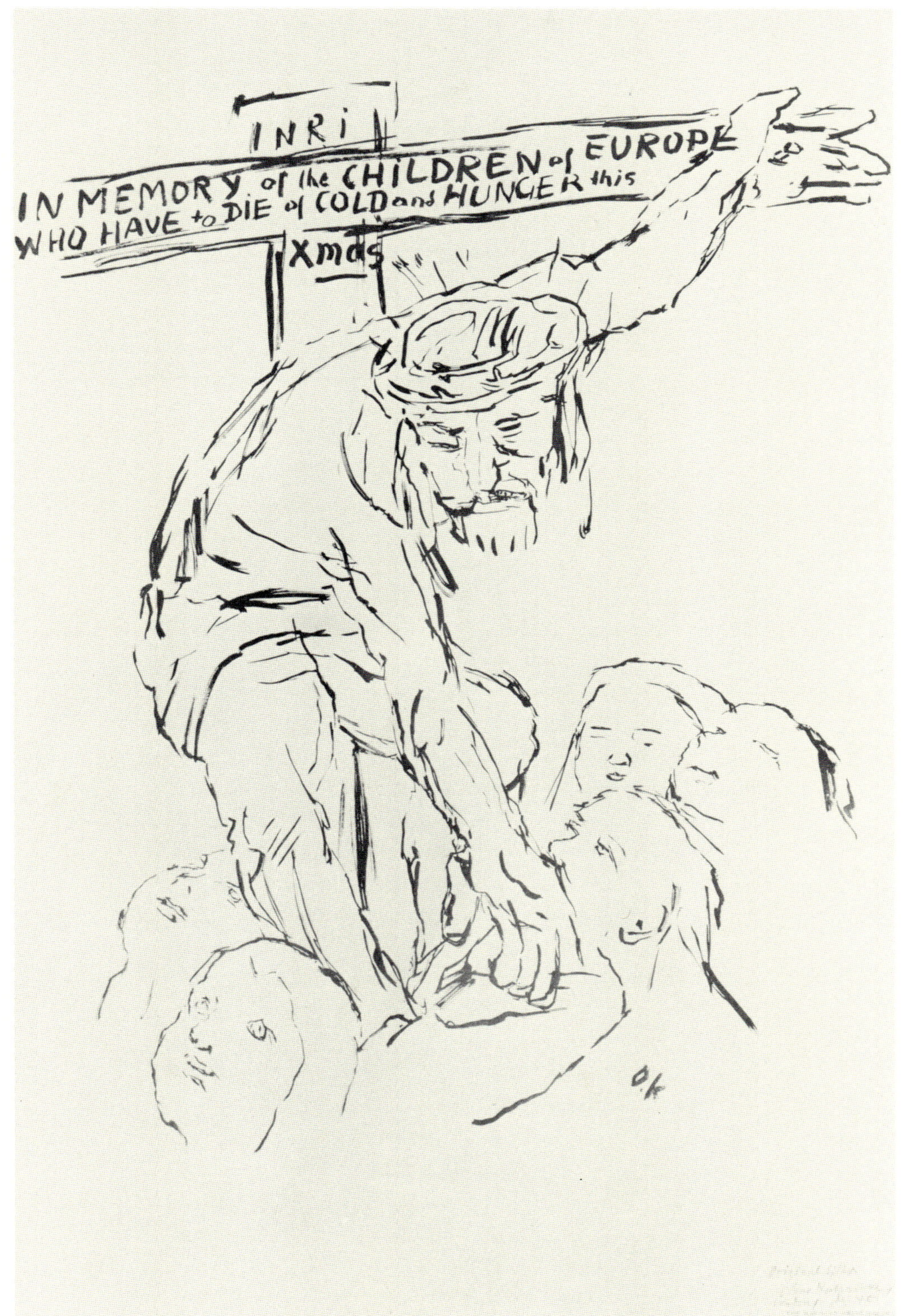

Cat. 49 *Christ Helping the Starving Children*, 1945–46 (WW 180)

side, peers up out of the grave in the lower foreground. Surrounding the two is an expansive landscape. Culminating the composition are the female-male symbols of a crescent moon and, on the horizon, the sun. In comparison to a scene from *The Fettered Columbus*, "Woman Strides Triumphantly over the Dead Man's Bier" (WW 53), where the notion of the triumph of one sex over the other is explicit, in the present scene, there is a lack of sexual tension between the two, even as the artist addresses the question of their sexual identity. The woman, seated on a grave rather than being in it, symbolizes her immortal nature—a condition which Kokoschka established in his earliest works. Yet by being on the grave close to the man, she shares in his predicament. The expression on her face is questioning and melancholy, and her right hand reaches down toward him. Significantly, the features of the woman's face here least resemble those of Alma Mahler. Kokoschka's later assessment of his dilemma shown in the scene lays the blame on fate and on himself: "I am in the grave slain by my own jealousy, like Hyacinthus by the discus that a treacherous fate turned back upon him."[23]

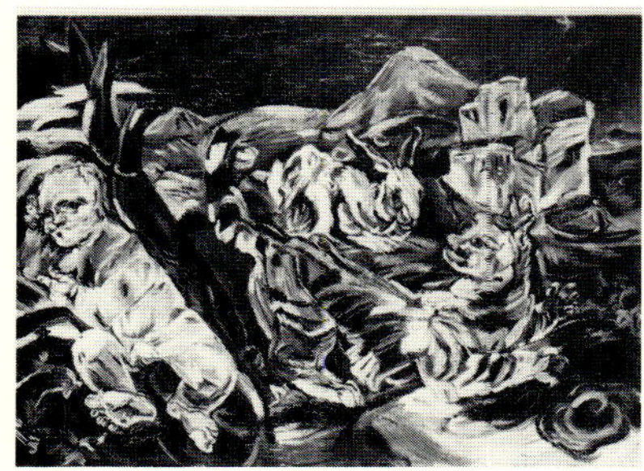

Fig. 16 *Still-Life with Cat, Rabbit and Child*, 1914

In a preparatory drawing for the lithograph, the artist included on the grave an inscription from Dante's *Divine Comedy* which is traditionally found on gravestones: "Lasciate ogni speranza/che voi entrate" (Leave all hope, you who enter). Kokoschka omits the dour epitaph in the print and thus opens to interpretation the scene's meaning which is, in fact, associated with a hopeful passage from the cantata: "I shall exist in bliss from now on."

The artist in the grave is not dead—the uplifted hands may be interpreted as the initial gesture of his rebirth. The sun in the background may be seen as a rising sun, most often associated with Resurrection scenes. If the head initiates artistic creative impulses, then the hands are the tools through which they are translated into visual reality. Through his creative power man will be reborn. It is precisely at this time and in this cycle that Kokoschka depicts himself in a self-portrait (Figure 19) in an explicit, not symbolic, act of creating in which his hands actively participate in establishing his artistic identity as his eyes search out intently his inner vision.

The *Bach Cantata* represents a new stylistic and thematic language in Kokoschka's art. The human form and its setting is rendered with a bold, powerful use of light and dark which enhances the visual intensity of the image and thus its emotional impact on the viewer. In the guise of Fear and Hope, it is the human spirit that is attempting to redefine itself in the context of a new, harsher reality outside Eden's gates. The cycle aspires to a monumentality of form and grandeur of spirit which point to such seminal works as *The Tempest*.

Allos Makar, The Passion, Job

The years that followed the completion of the above cycles proved to be pivotal ones for Kokoschka. While the affair with Alma Mahler was coming to an end, the artist joined a prestigious cavalry regiment at the outset of 1915 and went off to war—as if searching for an alternative condition which was also replete with danger

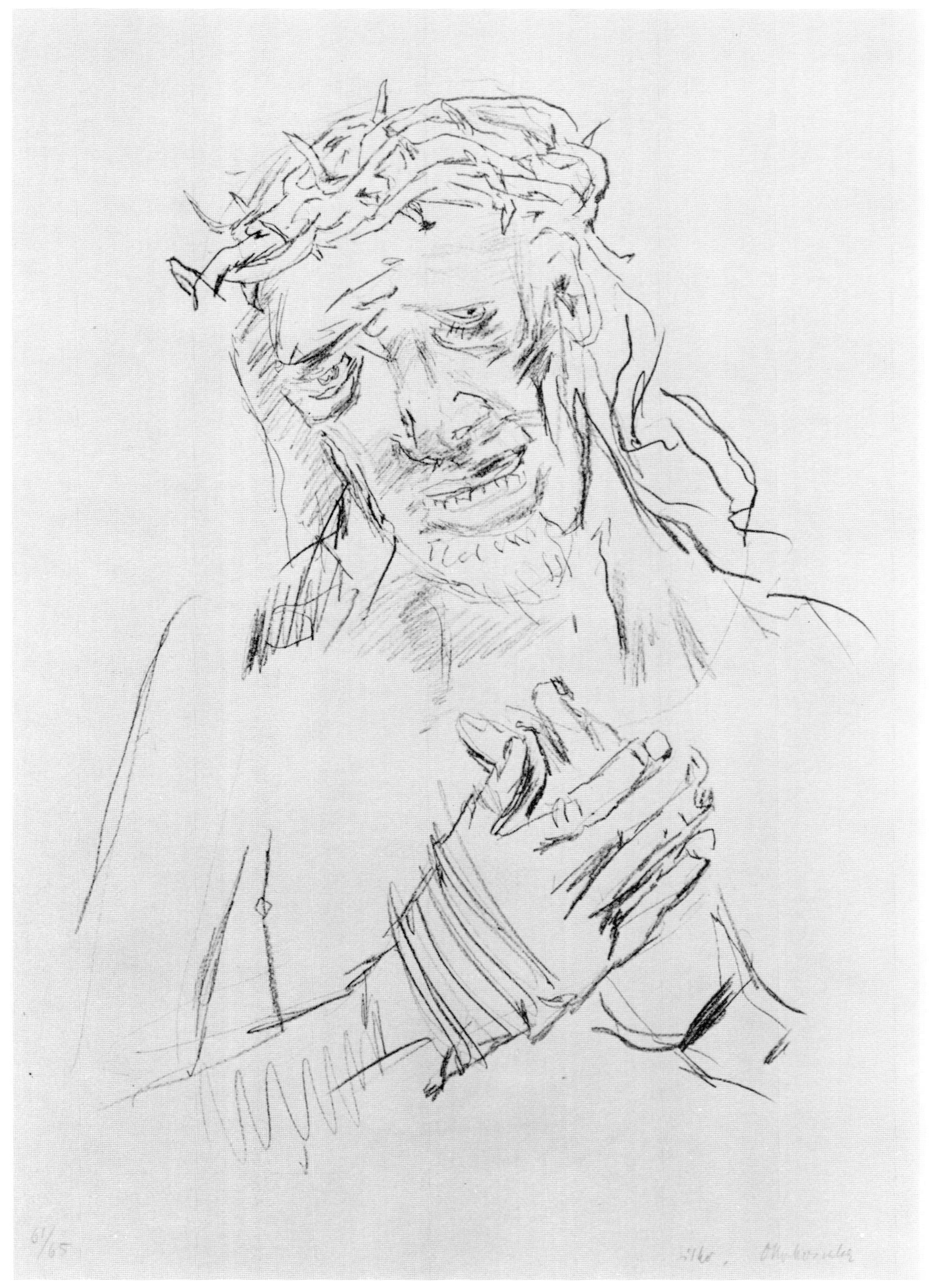

Cat. 59 *Christ Crowned with Thorns*, 1956

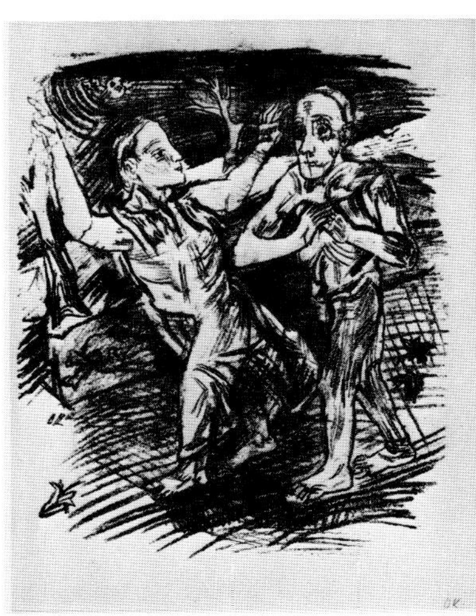

Fig. 17 *Woman Guides Man*, 1914 (WW 61)

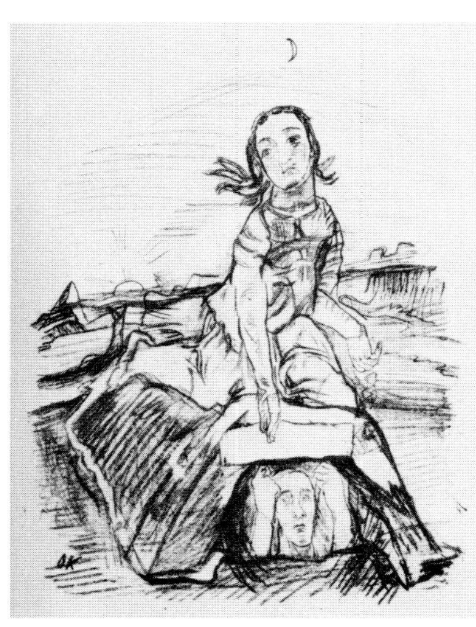

Fig. 18 *The Man Raises His Head from the Grave on Which the Woman is Seated*, 1914 (WW 67)

and excitement. Later that year, Kokoschka was severely wounded on the Galician front; and, after a period of recuperation, he moved for further convalescence to Dresden in 1917. There he established a rapport with the city's intellectuals, many of whose portraits he rendered—some in oil but also, and especially, as lithographs. In 1919, he became a professor at the Dresden Academy where he taught until 1923—only to leave abruptly and without an explanation.

This period of Kokoschka's life was rich in creativity and accomplishment. For example, Paul Westheim's book on the artist came out in 1918—the second book to be published on him in five years. Interwoven through these years was the painful and lingering aftereffect of his relationship with Alma Mahler. Already in June of 1915, the artist published in the Munich-based *Zeit-Echo* a poem along with five lithographs under the title *Allos Makar*, a near anagram for their combined first names which also translates from Greek "something else is happy." The poem, written in 1913, is a bittersweet reflection upon the torturous nature of their futile struggle in which the artist senses its eventual dissolution. In the major scene of the series, "Sun Over a Birdlike Pair" (Cat. 25),* the two winged creatures have the facial features of Kokoschka and Mahler as they confront each other in a craggy, mountainous environment each holding a worm in the mouth, reflecting a passage in the poem:

> One looks at the other's eminence fearfully. And one lost power because of the other. And now the worm wriggles out from shrieking beaks.

The poem concludes:

> The lips laugh at deceptive repose,
> "Something else is happy."[24]

In its setting and confrontational nature the illustration echoes works such as Ingres' *Oedipus and the Sphinx* of 1808 and its many transformations among symbolist artists like Gustave Moreau and, later, Fernand Khnopff. Yet the primary source for the winged creatures in Kokoschka's work is to be found in Goya, to whom the artist had turned earlier in his illustrations of Kraus's *The Chinese Wall*. In the nineteenth plate of the *Los Caprichos* suite of 1799, titled "Todos Caerán" (All Will Fall) (Figure 20), Goya includes half-human, half-bird creatures similar to those in the above poem illustration and also set in a sexually taunting context.

Kokoschka focuses once more on the affair in his deeply personal drama based on the legendary lovers *Orpheus and Eurydice*. The play was written in part while the artist, recuperating from war wounds, was still in a state of high tension. The few inconclusive illustrations for it are among Kokoschka's rare experiments in etching—a medium he found too confining. The drama itself is a deeply revealing one in which, in the context of the ancient legend, the artist reflects on the nature of the affair and the reason for its dissolution. In the initial stages Kokoschka adheres to the original story but then in the second act introduces a scene in which Eurydice aborts their child. This personal inclusion, not found in the original, refers to one of the most difficult moments of his relationship with Alma Mahler and one of the precipitating events for

*Refer to catalogue entries (p. 97) for page number of illustrations.

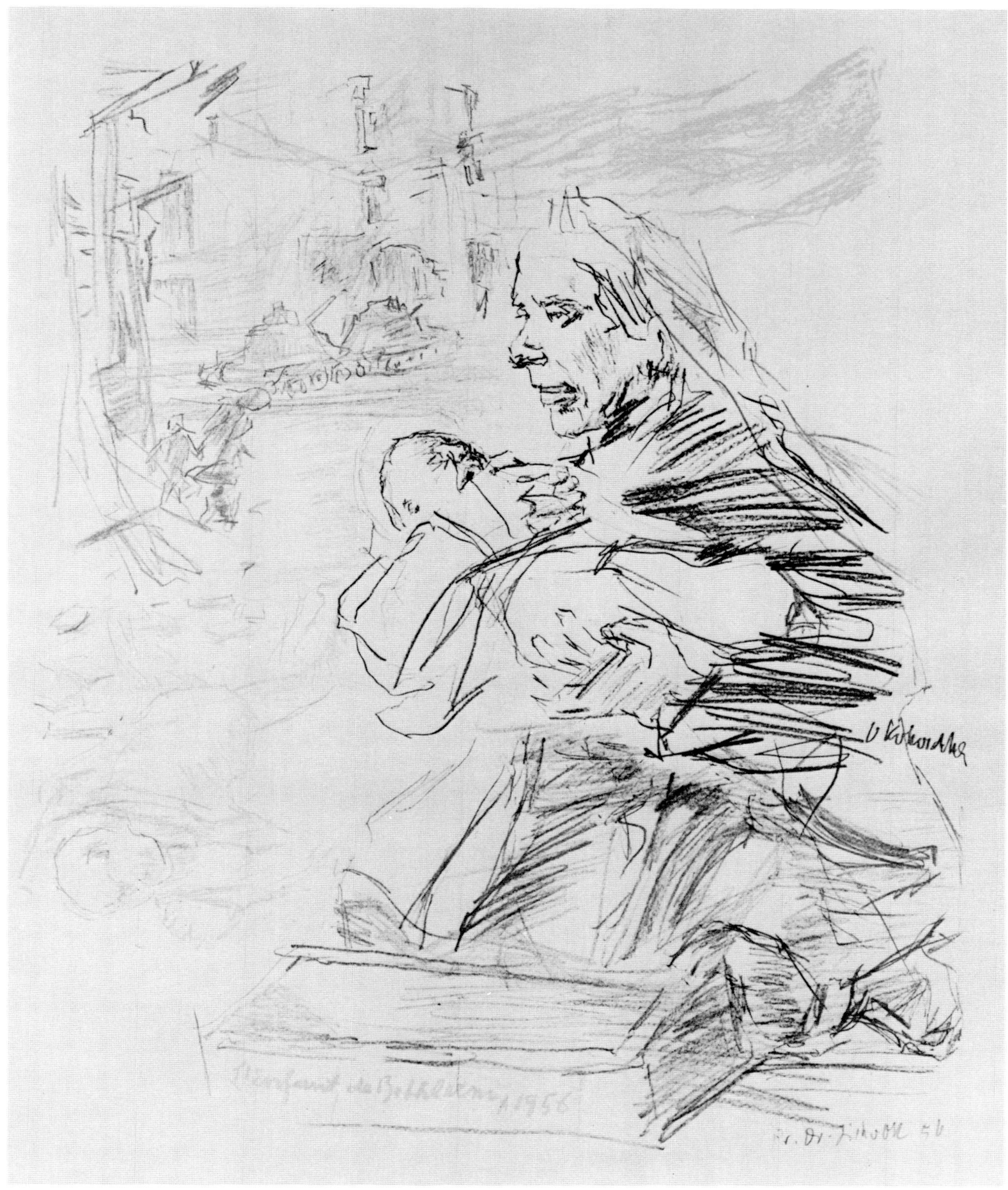

Cat. 58 *L'Enfant de Bethléem*, 1956

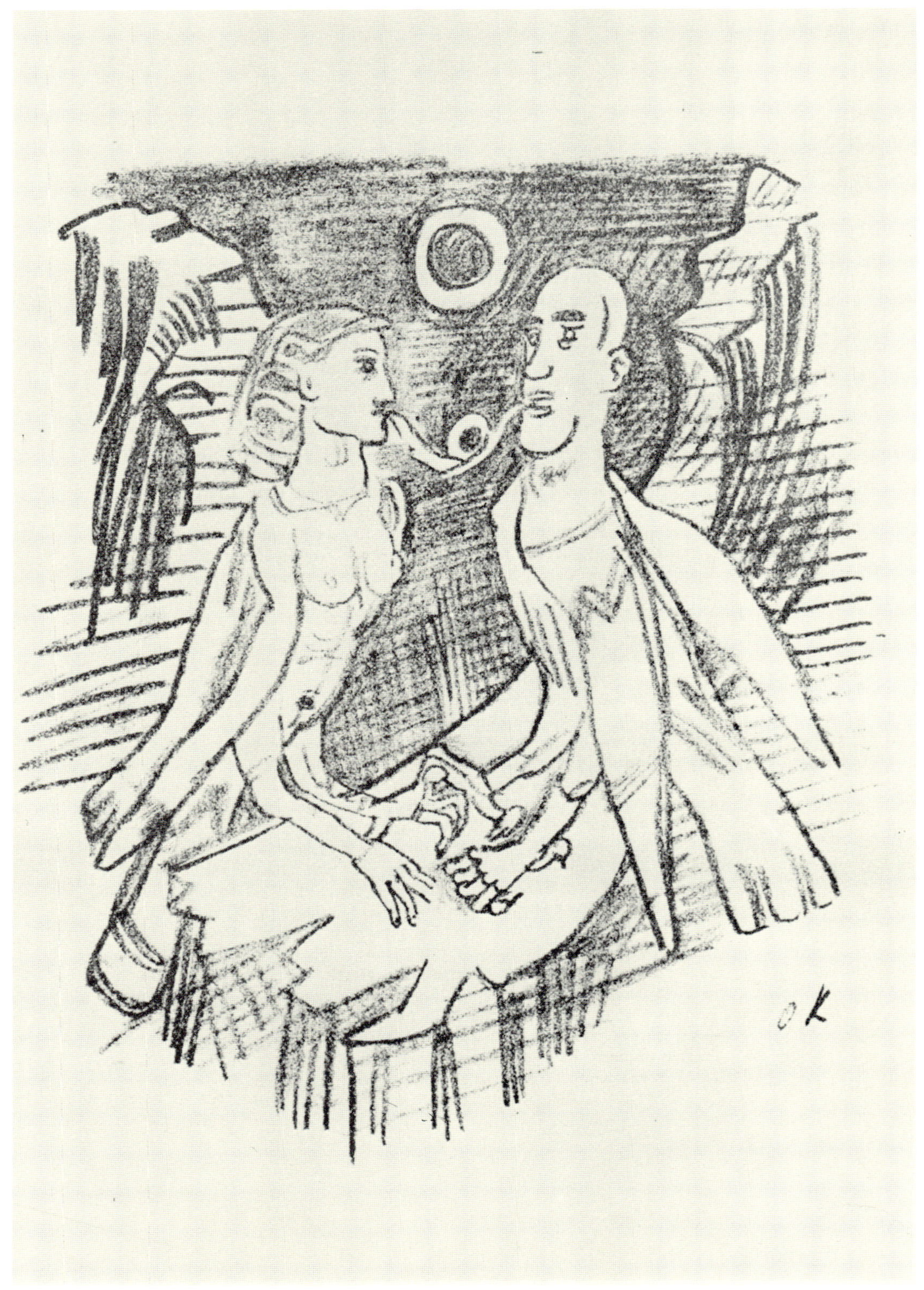

Cat. 25 *Sun Over a Birdlike Pair,* 1914

its eventual termination.

In 1917, Kokoschka turned his attention to a reworking of an earlier play, *Sphinx und Strohmann (Sphinx and Strawman)* of 1907. The result was *Hiob (Job),* a play which had its première in Dresden on July 3, 1917. In it the artist reinvestigates a group of characters he introduced in the earlier work and to whom he gives new identities. They are among Kokoschka's most fanciful protagonists—full of verbal and visual puns—like the main character, Job, whose head has been "turned by a woman" so that it is on backwards, not allowing him to see Anima's (she is the woman principal) indiscretions with Mr. Rubberman, the sly, demonic seducer.

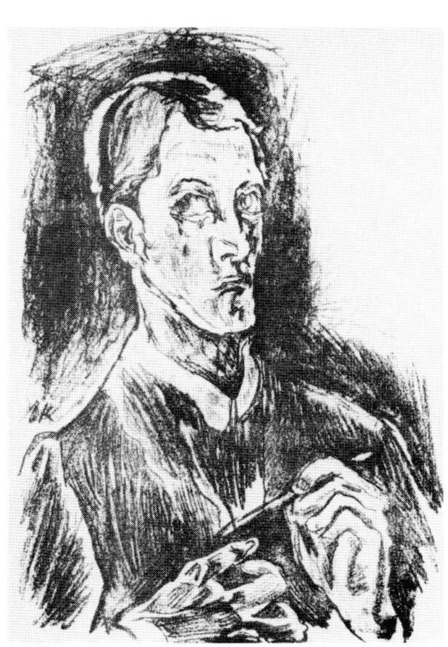

Fig. 19 *Self-Portrait with a Drawing Crayon,* 1914 (WW 58)

In the final analysis, *Job* is a profoundly ironic, cynical assessment of the conflict between man and woman which certainly reflects Kokoschka's by now bitter recollection of his relationship with Alma Mahler. Significant in this context is the fact that soon after Kokoschka had enlisted into the service, Alma Mahler married Walter Gropius, the renowned architect, with whom she had been seriously and secretly involved even while still seeing the artist. Man as cuckold plays a central role in the above play.

Kokoschka produced a suite of fourteen lithographs for *Job* which, if not achieving the high level of the three cycles considered earlier, are nevertheless compelling evidence of the continued strength of his graphic imagery. The style of the illustrations is rather dense and compact, using an ample, undulating line to emphasize the figures' exaggerated and grotesque features. Many of the scenes have about them a sense of stage-set—so much so that Edith Hoffmann has drawn a parallel between them and the Yiddish theatre tradition.[25]

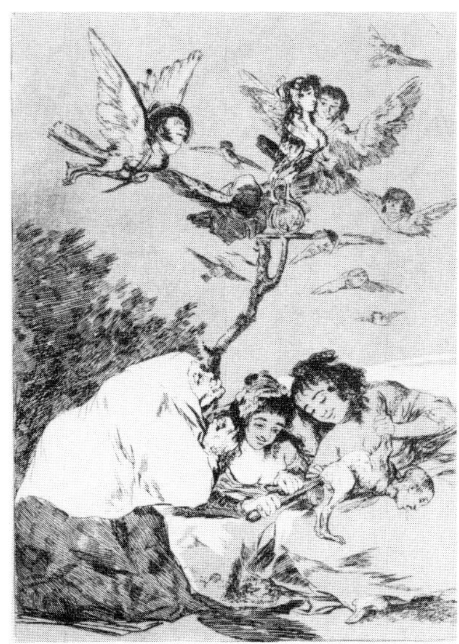

Fig. 20 Francesco Goya, *Todos Caerán,* etching, 1799

As the play itself refers to Kokoschka's earlier literary imagery, thus many of the illustrations in *Job* echo archetypes the artist has established in earlier works. In one of the visually more striking scenes, "Job with Antlers" (Figure 21), Kokoschka depicts Job on all fours with antlers growing out of his head—a poignant, melancholy transformation of the reindeer motif, often found in his early works, which he associated with the male principle. Anima is shown, falling from a window naked, about to "land with her buttock" on Job's antlers and thus kill him. The visual arrangement of a woman on top of a man who is on all fours, reinvestigates Kokoschka's treatment of the Phyllis and Aristotle story in one of the illustrations for Ehrenstein's *Tubutsch* and again in a scene for *The Chinese Wall,* (WW 36). In the latter two, man is also shown on all fours with woman "riding" on top of him—thus a visual and iconographic juxtaposition similar to the present scene. An even more direct reference to an earlier work is in the last image of the series, "Anima and Job" (WW 100). Job has just died—he is lying in the foreground, his head thrust forward. Next to him is the kneeling Anima, who places her foot on Job's neck as if to reconfirm her triumph. Behind them are a series of top-hatted mourners. The stark brutality of the scene represents in reverse the conflict in the drawing for *Murderer, Hope of Women* (Figure 6) where it is the man who plants his foot on the prostrate woman as they engage in a struggle for supremacy. In the earlier drawing there is, as in the *Job* lithographs, a group of figures in the background observing the scene. Through the prism of irony, then, Kokoschka explores in the *Job* scenes many of the same man-woman tensions of his earlier cycles, giving them here a wry grimace.

In 1916 Kokoschka produced a series of six lithographs with a religious subject, titled *Die Passion (The Passion)*, which was to have been part of a larger project. While they are similar in style to the *Job* illustrations, they lack the latter's sense of the grotesque and are, instead, imbued with a spirituality that is achieved by a dramatic use of light and dark which has been correctly associated with Rembrandt's religious prints. Iconographically, it may have been Dürer's *Great Passion* which inspired the artist in this project. According to Kokoschka's own testimony, they were produced as a direct result of the artist's revulsion to the carnage of the world war which he had personally experienced:

> . . . I was horrified by that aspect of human personality which made it possible for hundreds and thousands of men to stick bayonets into each other's bodies. I simply couldn't understand it, and this shock, this profound depression, this agony brought on by my fellow human beings was the experience which formed the background to the *Passion*. In this deeper sense, then, you can say that the various themes, the crowning of thorns, Christ on the Mount of Olives and so on, are connected with the profound shock I experienced in the First World War. I was badly wounded myself, of course.[26]

Kokoschka's reference above to "Christ on the Mount of Olives" (Cat. 27), focuses on one of the more unusual scenes in the cycle in which the artist otherwise treats the various moments in Christ's Passion in a straightforward fashion.

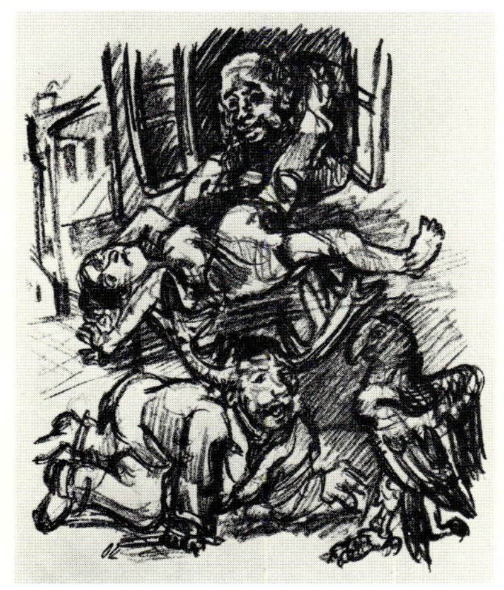

Fig. 21 *Job with Antlers*, 1916–17 (WW 97)

The above scene represents Christ on the left with an angel hovering above. At the right are two figures—the one on the extreme right bears close resemblance to the artist while the other thrusts an arm in front of and around the former in a gesture pointing to heaven. Dividing the two halves is a shape which, in the context of the scene, one wants to read as a rocky hill, but which looks more like a dark, draped partition that creates the critical contrast of light and dark between the two halves. In the division of the scene and placement of figures, Kokoschka seems to be evoking "The Eavesdropper" (Figure 8) from *The Chinese Wall*, where a figure of Death hides behind the partition from the two lovers. The present scene reverses the earlier image in nearly every respect—compositionally and iconographically, and in that sense Kokoschka may be addressing the new reality of his life. By his presence in a scene of Christ's suffering, the artist identifies himself with the predicament and reflects, as well, on his own state of vulnerability at this time. The explicitness of the connection with the suffering Christ is demonstrated in a drawing which Kokoschka executed in 1916, as a possible study for the *Passion* cycle, entitled "The Agony in the Garden," (Cat. 180) in which the features of the kneeling Christ are those of the artist. Kokoschka introduces this important archetype as early as 1910 when he represents himself in a poster for *Der Sturm*

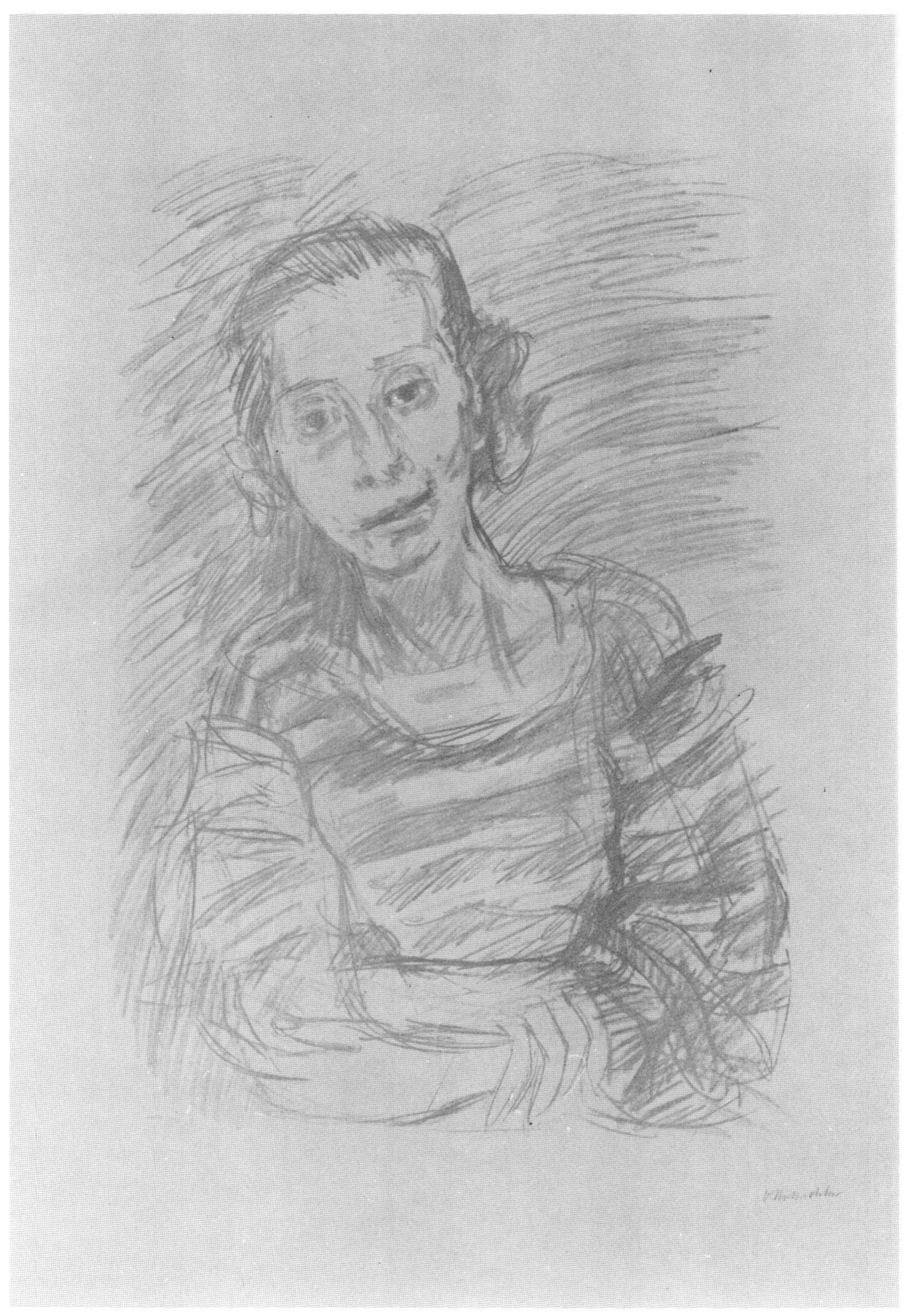

Cat. 41 *The Concert I (Naomi)*, 1920

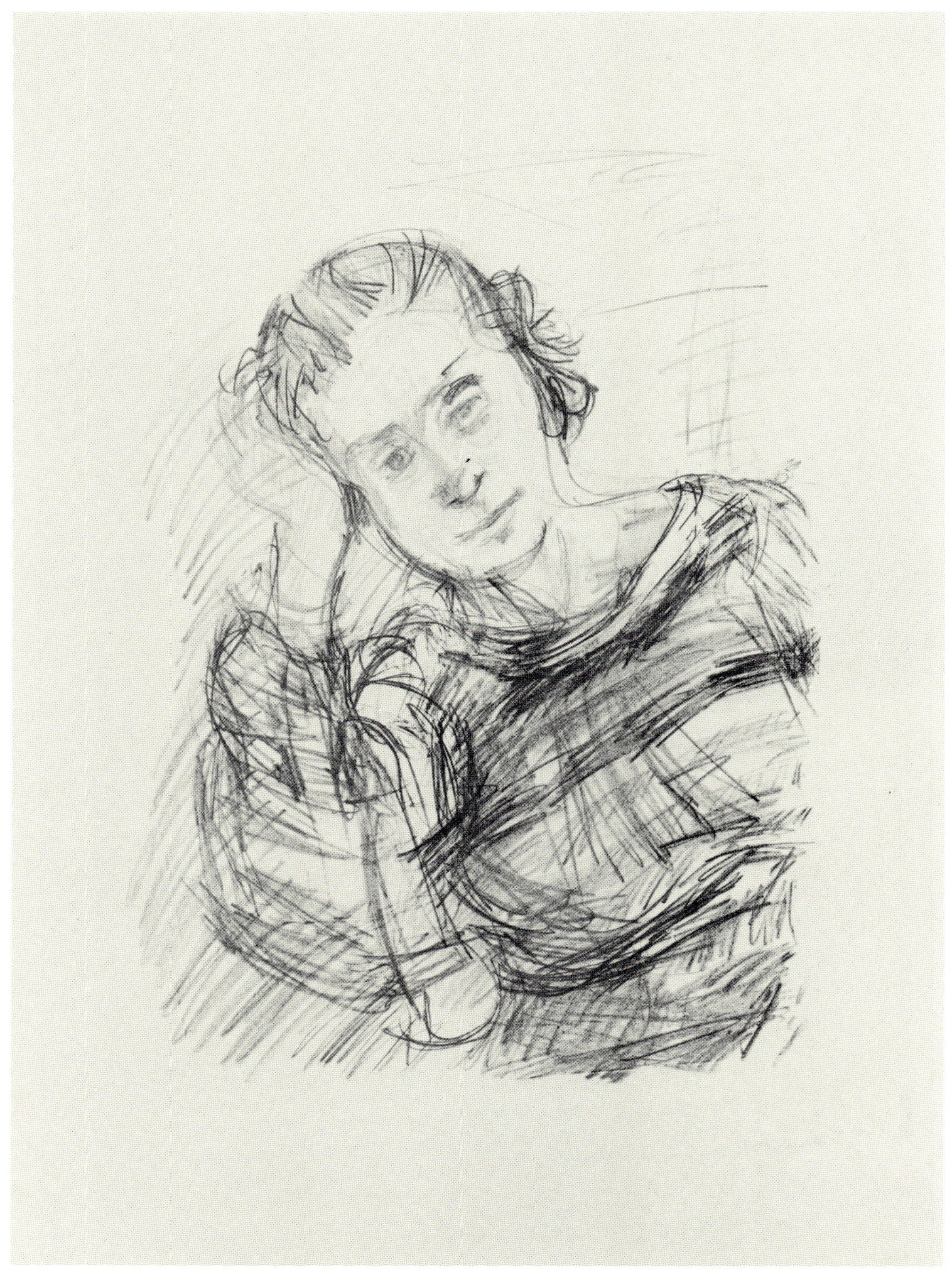

Cat. 42 *The Concert* II *(Hagar)*, 1920

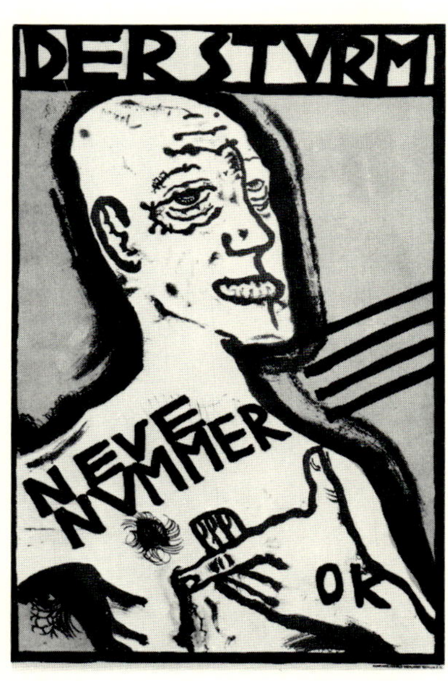

Fig. 22 *Self-Portrait Pointing to Breast,* 1910 (WW 32)

entitled *Self-Portrait Pointing to Breast* (Figure 22); and, as such, evokes a long tradition of artists identifying with Christ which goes back at least to Dürer, and is an especially important element in the imagery of artists working at the end of the nineteenth and the beginning of the twentieth century—among them Van Gogh, Gauguin and James Ensor.

Kokoschka's statement about *The Passion* reflecting his revulsion toward the war becomes important also in the context of the artist's career as a whole during which, whenever he addressed the general public in a moment of profound personal commitment to a cause, he would often use religious imagery associated with suffering to convey his point. A telling example of this is his poster, *Christ Helping the Starving Children,* 1945–46 (Cat. 49), in which the crucified image of Christ extends his right hand toward the hungry children huddled around him. The image was printed in a large (5,000) edition at the expense of the artist and was posted by him throughout London in a deeply felt humanitarian gesture.

In 1956, the artist produced a lithograph, *Christ Crowned with Thorns* (Cat. 59), the proceeds from which were to be given to the victims of the aborted Hungarian Revolution. It is an Ecce Homo in which the pained grimace of Christ reflects, on one level, sympathy for those who suffered during these tragic events and, on another, pain and sadness because the purpose of His suffering has been so completely ignored.

In another image, *L'Enfant de Bethleém* of 1956 (Cat. 58), Kokoschka depicts the Madonna holding the infant, who is crying as if in response to the scene around him—a city, invaded by firing tanks, with people trying to hide or already dead—a graphic reference to the invasion of Hungary. The image was made for the Swiss Lithographers Society to aid Hungarian refugees.

The above images, the six lithographs for *The Passion* cycle, the artist's religious paintings from 1911, and his frequent self-identification with the image of Christ, indicate that religious imagery was for him an important form of self-expression to which he often turned in a moment of crisis.

Before proceeding in our discussion of Kokoschka's portraiture and his later works, it is important to reflect on the long hiatus which the artist took from the graphic medium.

The fact that from 1923 for nearly twenty years Kokoschka produced only a few prints is often acknowledged but never satisfactorily explained in the literature on the artist, and there is no hard testimony from him that would shed light on this important point. Viewed in a broader historical context, there are reasons for this hiatus that Kokoschka shares with a number of other artists of the period. In the previously cited catalogue, *The Print in Germany 1880–1933,* the authors suggest the economic circumstances of that period as one likely reason for this phenomenon: "With the end of the inflation the impetus collapsed behind the printmaking activities of the majority of post-war artists . . ."[27] Besides Kokoschka's cessation of activity, such others as Max Beckmann, Otto Dix, El Lissitsky, Laszlo Moholy-Nagy, Kurt Schwitters—and to a somewhat lesser extent, Paul Klee and Wassily Kandinsky, also stopped producing prints. Suggested, too, are other reasons: "There were, of course, artistic as well as economic reasons for the decline in original printmaking, first and foremost of which was the exhaustion of the Expressionist tradition which had endowed this activity with so much importance."[28]

Kokoschka's position in the broad spectrum of early twentieth-century printmaking is unique enough so that the above statement needs to be qualified at least in part. For Kokoschka, the print medium never carried with it the rich and special aesthetic resonance that it did for the artists of *Die Brücke* and, to an only slightly lesser extent, those of *Der Blaue Reiter* group. Rather, the print remained primarily a communicative medium, and it is especially in his prints that Kokoschka establishes himself as a consummate storyteller. More often than not, he associates his print with the written word—his or that of other writers; and the dominant theme of nearly all his writings and prints of his early years (up to 1923) reflected, in one way or another, the dominant concern of the relationship between the sexes. It may be argued that what Kokoschka did exhaust by 1923 was this central theme of his early career as his affair with Alma Mahler faded into a bittersweet memory.

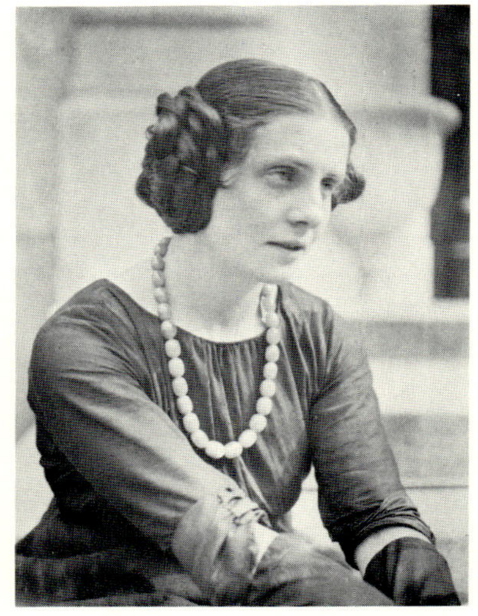
Camilla Swoboda, 1920

After leaving Dresden, Kokoschka would travel extensively during the next decade. Initiated in part by the artist's desire to leave behind his memories of the affair and the experience of war, this ambitious peripatetic undertaking was fueled by a very generous contract from his dealer, Paul Cassirer, and by Kokoschka's strong desire to establish an international reputation.

Cassirer's contract called for a sustained production of paintings of locales—important sites and famous cities that the artist visited. While the contract did not preclude the production of prints, the emphasis was clearly on painting. Beyond that, the artist's constant, often frequent, change of locale did not always provide the conducive opportunity for printmaking. If the wanderlust period of Kokoschka's travels was, to a large extent, self-motivated, soon external events would once again determine his venue. Political realities necessitated his moves—first to Prague, where he lived from 1934 to 1938 and where he met his future wife, Olda, then to London, where he remained off and on from 1938 to 1946, the war years. Kokoschka eventually settled in 1950 in Villeneuve, Switzerland, where he lived for the rest of his life. Significantly, it was only after things had stabilized both politically and in his own life that Kokoschka returned in earnest to the graphic medium which in the late phase of his career, as will be shown, became an important form of expression for the artist.

The Concert Series

In the summer of 1920, while visiting Vienna, Kokoschka produced over twenty drawings in black chalk—an exceptional spurt of activity even for him. What makes these works especially unique is that they are all of the same sitter, Camilla Swoboda, shown in a variety of closely related poses and reflecting different moods as

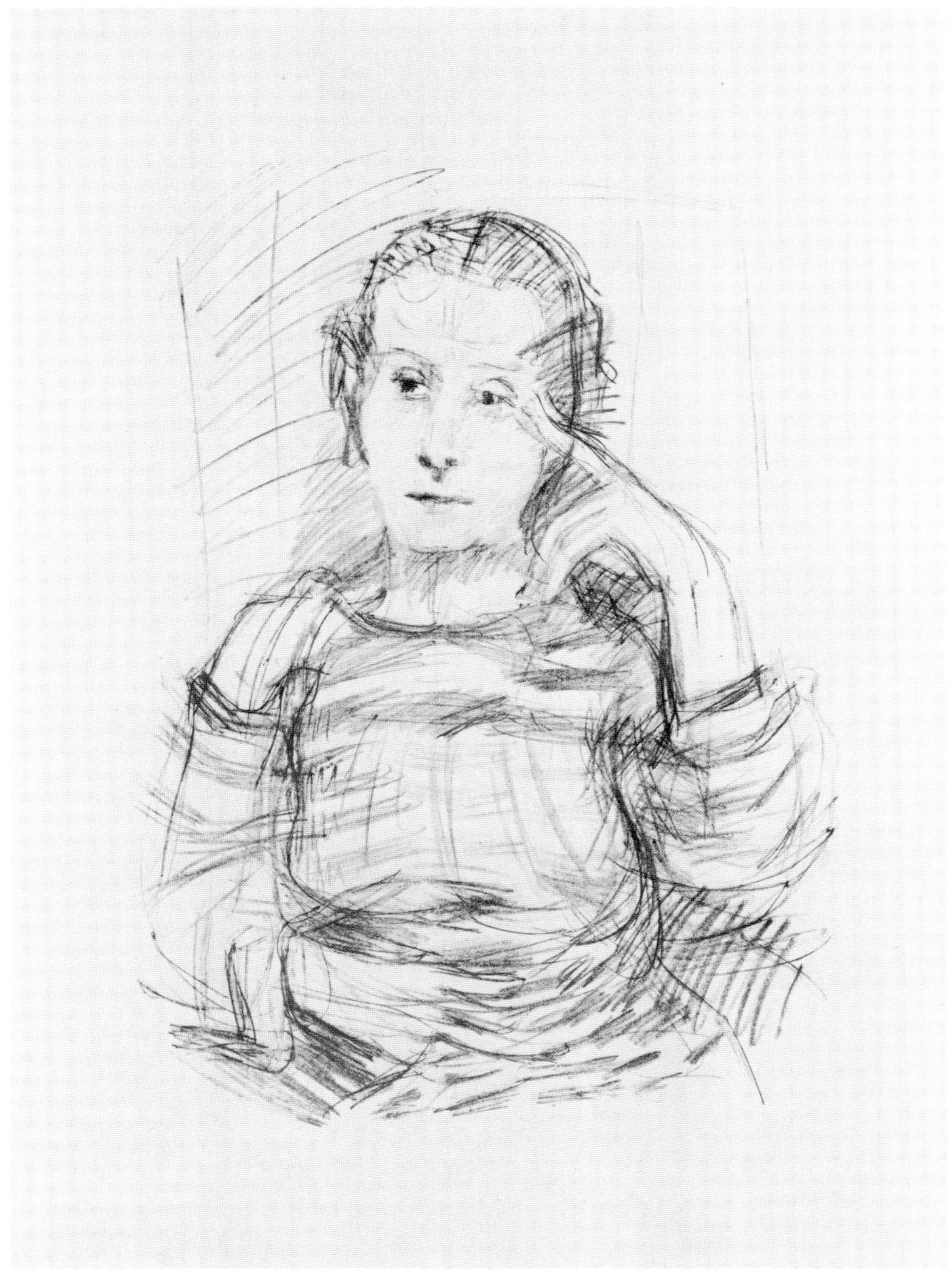

Cat. 43 *The Concert* IV *(Miriam)*, 1920

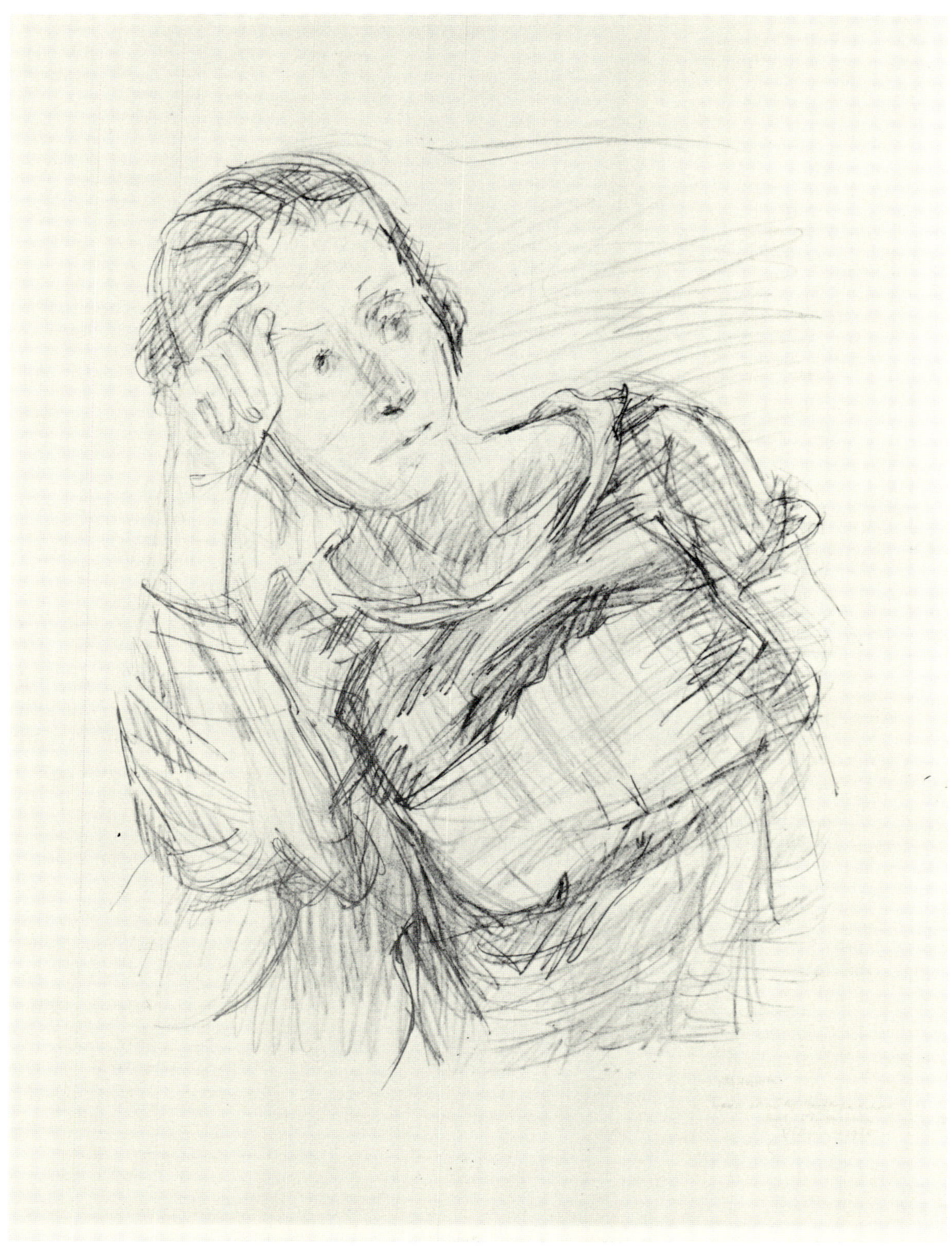

Cat. 44 *The Concert V (Deborah)*, 1920

she listens to music of various composers played on the piano by her husband, art historian Karl Swoboda. Of these drawings, ten were reproduced in a portfolio, *Variation on a Theme,* published in 1921, and five of these were made into lithographs and published as *The Concert,* also in 1921. Four of the latter are in the present exhibition.

Max Dvořak, whom Karl Swoboda assisted at the Kunsthistorisches Institut of the University of Vienna, wrote a preface to the *Variation* portfolio in which he correctly removes the series from the impressionist aesthetic:

> Her ever-changing appearance derives neither from the discovery of new external features in the model, nor from the changes caused by the influence of light and atmosphere, but from the inexhaustible variety and ceaseless flow of expression animated by a human soul.[29]

When Edith Hoffmann refers to these variations of the highly sensitive sitter as culminations of the psychological phase of Kokoschka's portraiture, she basically concurs with Dvořak's reading of these works. Hoffmann concludes her assessment by comparing them to Kokoschka's earlier portraits:

> In his youth, he had seen the expression of one dominating disposition in each human face, had conceived each one of his models as an actor in one rôle only. Now he has come to see countless moods in a single human being and has recognized the innumerable artistic possibilities in one face.[30]

In comparing these nuanced renditions of a single sitter to the early portraits, Hoffmann draws our attention especially to works done between 1909 and 1911, of individuals who were, to a large extent, the embodiment of the intellectual life of the period.

Kokoschka's development as a portraitist dates back to the years 1908–1909 to his friendship with the architect, Adolf Loos, who introduced the young artist not only to most of the intelligentsia of Vienna, but also to many prominent figures outside its borders—and whose portraits he insisted Kokoschka should paint.

Through a special mix of insight, intuition and empathy for his sitters, Kokoschka depicted the visual equivalent of the unique intellectual gift of each of these individuals.

The challenge that Loos thrust on the artist was immense. To ask a young, as yet untried, talent to make his way in the rarified stratum of the period's intellectual olympians was daunting enough. But to insist that he render their portraits—thus defining and revealing their essential characteristics before really knowing them well or fully comprehending the special world that they created for themselves—was a compelling task. Through a special mix of insight, intuition and empathy for his sitters, Kokoschka depicted the visual equivalent of the unique intellectual gift of each of these individuals. In trying to unravel and understand the essence of their talents and translating these into a pictorial context, the artist also tried to gain insight into his own creative gifts as they related to, indeed, compared with, that of his sitters.

What emerged was a penetrating series of painted portraits which included: Karl Kraus, the editor and guiding force of the literary journal *Die Fackel (The Torch),* the poet Peter Altenberg, the art historians, Dr. Hans Tietze and Erica Tietze-Conrat, the scientist Auguste Forel, Herwarth Walden of *Der Sturm,* and Loos himself,

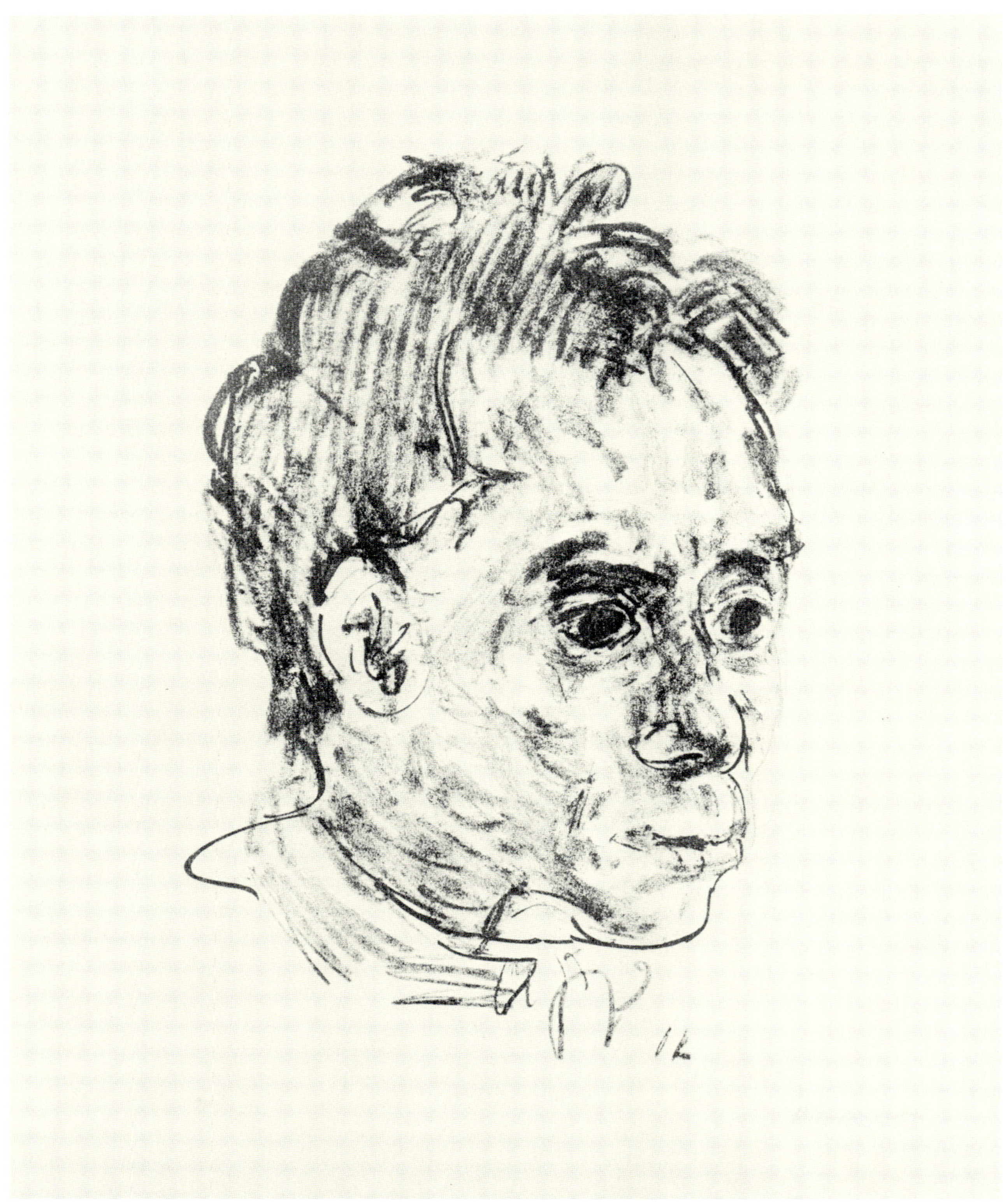

Cat. 35 *Walter Hasenclever*, 1917

Kokoschka's early portraits are of such pictorial and psychological intensity and complexity that no clear, single role in interpreting them readily manifests itself . . .

among others.

The power and maturity that these works and his other early portraits display is that much more impressive since they are among the first paintings created by Kokoschka, who was, as mentioned, never trained in oil painting as a member of the Kunstgewerbeschule and the Wiener Werkstätte. Complementing many of the portraits in oil were drawings of certain sitters, especially those close to the artist. Many of these drawn portraits, significantly different from the oils, were then reproduced in Walden's *Der Sturm*. As a result, some of them, portraits of such individuals as Loos, Kraus and Walden, became better known than the oil portraits.

The Concert and *Variation* series are, in many ways, exceptional in the history of early twentieth-century art, and, indeed, in Kokoschka's own development. However, we can see already in the early portraits a predisposition to reinvestigate a single sitter within a close timespan as the drawn portraits mentioned above indicate. Also, Kokoschka's experimentation with simultaneously rendered full-face and profile views in some of his prints and drawings of the period is yet another example of his ability to explore the complexity of the sitter's character.

Ultimately, Kokoschka's early portraits are of such pictorial and psychological intensity and complexity that no clear, single role in interpreting them readily manifests itself—indeed, it is precisely their complexity and suggestiveness of a variety of interpretations that hold our interest and make of these works some of the most penetrating portraits of the twentieth century.

An even more emphatic reinvestigation of a single sitter can be seen in his treatment of the features of Alma Mahler between 1912 and 1914. Kokoschka's representation of her was obsessive; she appears as a central figure not only in his painting, but also in his drawings, graphic cycles and dramas. Among these are a number of actual portraits, both painted and in print, which focus on the various physical aspects and psychological phases of the sitter.

There are, then, many precedents in Kokoschka's earlier portraiture to lay the groundwork for *The Concert* series. Yet the series has enough characteristics that are uniquely its own to make of it a rather distinct experiment in the artist's oeuvre. To begin with, variations of the image were done over a relatively brief span of time during which the sitter was engaged in the same activity. Thus, the circumstances consciously chosen by the artist are limited to the minimum possibilities of major shifts of pose and gesture.

Critical, too, is the presence in the series of a discernable outside stimulus—music, which subtly plays on the emotional and intellectual responses of the sitter. Whereas in his early portraits the stimulus for certain gestures and attitudes remains in large part the unknown, mysterious essence of the work, here we are presented with the knowledge, or awareness, that the sitter is engaged in a specific activity and thus becomes the embodiment of certain values we associate with this process.

The five images which comprise *The Concert* series share a general mood and attitude which pervades them all. They are, at the same time, distinctive; and each expresses a shift of mood as the artist varies the pose of the figure, its relationship to the background, as well as the representation of the facial features.

In the first of the series (Cat. 41), Kokoschka shows the half-length figure of the sitter with her hands folded in front of her. Her head, tilted to the left, culminates a diagonal axis of the figure and accents the assymetrical features of the face. Of these features, the most compelling is the contrast between the strongly defined left eye and the less distinct treatment of the right, implying a critical juncture—a moment in which the sitter shifts from an active into a contemplative state and becomes immersed in the music's impulse. The slight twist of the mouth forms a smile suggestive of quiet reverie and pleasure—a mood which the delicately folded arms enhance and conclude. The fluid, repetitive stroke which makes up a neutral background becomes a visual metaphor for music's sound as it gently envelops the figure.

In the second print of the series (Cat. 42), Kokoschka shows the figure deeply absorbed in the experience of music. The introspective nature of this experience is especially evident in the self-absorbed features of the face. The whole figure tilts to the left even more than in the first print as the head rests in her hand in a pose which has such powerful resonance in western art and is so often associated with contemplation that its meaning becomes at once obvious and profound.

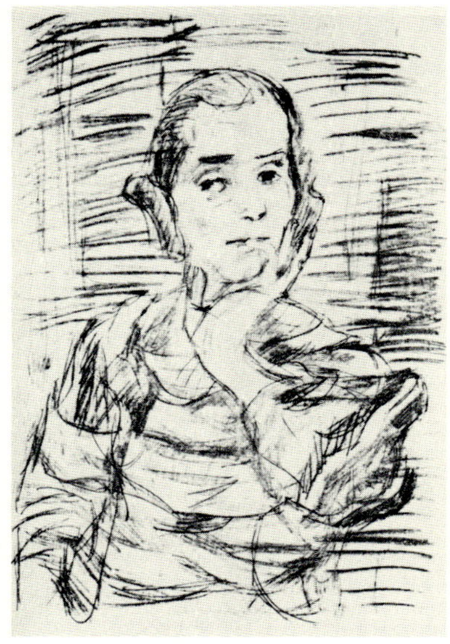

Fig. 23 *The Concert* III (*Ruth* I), 1920, (WW 142)

There is a density of stroke and an intensity of execution in this print which complements the introspective pose and spirit of Camilla. This is evident around the nose and especially the eyes whose reflective gaze is enhanced by the rich pools of shadow around it. The vigorous, gestural strokes in the upper torso which articulate the dress, on another level, seem also to be defining the deep emotional involvement of the sitter with the power of music.

Kokoschka worked on *The Variation* series over a period of a few weeks as he "continued to study his new model."[31]

The equation of the sitter's cónscious awareness of the artist's presence is seen most clearly in the third print (Figure 23). Camilla sits erect, her face cupped in an open-palmed hand, looking directly out at the observer-artist, as if bemused by his attention and scrutiny. The artist, in turn, focuses here on aspects of the sitter that are more physical than metaphysical.

Camilla appears here more beautiful than in the other prints. Such features as her carefully coiffed hair and the lavishly undulating sweep of her left sleeve suggest stylishness and aplomb. Both artist and sitter seem to be addressing here the question of decorum associated with the civilizing activity of listening to music.

Of the five prints comprising *The Concert* series, the fourth (Cat. 43) is the most eloquent and imposing. Here, too, the figure sits erect, and we respond to her alertness. The stylishness of the previous image is here replaced by a more compelling serious presence. The forefinger of her left hand touches the temple in a gesture reminiscent of Ingres' portrait of Madame Moitessier of 1856, and is made even more

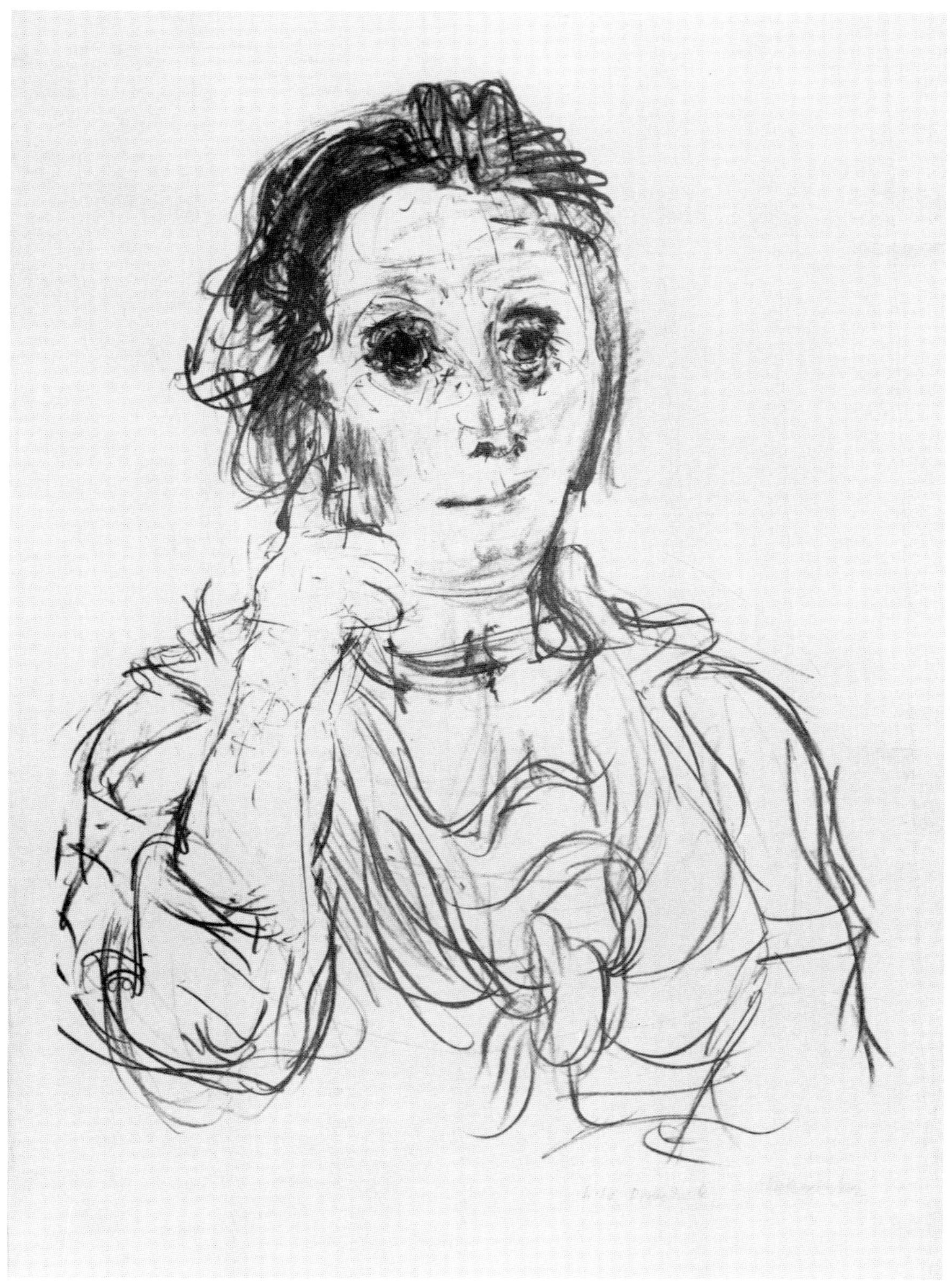

Cat. 39 *Hermine Körner*, 1920

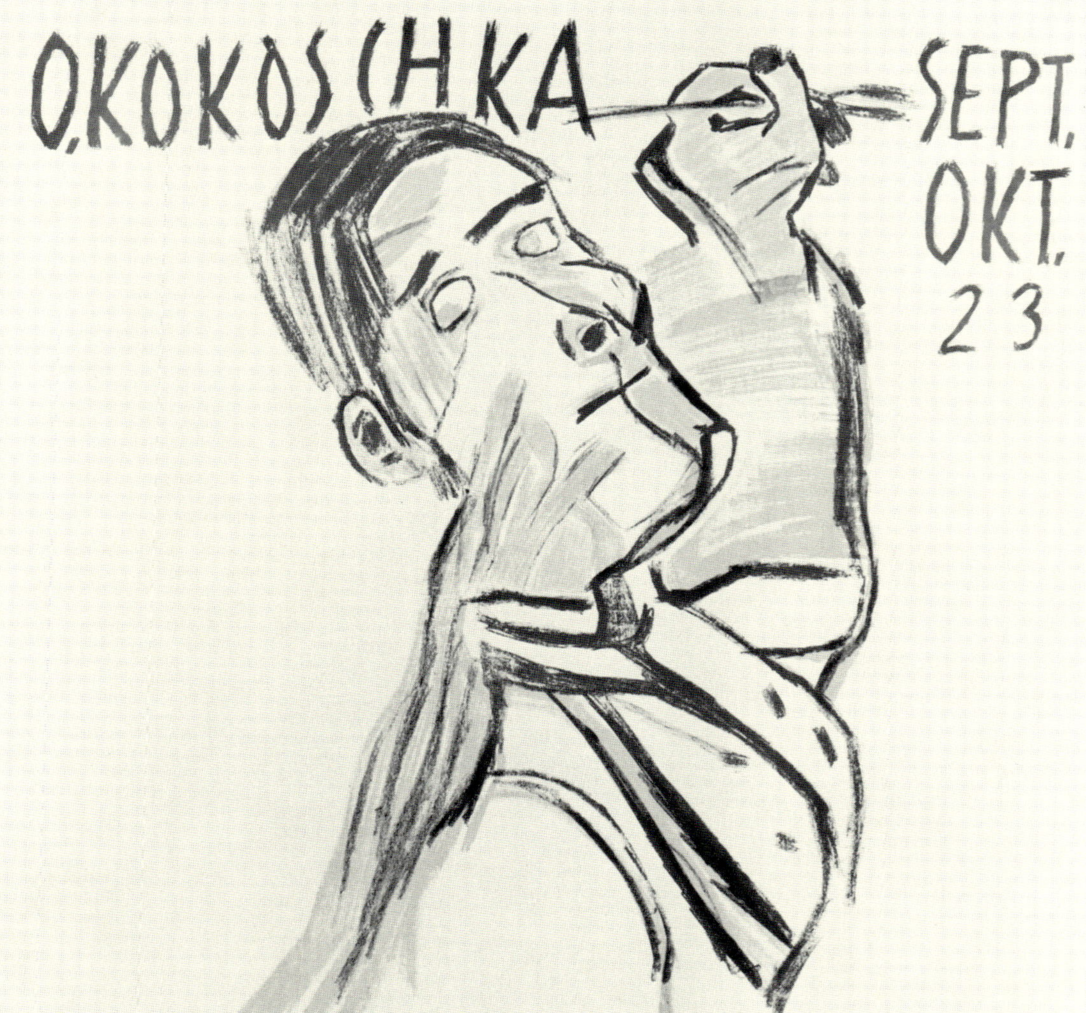

Cat. 47 *Self-Portrait from Two Sides as Painter*, 1923

prominent because the right hand is nearly subsumed in a series of sweeping strokes in the lower portion of the print. Here, too, the eyes are assymetrical and pensive, but they are lodged within a head that is a clearly defined, assertive presence. More so than in any other image in the series, the sitter's psychological depth manifests itself here. We want to suspend our assessment of the sitter as the embodiment of the music's impulses and instead wonder who she is and what she is thinking.

The fifth print of the series (Cat. 44), is, in many ways, the most disquieting. The overt manifestation of this mood may be seen in the troubled, saddened features of the face. The expansive, sweeping stroke that the artist employed in the previous four prints has here been shortened, intensified, and becomes a pervasive element which envelops the figure both physically and psychologically as she appears darkened by its onslaught. The artist returns here to a diagonal disposition of the figure, and once more the head is propped up by the hand. In this case, the gesture of the hand, a pinched configuration of index finger and thumb, becomes a telling symbol of the new mood. In Kokoschka's portraits, the gesture and placement of hands is second only to the treatment of the head in establishing the psychology of the sitter. Thus the artist here reverts to a sign which he utilized often in his oeuvre specifically to express vulnerability and suffering.

Given the context of *The Concert* series, we may speculate if the sense of disquietude in this work is a result of listening to a difficult, even disturbing, piece of music or whether we are witness to some inner anxiety brought on by different impulses.

In writing about one of his most admired works by Dürer, *Melancholia,* in which the pose of the female figure is similar to that in his own print, Kokoschka states: "This engraving represents the human reaction to fear" and concludes "She is not gazing into space, she is staring into emptiness."

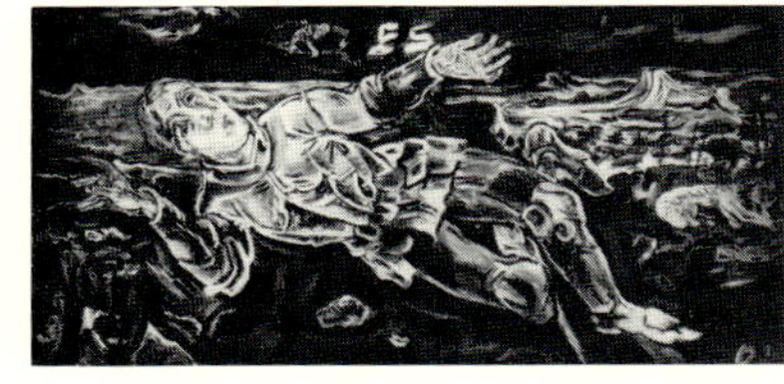

Fig. 24 *Knight Errant,* 1915

There are moments in Kokoschka's career where he demonstrates in his works an uncanny ability to "predict" events, which, as mentioned previously, the artist felt he inherited from his mother. For example, his allegorical self-portrait, the *Knight Errant* of 1915, (Figure 24) in which the artist shows himself in armor, prostrate and vulnerable, was actually completed before Kokoschka entered the military service and was severely wounded on the Galician front. Kokoschka and many of his biographers have so often referred to this special gift, that one is reticent in addressing it for fear of perpetuating something which is nearly impossible to prove or disprove. Art history is an inexact enough science. Yet it is difficult to consider this last print of *The Concert* series without recalling the words of J. P. Hodin who writes in his biography of Kokoschka:

> We can understand Kokoschka's surprise and sorrow when he learned in 1947 on a visit to Prague that Swoboda's wife had died at Auschwitz, for Kokoschka had a clear insight into her destiny.[32]

Ultimately, the compelling quality of *The Concert* series lies in the fact that it brings together, uniquely and forcefully, two powerful strains of Kokoschka's creativity:

his strength as a portraitist and his deep association with music.

To grow up in Vienna is to be touched deeply by music. There is no period in Kokoschka's life or art which does not reflect this important stimulus. His *Bach Cantata* cycle of 1914, and his painting, *The Power of Music* of 1918–1919, are only two among numerous examples which underscore this point. At times music has a profoundly personal resonance for the artist. During Kokoschka's intense affair with Alma Mahler, the artist recollects the powerful impact of the performance of Wagner's *Tristan und Isolde* on the two of them—an association which helps us to understand more fully the image of the two lovers in his most famous and important painting, *The Tempest* of 1914.

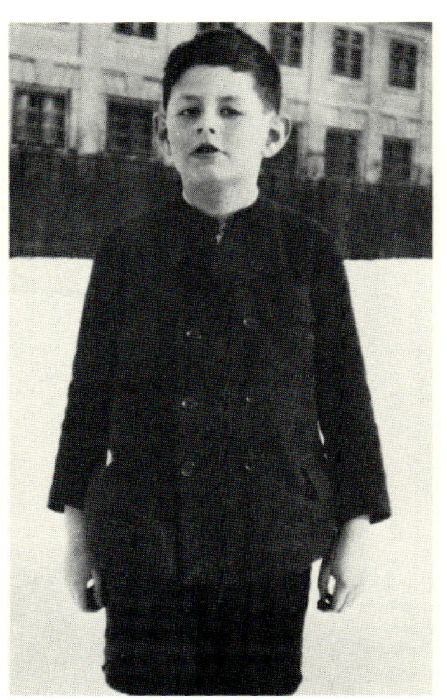

Michael Swoboda in 1920

"The rhythm of his life and the dream-like, anti-logical, dynamically unbounded nature of his character all signify a close relationship with music."[33] These words by Hodin capture the essential, unrelenting power that music held for the artist.

The fusion of music and portraiture may be unique in Kokoschka's oeuvre, but it underscores once more the close and rich interconnectedness of all his creative impulses.

Portraiture

The Concert series draws our attention to the artist's maturity as a portraitist in the graphic medium. Although painted portraits dominate his early output, the few drawn portraits such as those of Loos, Kraus and Walden, for example, indicate the expressive power and variability of his draftsmanship.

Kokoschka's first portrait in the print medium is a dramatically public one—the poster, *Self-Portrait Pointing to Breast* (Figure 22), for *Der Sturm* of 1910. In this powerful image he addresses us in "a kind of barbarian mask."[34] The gesture of his hand is explicit as he points to the open wound in his chest, which is indicative of his suffering. The allusion to Christ's wounds and suffering is evident. In transforming his visage into a "barbarian mask," though his features are still recognizable, and in pointing to the wound, Kokoschka, like Christ, reveals his anguish openly before the public that has vilified him. But at the same time, in creating an expressive image—crudely executed with violent, brutal distortions—Kokoschka willingly provides the evidence and reason for his vilification. In depicting himself with a shaven head, his actual appearance at that time, he much more insistently presents himself as a criminal type—an epitaph which the public had used against him. In other words, here he consciously establishes the terms of his own artistic and personal condition—a condition which he knew well would outrage his enemies and delight his supporters.

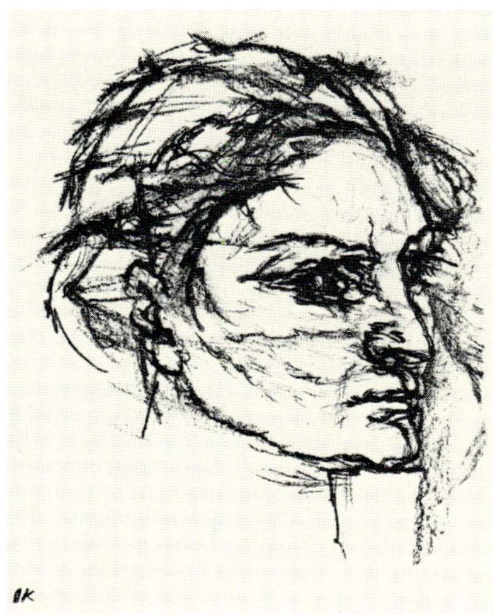

Fig. 25 *Portrait of a Woman (Alma Mahler)*, 1914 (WW 43)

Like the poster, Kokoschka's initial forays into portraiture in the graphic medium exist in a larger context. The two most compelling images date from 1913–1914, and are, not surprisingly, of Alma Mahler and himself. In each case, the portrait is associated with a cycle—Alma Mahler's image (Figure 25) initiates *The Fettered Columbus* and the "Self-Portrait with a Drawing Crayon" (Figure 19) is among the first prints in the *Bach Cantata*. Thus in the four years between 1910 and 1914, there are only a handful of

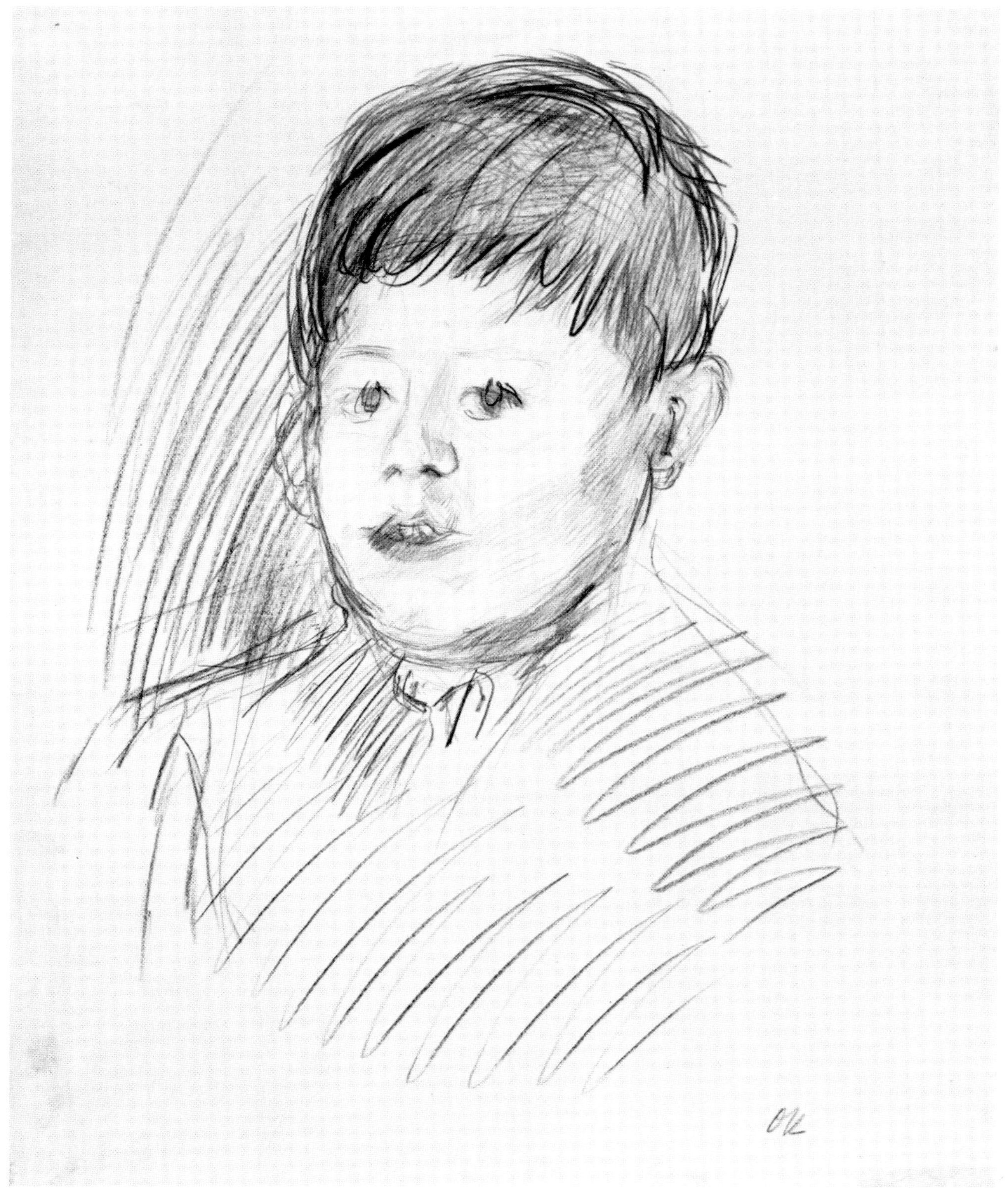

Cat. 181 *Michael Swoboda*, 1920

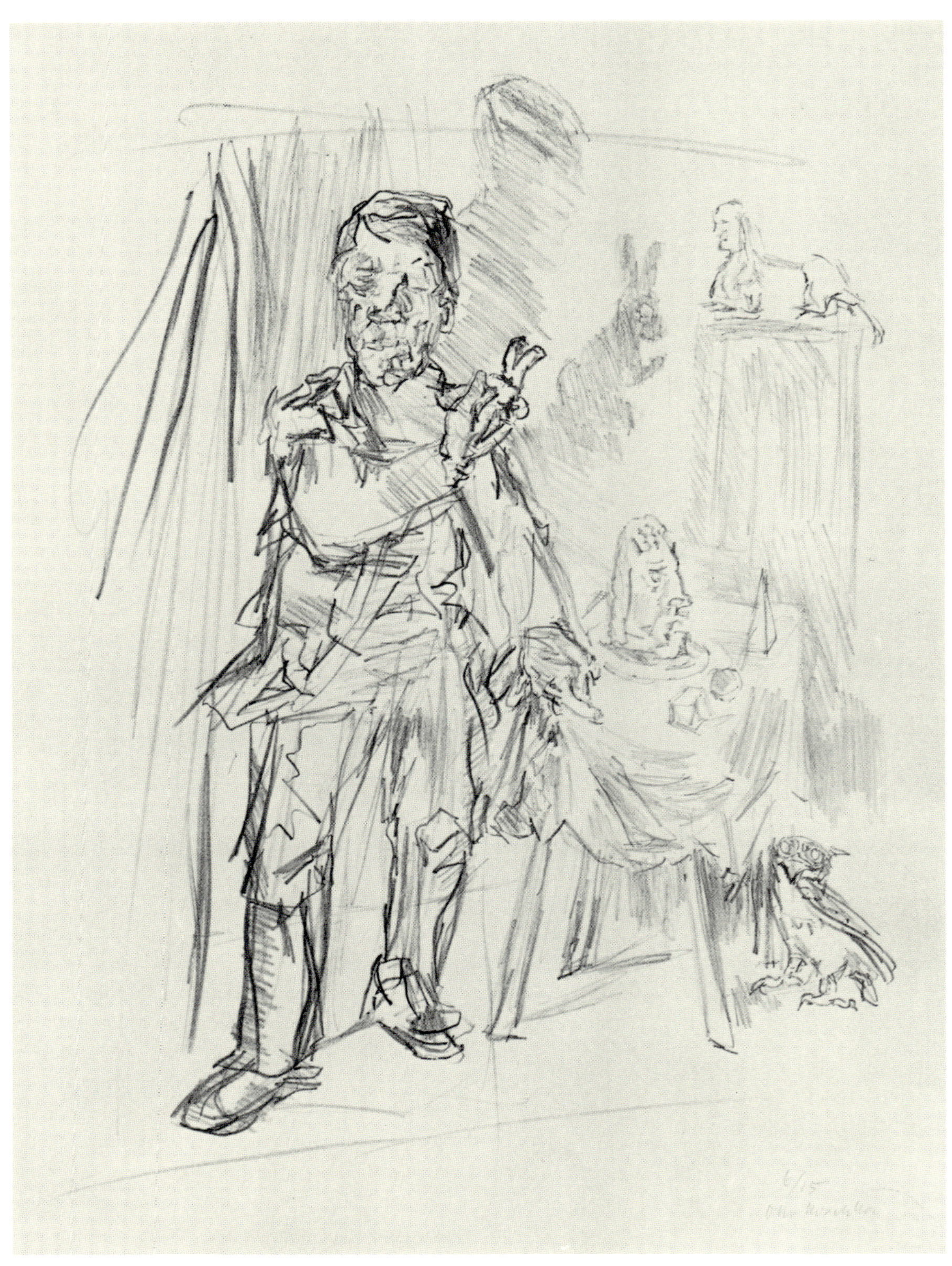

Cat. 51 *Magical Form (The Magician)*, 1951

portraits in the graphic medium, yet they are among the artist's most important.

The "Self-Portrait with a Drawing Crayon" belongs to a small group of self-portraits that the artist undertook between 1912 and 1914 and is the only print among them. The artist faces us in three-quarter view, the tool of his trade in his left hand (it is a mirror image). His hands are turned inward, toward the torso, creating an expressive counterpoint; the left hand holds the crayon in a rather formal, almost delicate gesture, while the right hand is shown tensed, somewhat distorted, as if a metaphor for the creative act. The head is slightly tilted and the body is a reticent presence—only the large eyes which stare out of the side of the socket make strong, psychologically probing contact with the viewer. The image was a successful one for the artist because he repeated it in an oil painting of the same year. He makes clear in the painting his intention to establish a dialogue with the viewer by an inscription written on the back of the canvas which is equally valid for the print:

Looking out of the picture am I
Looking at me are you

Another self-portrait which compares readily with the above work is his painting, *Self-Portrait Pointing to Breast* of 1913, one of the artist's best known images. In pose and gesture as well as in the elongated features, it is similar to the lithographic portrait. Yet the conscious act of interaction with the viewer and the physical act of creation evident in the lithograph have here been substituted for a more elusive, spiritual countenance.

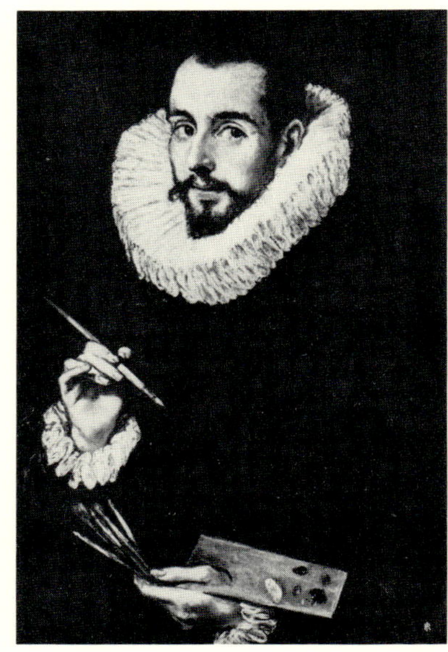

Fig. 26 Domenico Theotocopuli, called El Greco, *Self-Portrait*, c1600

When Herbert Read wrote in the introduction to Edith Hoffmann's book "... there is no artist of the present time so near to El Greco as Kokoschka,"[35] he could certainly have been referring to the above images. In the elongation of the bodies as well as the intensification of the psychological and spiritual state, the above images share an affinity with the mannerist master. More specifically, El Greco's painting, often identified as a self-portrait, of c. 1600 (Figure 26) may have, in fact, directly influenced Kokoschka's lithographic self-portrait. It is especially in the side glance and in the treatment of the hands that the latter's work comes closest to the El Greco.

It could be argued that the artist's powerful lithographic portraiture of Alma Mahler for *The Fettered Columbus* is among the most compelling images of her that he produced. It is an impressive portrait of an impressive person—her awesome beauty which is defined not only in physical terms but in her strength of character, evident in the face which is at once refined, strong-willed, determined if not domineering. A degree of respect and admiration of the artist toward his formidable partner emanates from it. In the context of the development of Kokoschka's graphic portraits, Alma Mahler's portrait establishes a precedent of defining the sitter exclusively in the context of the head. This image is not a first for the artist from that point of view, since already in his portrait drawings for *Der Sturm* during 1910, he often focuses exclusively on the head, eschewing the incorporation of the hands as an expressive vehicle. The most brilliant among these is, in fact, the portrait of Herwarth Walden, a calligraphic tour-de-force in which the likeness and essence of the sitter is sought out through the vigorous, thin line of a pen. Alma Mahler's portrait, done in crayon, is softer in execution but also defines the corporeality of the sitter more concretely. It will be the latter quality that Kokoschka's portraits of the late teens and early 1920's will develop.

An excellent example is the portrait of the artist's mother, Romana Kokoschka, (Cat. 33) of 1917. Like the Alma Mahler portrait, it is rendered in three-quarter view. Here it faces in the opposite direction, to the left, as if a pendant to it. The rapport Kokoschka attempts to establish with the sitter is, however, significantly different from the Mahler work where the latter's presence is nearly overpowering. In the portrait of his mother, Kokoschka establishes an empathy that is both physical and psychological. We can, for example, recognize a familial likeness especially in the lower portion of the face—from the nose to the mouth and chin. The artist searches out even more intently the quality for which he admired his mother the most—her visionary gift—which, he felt he shared with her. The intense, glistening eyes stare off to the left as if, in fact, seeing something beyond. The image is an act of respect and admiration by the artist toward a person who played a critical role in his life. It is also a unique document in the sense that through it, Kokoschka attempts to define and understand his own identity.

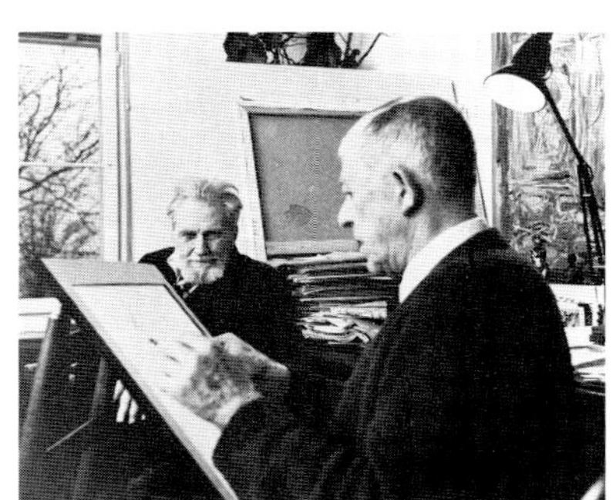

Kokoschka drawing Ezra Pound's portrait, 1964

Romana Kokoschka is among the first portraits from this period and initiates a quantitative shift in Kokoschka's output. For the next number of years, through 1923, he would increase the number of lithographic portraits to the point that they exceeded his portraits in oil. Certainly among the reasons for this is that the artist had mastered the expressive potential of the medium and now felt at ease with it. It is also at this time that Kokoschka was experimenting in his painting with the very fiber of the medium, searching out its sonorous potential. Paul Westheim writes in his 1918 book on the artist: "What Kokoschka is now aiming at . . . is 'beautiful painting,' exquisite workmanship turning color into a jewel for the senses."[36]

While this approach produced out of paint "a precious object in itself," the psychological density of Kokoschka's painted portraits diminished in the process and was, in an important sense, picked up in his prints since lithography offered a process whose inherent possibilities were not as plentiful or alluring and provided a vehicle for directness of observation of the sitter which was more focused.

In fact, a vivid example of the type of painting Westheim describes above is Kokoschka's three-quarter-length portrait of his mother, also of 1917, which depicts her sitting in a room in front of a window, her hands folded in front of her in a pose reminiscent of Van Gogh's *La Berceuse.* The quality of the portrait is achieved by a rich layering of color, mainly blue and green, in gently undulating thick lines. The visible movement of the brushstroke, which in the artist's earlier works carried an intense psychic energy, is here a lyrical, sumptuous presence. The portrait, ambitious and attractive, does not possess the penetrating quality of its lithographic counterpart. Westheim recognizes the unique quality of Kokoschka's lithographic portraiture from

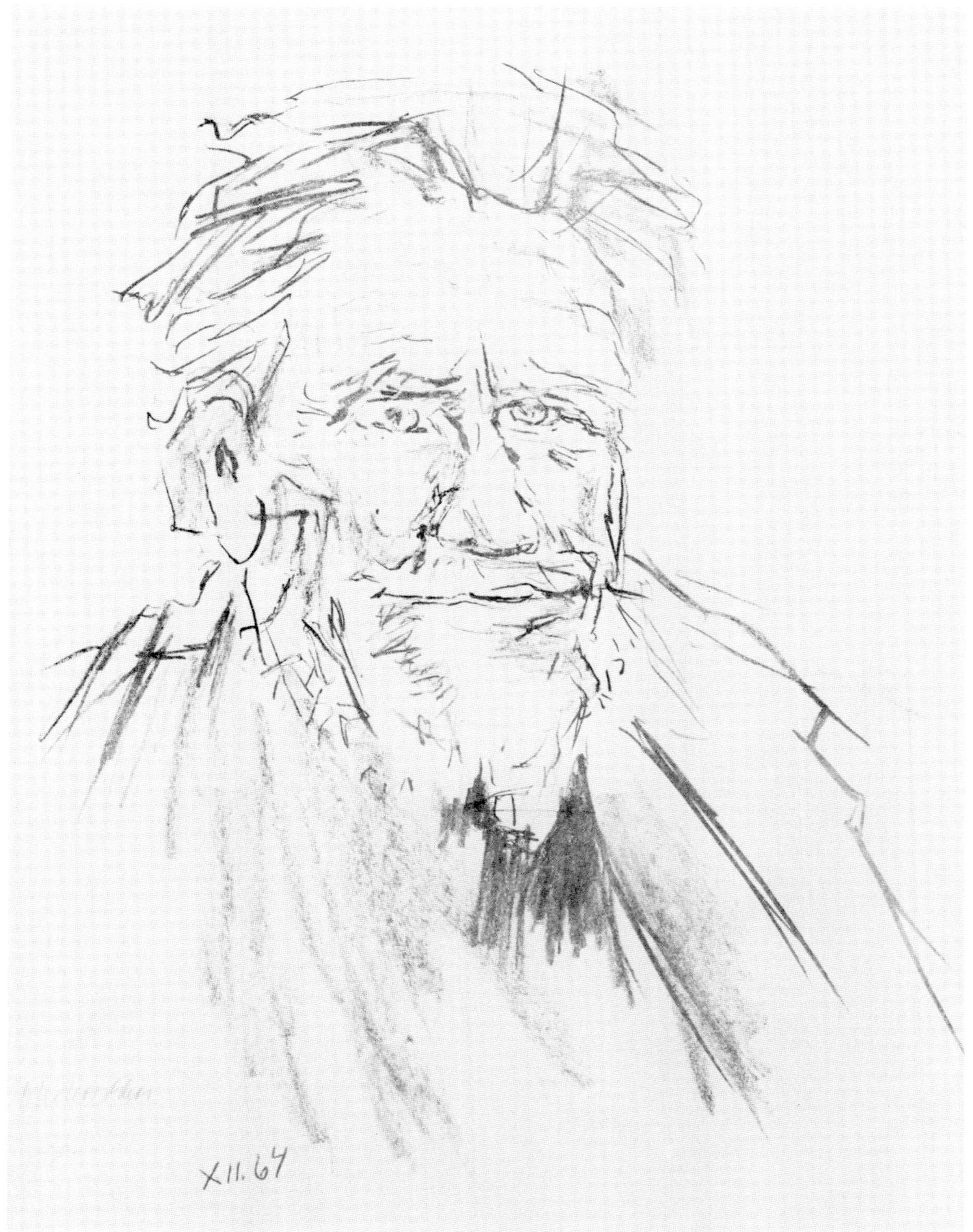

Cat. 82 *Ezra Pound*, 1964

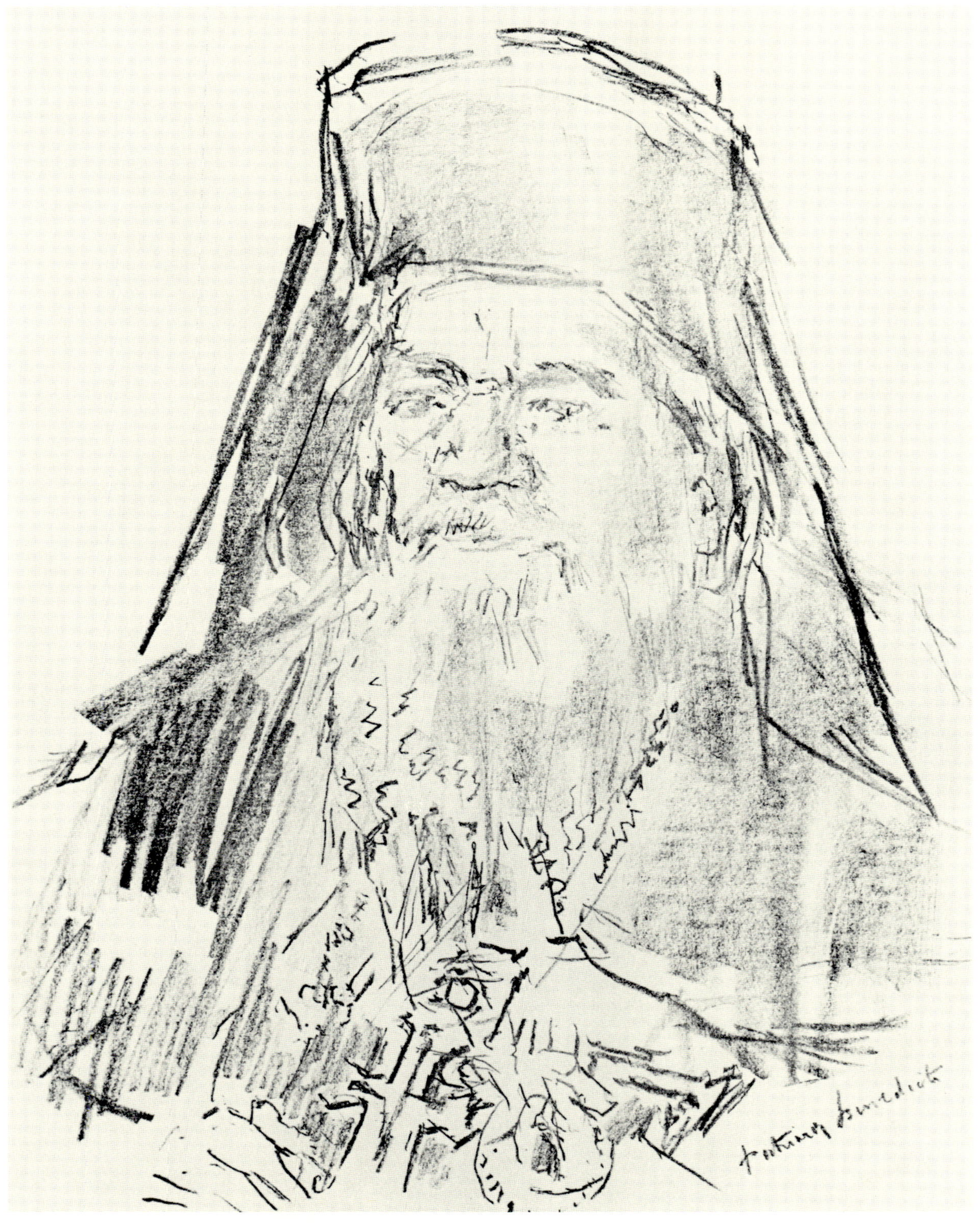

Cat. 157 *His Beatitude Benedictos I, Greek Orthodox Patriarch of Jerusalem,* 1973

this period when he writes:

> Reality has now acquired a compelling power. Each stroke is inspired by the most intense and loving experience of the essential nature of everything.[37]

In this all-encompassing comment, the author attempts to define the special quality of these works in which the intensely physical representation of the sitter coexists in an exceptional balance with a psychologically penetrating one.

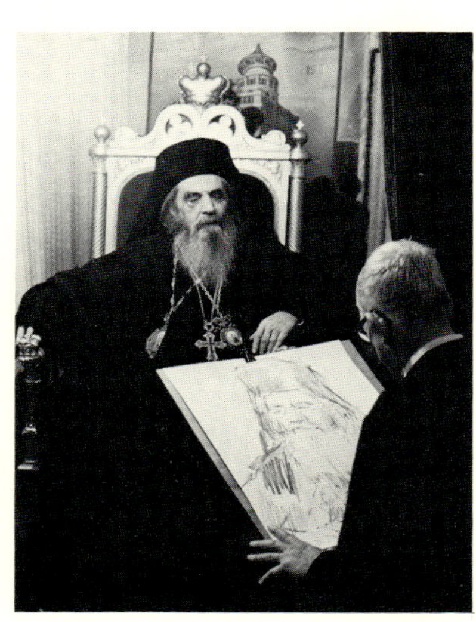

Kokoschka drawing Benedictos I, Jerusalem, 1973

These works are as forthright a group of portraits as the artist will produce in his career. Not all are focused exclusively on the head like the portrait of the artist's mother or the portrait of one of Kokoschka's closest friends, the expressionist poet, Walter Hasenclever, (Cat. 35) of 1917, which in its resolution is nearly identical to the former. In fact, the artist did another lithographic portrait of Hasenclever (WW 118) a year later in which he includes the upper torso and right hand propping up the poet's head—elements that are treated naturalistically, even as the gesture of the lithographic crayon sustains an expressionist syntax.

Other works of this period share this quality. In the half-length portrait of the eminent actress, Hermine Körner, (Cat. 39) of 1920, the undulating line which articulates the lower torso is even more free and expressive than in the 1918 Hasenclever portrait. Her frontal pose, the gesture of her hand against her head, and the sensitive resolution of the facial features are all elements which form the basis for the artist's *Concert* series.

Kokoschka's self-portraits of 1910 and 1914, considered earlier, initiate an avenue of self-investigation and self-revelation which the artist would essay in his prints throughout his career. These works are not merely afterthoughts to the painted self-portraits, but are, instead, highly independent probings of self which are often more spontaneous and direct than the latter and in which the artist is willing to investigate features that he does not address in his paintings.

For example, in his *Self-Portrait from Two Sides* of 1923 (Cat. 47), a poster for an exhibition of the artist's work in the Kunstsalon Wolfsberg, Zürich, he views himself simultaneously from profile and nearly full face—a formal experiment which he initiated in 1909/10 in his drawings for *Murderer, Hope of Women* and repeated in other works like the *Der Sturm* poster and his drawing of Karl Kraus of 1912. Significantly, this device does not occur in the artist's paintings with such explicitness. In the 1923 poster, Kokoschka shows himself in the process of painting, his head tilted to the side as he turns and glances out toward the viewer. His face, strained in appearance, is faceted into a sequence of boldly colored and delineated expressive geometries which capture our attention as much as the insistent line which divides the face and identifies the dual views of it. To the extent that a poster is destined for a more general audience, this portrait is a vivid example of Kokoschka's continuing ability to engage the public with dramatic self images.

It would be over thirty years until Kokoschka produced his next *Self-Portrait* of 1956 (Cat. 56)—a gap which is only partially explained by his general hiatus from print-

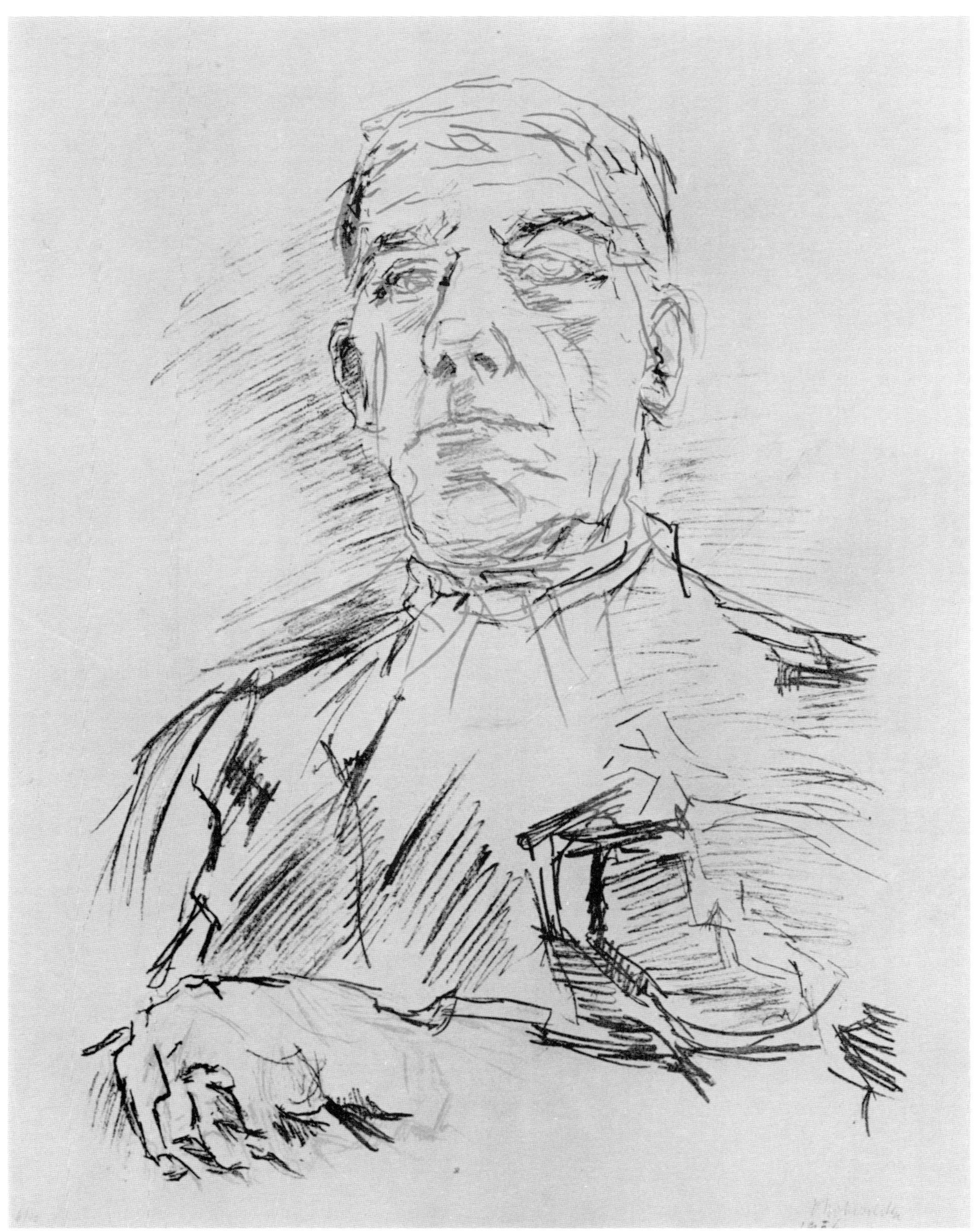

Cat. 56 *Self-Portrait,* 1956

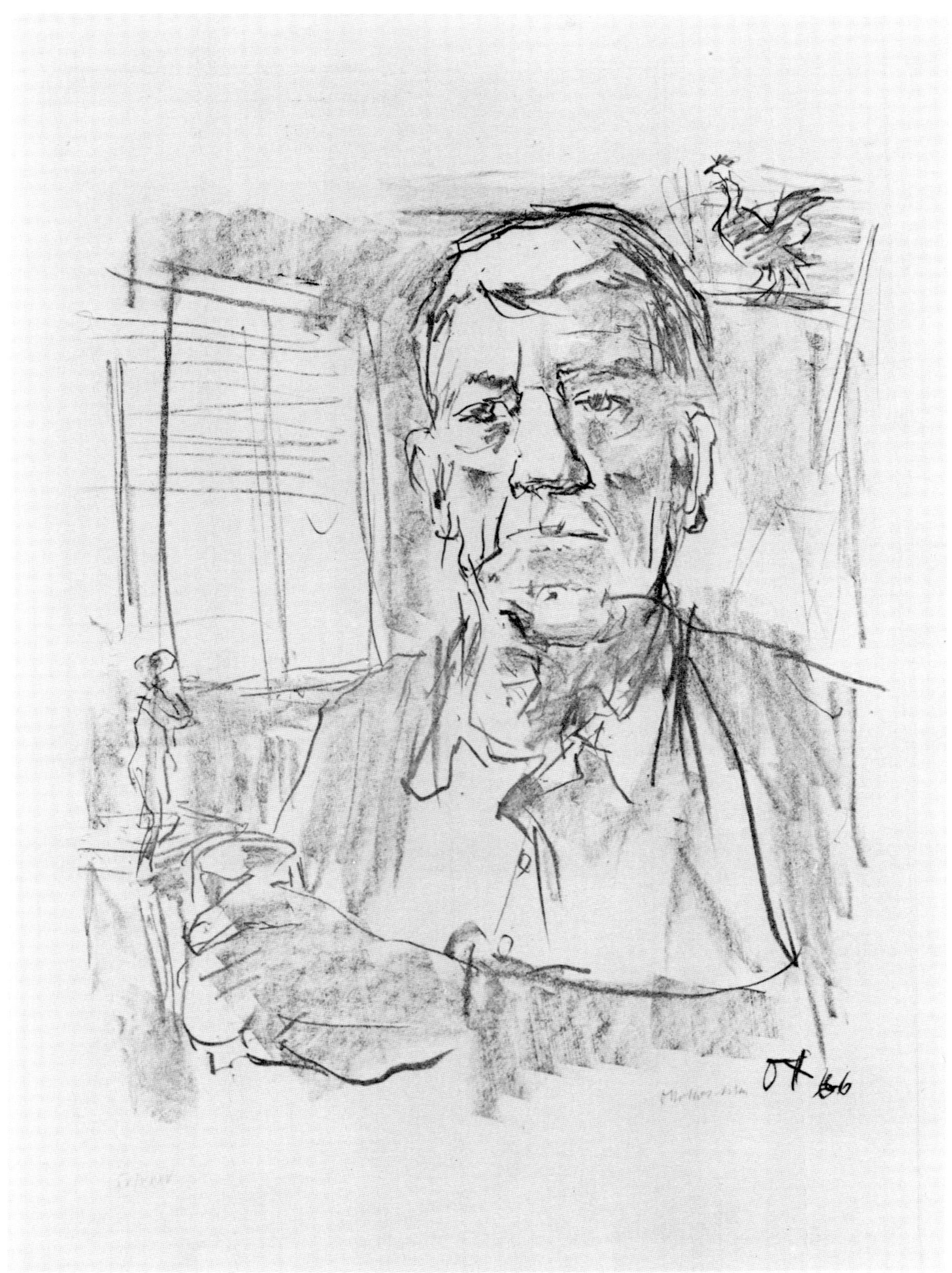

Cat. 103 *Self-Portrait with Statuette,* 1966

making. The work is among the artist's rare color lithographs in which he manipulates expressively the three colors by generally separating them and then accenting the various parts of the image—the face is mainly green, the torso blue and the hand a mixture of blue and red.

The significance of this work lies in the fact that the artist establishes here a compositional and psychological prototype for the best of his late graphic portraits of himself and others.

The low vantage point from which we view the figure of the artist distances us from it. The hand in the foreground concludes a powerful pyramidal structure which culminates in an imposing head. The face is an image of maturity and experience—the artist here seems to come to grips with the moment of old age (he was seventy at the time)—and the brilliant posturings of his earlier self-portraits are replaced by an image that is both sober and serene.

His *Self-Portrait with Statuette* (Cat. 103) of 1966 is similarly disposed, yet also less hieratic and more accessible. It is one of the artist's most resolved, thoughtful interpretations of himself in his whole oeuvre. The image is closer to us, and the vantage point from which we view it is nearer our eye level. Such details as the glass the artist holds in his hand also make the image less formal. The generalized background of the earlier work is here replaced with a discernible spatial setting dominated by a window at the left which provides the light source for the articulation of the figure. The small statuette of a female nude in the lower left and its counterpoint in the figure of the cock in the upper right above the artist's head are evocative symbols of the artist's earlier concerns.

The direct, forthright, imposing quality of the above self-portraits is also evident in the portrait of "His Beatitude Benedictos I, Greek Orthodox Patriarch of Jerusalem" of 1973 (Cat. 157), the strongest image in a suite of six portraits known as *Jerusalem Faces* that Kokoschka did during his visit to the Holy City in April of that year. The features of the face, intensified by the surrounding darkness of the headdress and garment, reflect wisdom, intelligence and grace. The whole image is almost an archetype of what one would expect a Patriarch's portrait to look like.

The artist's immense empathetic sense toward his sitters produces a variety of interpretations of character.

The sense of heroic dignity which emanates from these portraits of himself and others should not suggest a sameness of type in Kokoschka's late portraits. The artist's immense empathetic sense toward his sitters produces a variety of interpretations of character. An example of this is his extraordinary portrait of *Ezra Pound* of 1964 (Cat. 82), where the artist addresses with great sensitivity that delicate balance between genius and madness. He places the figure in the middle of the page surrounded by empty space, which therefore intensifies the sitter's isolation and our focus on him. The peripheral feature of dress, even hair, are treated summarily so that our attention rivets immediately on the face and more specifically on the eyes which make contact not with the outside world but with the poet's profoundly complex inner self.

Among Kokoschka's more unusual self-portraits is *Magical Form* (Cat. 51),

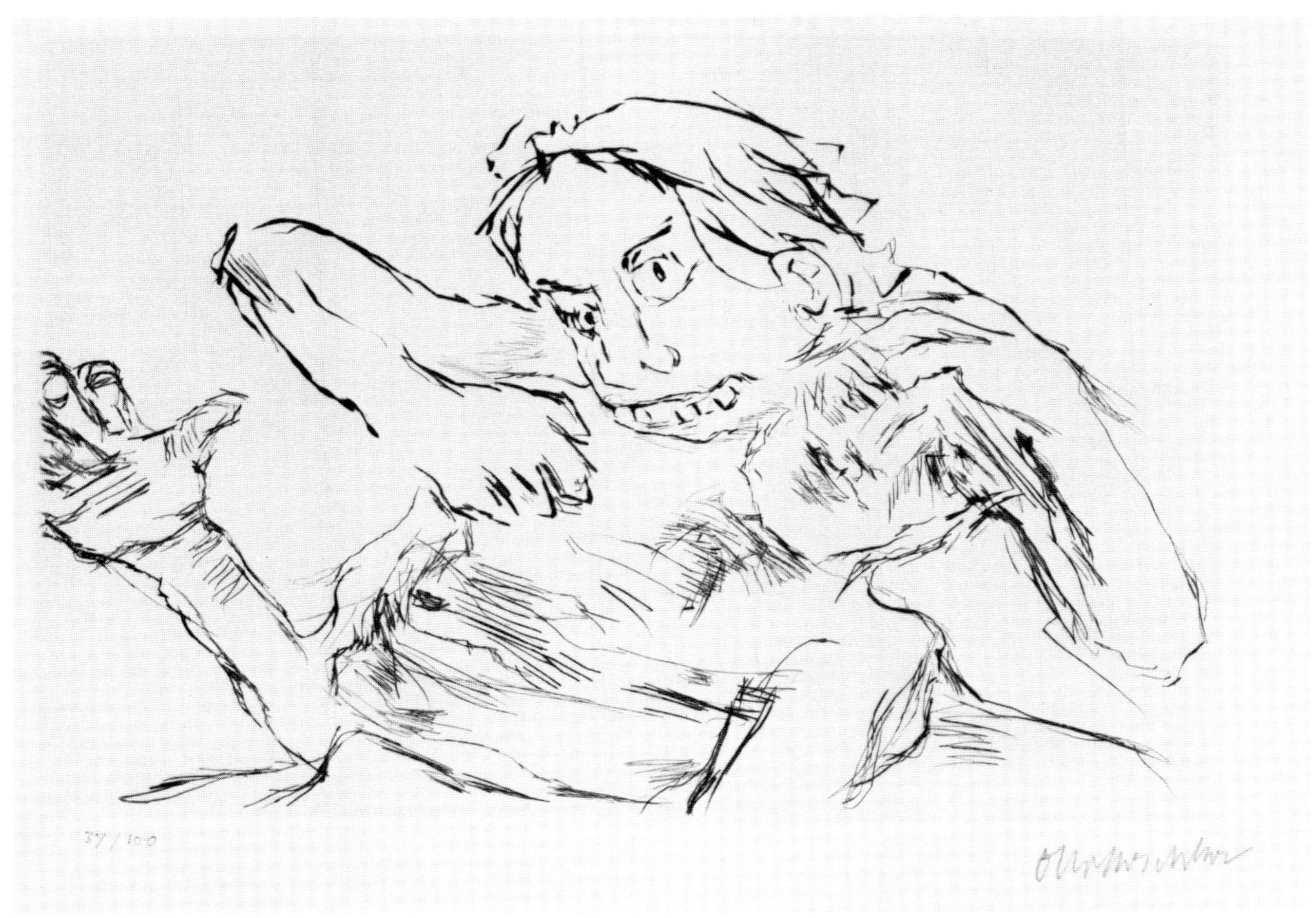

Cat. 138 *Penthesilea Tries to Eat the Dead Achilles*, 1969

Kokoschka serves notice that in his late works he will once again address a variety of concerns rich in personal meaning.

a lithograph of 1951 of which there is also a painted version where the image is reversed. The artist, left of center, stands in a room casting a shadow of a rabbit on the wall. Surrounding him are objects which visually and iconographically amplify the scene: on a table is a group of geometric shapes and a head, likely a drama mask—representations of the arts and sciences. In the lower right is an owl and in the background on a pedestal a figure of a sphinx—a juxtaposition of the intellectual and sensual.

In showing himself casting a shadow, Kokoschka refers to some of his earliest artistic experiences when he put on shadow plays like *The Speckled Eye* at the Café Fledermaus in Vienna. The artist further establishes the autobiographical nature of the scene by identifying himself with the rabbit who becomes an extension of the artist's own shadow. In having the rabbit confront the sphinx in the background, he repeats the juxtaposition in his painting *Still-Life with Cat, Rabbit and Child* of 1914. With this complex image, done at the outset of his return to active printmaking, Kokoschka serves notice that in his late works he will once again address a variety of concerns rich in personal meaning.

The Late Works

If there exists a consensus about Kokoschka's contribution to twentieth-century modernism, it is certainly focused on his early career. The artist's psychologically revealing early portraits, his revolutionary plays, the vivid, forceful graphic cycles and allegorical paintings which deal with his love affair with Alma Mahler, are all viewed as indispensible documents of early expressionism. For many historians, had Kokoschka's debilitating wound on the Galician front in 1915 been fatal, their assessment of his influence on twentieth-century art would not have changed much.

In a century which has delineated so clearly and insistently its "historicalisms," the above assessment is, in fact, a valid one. The expressionist movement, generally, developed and defined itself most completely prior to World War I, and its most important ideas as well as its greatest masterpieces—those which gave the movement its aesthetic underpinnings—were created during this period.

Yet while the war did, in fact, claim the lives of some key contributors to expressionism, like Franz Marc and August Macke, many others survived the conflict and went on to have long and varied artistic careers. This is certainly true of Kokoschka, who continued to create for another sixty-five years!

To follow a career of an artist after his historical moment has passed, is in part an act of faith and in part a manifestation of intellectual curiosity. Especially the late phases of artists who had lived long lives have always been a source of fascination for historians—we are, for example, intrigued with the late works of such titans as Michelangelo, Titian and Rembrandt. In our own century, the protean accomplishments of Picasso fascinate us beyond his most important historical achievement, the development of Cubism.

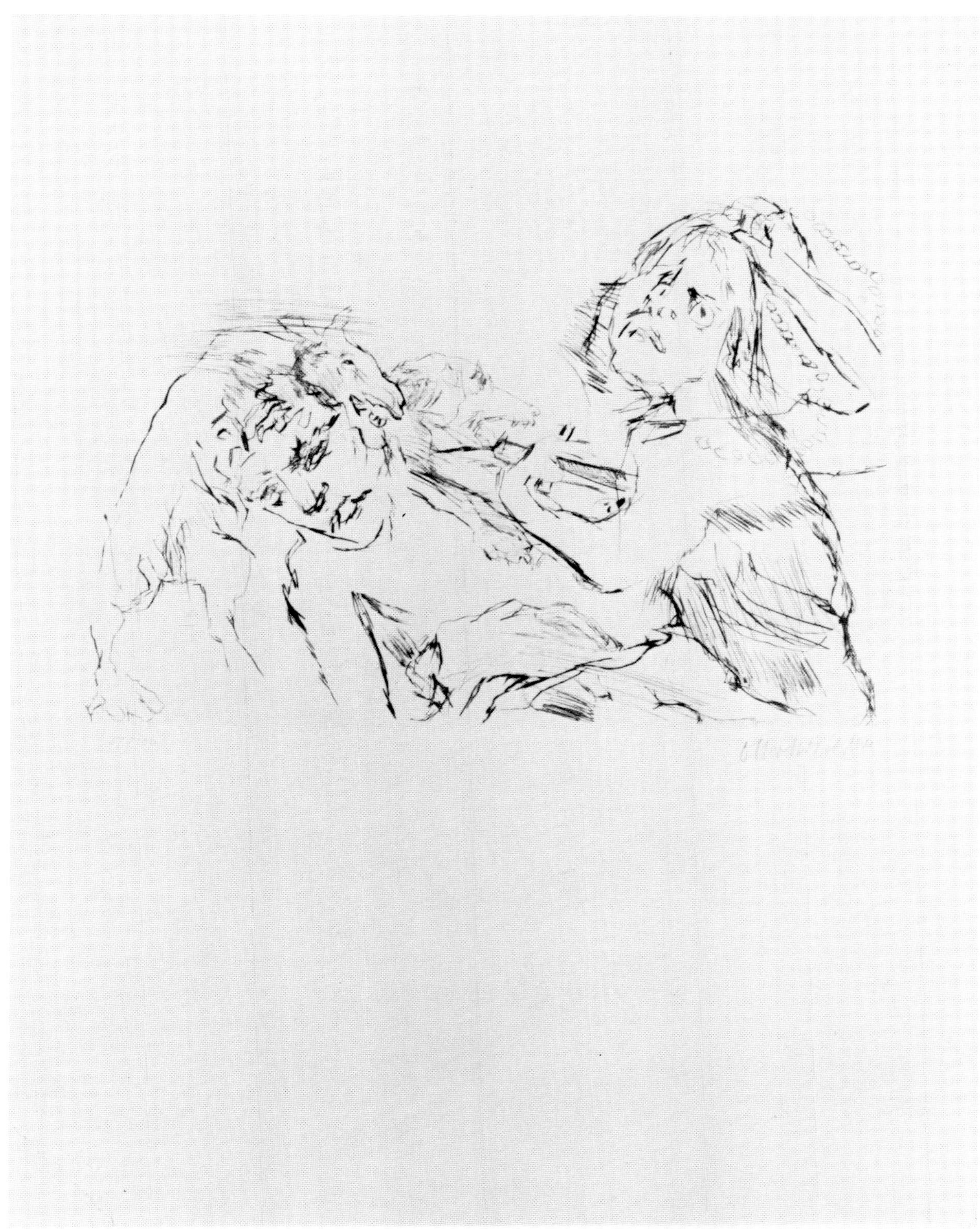

Cat. 139 *Penthesilea Kills Herself*, 1969

Kokoschka's art has never held center stage the way Picasso's has, thus the assessment of the former's late career has invariably been a source of interest to a smaller audience. For its supporters, Kokoschka's late career is a vivid example of the triumph of the humanist aspirations of twentieth-century art. In the face of the pervasive trend toward abstration, Kokoschka's art insistently focused on the human figure as the crucible of the human spirit. For the detractors, Kokoschka's late works, especially his large allegorical paintings, exhibit a lack of structure and aesthetic cohesiveness. Robert Hughes, in his review of Kokoschka's 1986 exhibition at the Tate, addresses the issue of the willful awkwardness of the late works, "In some of Kokoschka's last paintings there is a real sense of an old man's rage and an old man's freedom, the sense of the ludicrous posture, the gross energy of the old satyr that fires up our responses . . ." Drawing attention to the monumental *Theseus and Antiope* of 1958–1974, Hughes makes reference to its "strange, mocking intensity" and concludes, "If one can speak of neo-expressionism by an original expressionist, this painting is it."[38] In establishing a link between Kokoschka's late work and the dominant movement of the early 1980's—one which itself has been criticized for its excesses and lack of structure—Hughes brings into focus the rather compelling fact that the history of art is never definitively arranged and that the creative impulses of a new generation of artists often precipitate a reassessment of an earlier one. History is replete with such examples. Nineteenth century's evaluation of Velasquez was significantly tilted because of Manet's profound assimilation of his art. The reputation of El Greco, for example, was reestablished at the turn of the century as a result of a resurgence of interest in his art by a young generation of writers and artists, among them Picasso and, as we have seen, Kokoschka himself.

It may therefore very well be that the ultimate evaluation of Kokoschka's late work will be at least in some measure predicated on its relationship to the art of our own time.

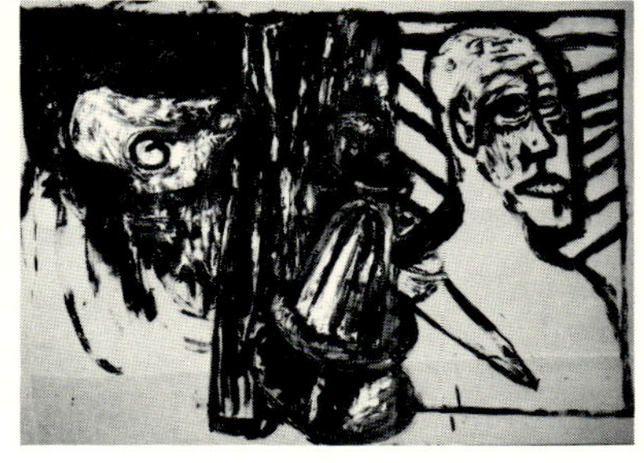

Fig. 27 Julian Schnabel, *Act of Faith*, 1981

An instance of Kokoschka's direct influence on an artist working in the neo-expressionist mode can be seen in Julian Schnabel's large oil on lavender velvet, *Act of Faith* of 1981 (Figure 27). The painting, divided into two dominant halves, depicts on the right an interpretation of Kokoschka's *Der Sturm* poster, *Self-Portrait Pointing to Breast*, of 1910. Schnabel responds to the expressive potency of Kokoschka's image—its intensity achieved by a rough, vigorous, abrupt line which defines the startling features of the face seen at once in profile and full view. Kokoschka depicts himself in the portrait pointing to an open wound in his chest—a gesture both of defiance and vulnerability. Schnabel omits the wound and pointing gesture and introduces in their place a diagonal shaft of paint. In doing so, he is objectifying this icon of early expressionism and focusing more on its defiant quality. In a larger sense, the battles won by the pioneers of expressionism in the twentieth century, Kokoschka among them, have made it possible for the new generation working today to feel less vulnerable and to be more openly defiant.

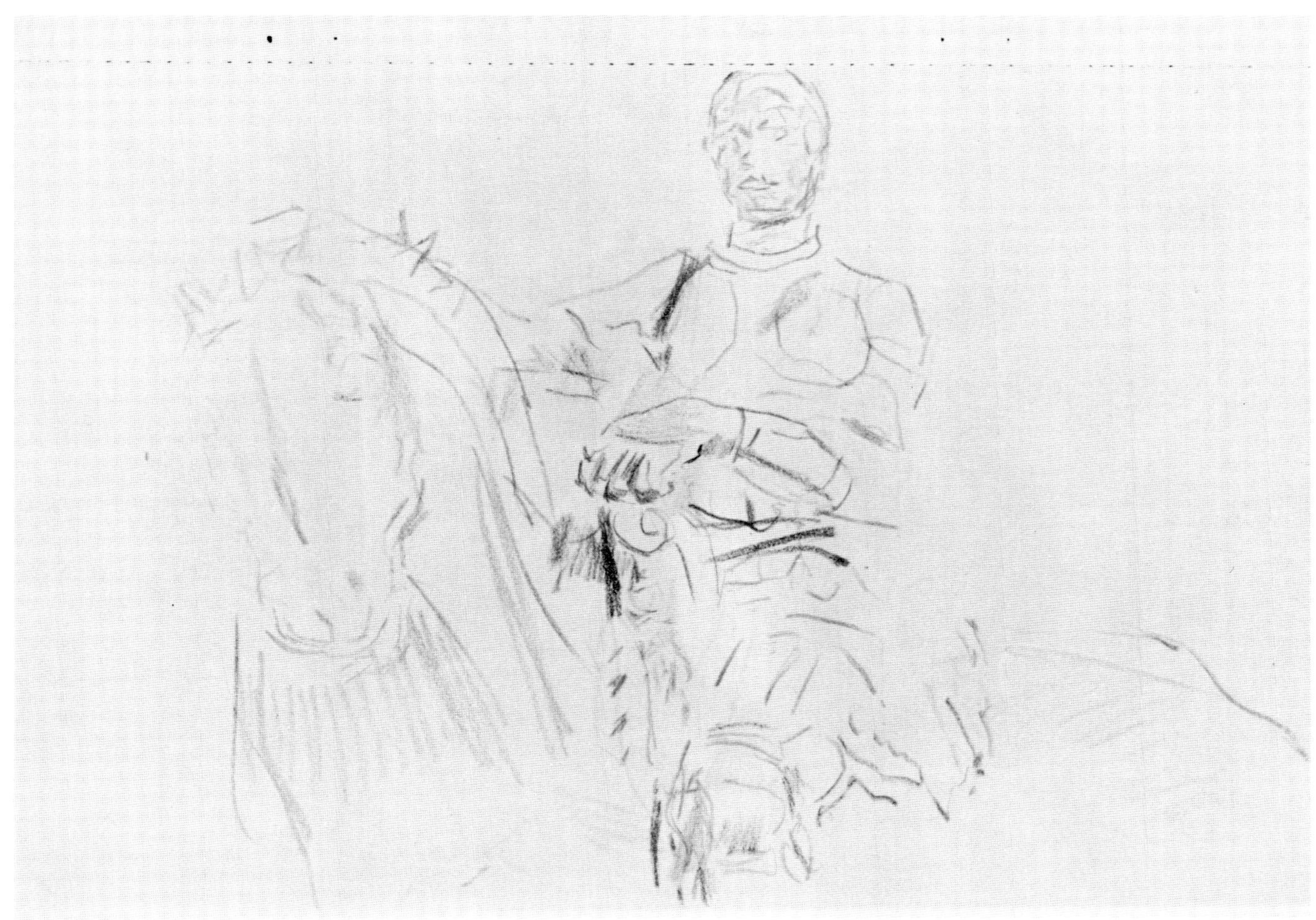

Cat. 183 *Gattamelata,* 1948

The single most qualifying aspect of the criticism of Kokoschka's late works is the limited consideration given to his graphic output. In his late prints, perhaps more fully than in his paintings, Kokoschka shows himself to be a master very much in control of his creative faculties, exploring themes and ideas which had preoccupied him most of his life.

When, for example, Kokoschka created a cycle of ten prints for Heinrich von Kleist's *Penthesilea* in 1969 (published in 1970), he was reinvestigating ideas which had riveted his attention from the time that he was introduced to the play as a young schoolboy. Karl Schorsky has convincingly shown the extent to which Kleist's work was central to the development of Kokoschka's earliest fully expressionist play, *Murderer, Hope of Women*: "Tearing off the decent draperies of Homeric mythology, he compressed Kleist's classic drama into short, stark, archetypal action."[39]

In an important sense, Kokoschka's illustrations for Kleist's 1808 work maintain that stark, elemental quality, never embellishing the mythological context but, instead, drawing from it its essential human quotient. In one scene, "Penthesilea Tries to Eat the Dead Achilles" (Cat. 138), Penthesilea, a crazed expression on her face, digs into the body of the dead Achilles with her fingers and with her teeth bites into his shoulder. In its dramatic confrontation between the two protagonists Kokoschka probes imagery with which he initiated his expressionism in the *Pietà* poster of 1909.

In the last illustration of the series, "Penthesilea Kills Herself" (Cat. 139), we see Penthesilea at the right plunging a knife into her breast, her face filled with anguish, head tilted back while the pearls which decorate her hair sweep expressively around it. To her left is the body of Achilles and hovering above it are two growling dogs. The elemental nature of this scene resurrects the torturous imagery from the artist's very beginning. We have already observed the howling dogs making threatening and anxious gestures in such works as *Lovers* of 1906, among others. Penthesilea's stabbing gesture reconsiders the most common form of violent death in Kokoschka's oeuvre, permeating both his literary and pictorial syntax.

In another example of the type, "Priam is Slain at the Altar in His Palace" (Cat. 150), one of the scenes for *The Women of Troy* of 1971–1972, Kokoschka depicts the anguished Priam in the foreground being stabbed with a dagger by a figure at the left identified as a soldier, whose profile is tantalizingly similar to that of the woman who dominated his early imagery.

It is not possible to view Kokoschka's late works without being aware of the profoundly personal quality of his art and the constant resonances with his past that they evoke.

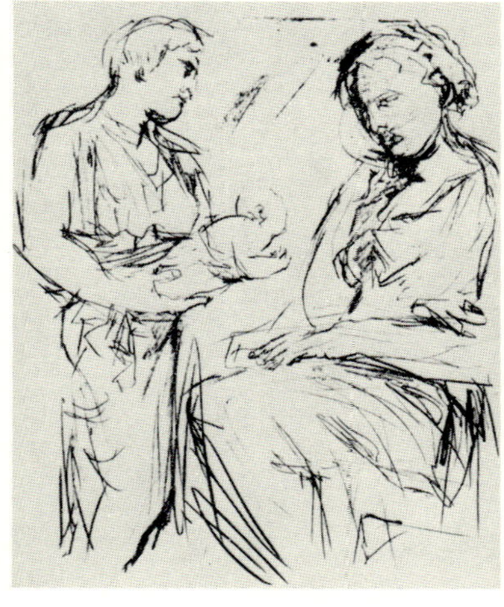

Fig. 28 *Funerary Stele with Child*, 1961 (WW 250)

For example, Kokoschka's depiction of an antique funerary stele from his 1961 *Bekenntnis zu Hellas (Homage to Hellas)* (Figure 28)—showing a standing figure on the left, probably a servant, holding out an infant toward the seated female figure on the right—can be seen on one level as a copy of a Greek work which the artist discovered in the National Museum in Athens and which appealed to him on a visual level alone.

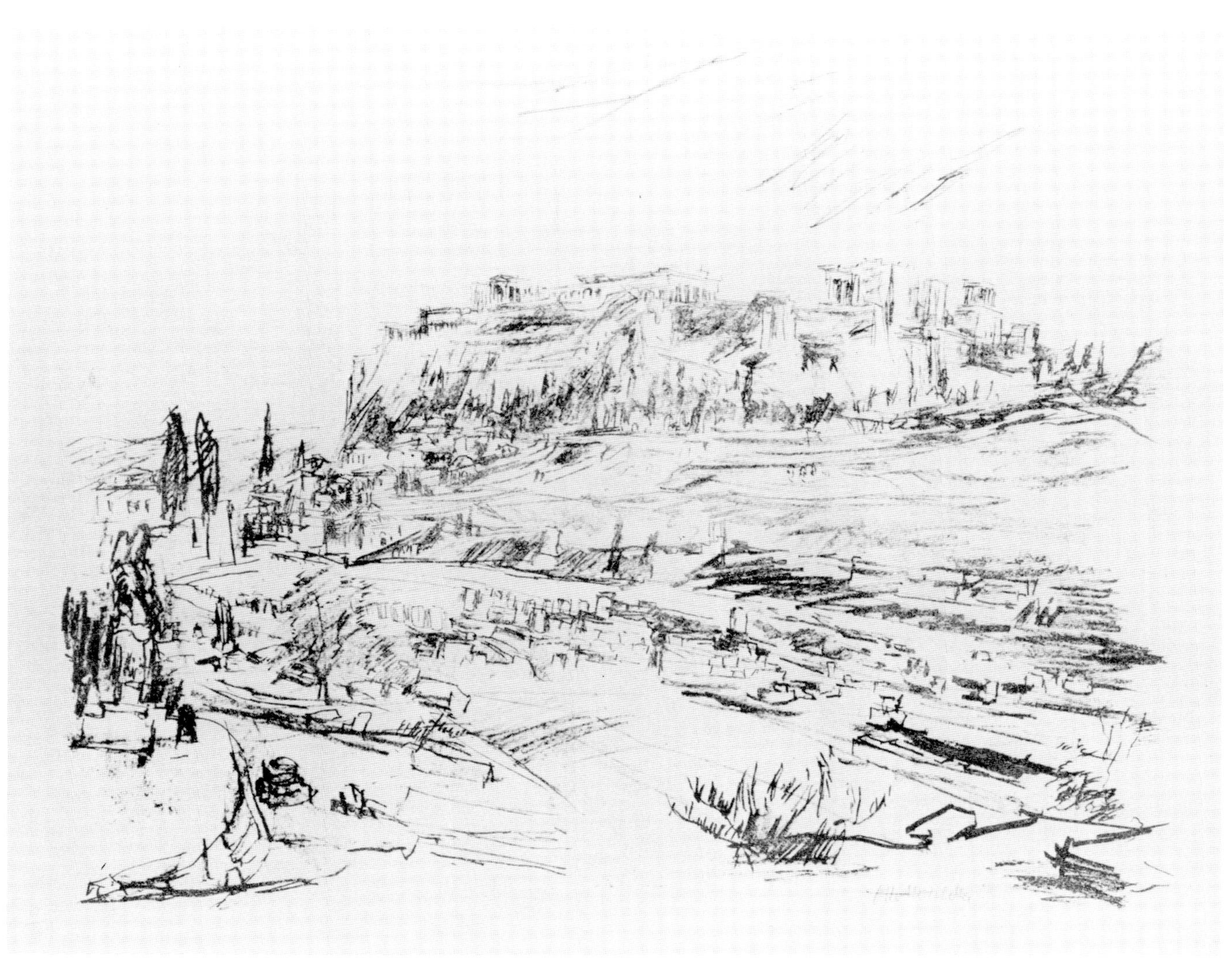

Cat. 71 *Acropolis* I, 1961

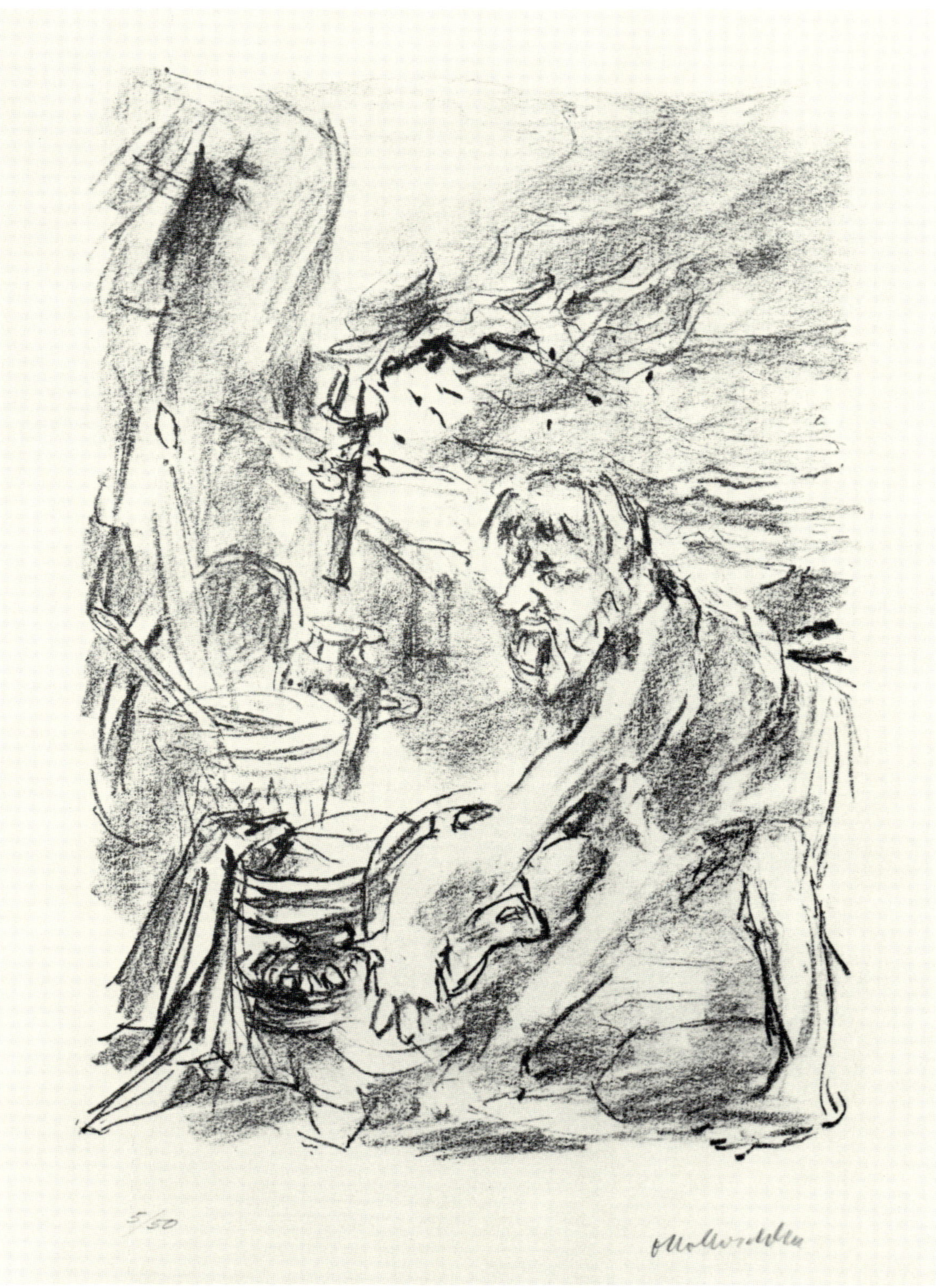

Cat. 88 *Ulysses Awakes after Landing on Ithaca,* 1963–65

This ability on Kokoschka's part to distill from other works of art a quality which in some way touches upon his own experience is a quality we find as a constant in his oeuvre.

But Kokoschka, in interpreting the scene, establishes a dramatic confrontation. The child, an indistinct, lightly outlined form in the center of the composition, is thrust toward the seated figure by the servant. With its outstretched arms it seems to reach out for the seated woman who does not reciprocate the gesture, and whose face, accentuated by a dark shadow around it, seems to reflect both grief and anxiety.

At the time of the creation of the above work, Kokoschka was a man of seventy-five. One of the regrets of his life was that he never fathered a child. In turning to this motif is the artist recalling once again Alma Mahler's abortion of their child? In 1915 Kokoschka had specifically addressed this tragic event in the context of a personal interpretation of the Greek legend of *Orpheus and Eurydice.*

This ability on Kokoschka's part to distill from other works of art a quality which in some way touches upon his own experience is a quality we find as a constant in his oeuvre. For example, there is in the present exhibition a pencil drawing by the artist of 1948 of Donatello's Paduan equestrian monument of the condottiere Erasmo da Narni, known more commonly as *Gattamelata* (Cat. 183). The artist returns once more to the theme of a knight-warrior in armor—an image which he had treated often throughout his career, most prominently and personally in his self-portrait, *Knight Errant* of 1915.

There is, of course, a difference between the earlier, deeply personal renderings of the motif and the present one in which Kokoschka is paying homage to one of the great monuments of the Quattrocento. Even so, the artist's choice of vantage point and focus in the drawing suggests his understanding of Donatello's most profound intent. Physically, the most compelling aspect of the sculptor's work, as well as the most public, is the imposing massiveness of the horse and the exquisite detail in the casting process evident in every part of the statue. Kokoschka, however, largely omits these elements in the drawing, suggesting, for example, the imposing bulk of the horse with only a few summary lines. Instead, he focuses on the least "public," yet the most compelling part of the work—the psychologically complex features of Gattamelata's head—for it is there that Donatello shows his greatest gift—an ability to probe the essence of a person as he explores in the features of the face the strengths, vulnerabilities, anxieties and ambitions of his complex personality. Kokoschka renders the head in a series of densely knit lines of color, which coalesce to make Gattamelata's facial features physically and psychologically the most expressive part of the drawing.

This ability to charge a monument with a special pulse is displayed brilliantly by Kokoschka in his crayon drawing of an ancient kouros, *Kouros* I of 1968 (Cat. 135). By viewing the work from a low vantage point and three-quarter view, the artist is able to extract from the archaic statue a silhouette which, rather than being rigid and symmetrical, becomes animated with life which, in the development of Greek art, will not yet occur for a number of decades. Enlivening the image, too, is the vigorously broken silhouette treated in a multitude of colors—as is the figure and the background. It is not surprising that this vibrant, life-enhancing image was made into a color serigraph

The classical context in which so much of Kokoschka's late imagery is explored shows his profound attachment to the principles of Greek art, literature and philosophy.

and used as the poster for the 1972 Munich Olympic Games.

It is in the *Homage to Hellas* series that Kokoschka's intoxication with the wide panorama of the Greek experience manifests itself most clearly.

In his "Acropolis I" (Cat. 71), the artist displays once again his strength as a landscapist. Through a sequence of broad, expressive sweeps of the crayon and a dramatic intensification of light and shade passages, he imbues the view with a pulsating energy and a sense of immediacy. The Acropolis is in the distance and culminates the composition. Its buildings, recognizable to us even from afar—the Erechtheum, the Parthenon and others—create a sequence of interrelated, vigorous geometries which exist like a thin crust of civilization which man has posited on earth between heaven and the dynamic chaos of the landscape beneath.

Kokoschka exhibits in this work an ability to capture the essential meaning of a locale, to interpret it not as a relic of history, but as something filled with the excitement and energy of life. One of Kokoschka's lasting contributions to twentieth-century art is his stirring series of landscapes, often of cities whose "portraits" the artist has rendered. The above lithograph belongs among the more stirring of these "portraits."

The classical context in which so much of Kokoschka's late imagery is explored shows his profound attachment to the principles of Greek art, literature and philosophy. It is an attitude which, in relation to this exhibition, created the richest bond between Kokoschka and Count Bethusy-Huc. And while Kokoschka travelled to Greece only later in his life, its impulse had been with him from the very outset when the young boy received from his father, along with Comenius's *Orbis pictus,* an illustrated volume of Greek legends.

By far the most ambitious of the cycles dealing with Greek subject matter is Kokoschka's illustration of forty-four lithographs for Homer's *Odyssey* on which he worked between 1963 and 1965. The artist immersed himself in the project and, of his own volition, expanded it to include the whole saga rather than just a part of it as was originally planned. The sheer number of prints suggests that he was loath to omit any significant moment of the story which he revelled in recounting for us, for Kokoschka's role here is best described as one of guide and narrator using his richly interpretive images instead of words. Yet clearly he is more, for his identification with the figure of Odysseus himself is powerful and self-evident, as the artist attests: "I could identify myself with this figure of Odysseus as a vagabond, as an eternal wanderer."[40] Gracing the cover of this catalogue is a postcard done by Kokoschka for the Wiener Werkstätte, *Rider and Sailing Ship* of 1907 (Cat. 4), in which we see the artist in a self-portrait as a rider, gesturing with his right hand in a sweeping, expansive manner. Surrounding him are symbols of youthful yearning—a hilly landscape and, in the distance a sailship. Already at this early date, Kokoschka manifests his sense of adventure and establishes a prototype which will experience many permutations throughout the artist's long career, finally culminating in the hero of the Odyssey saga.

Among the more exceptional aspects of Kokoschka's *Odyssey* is the strength

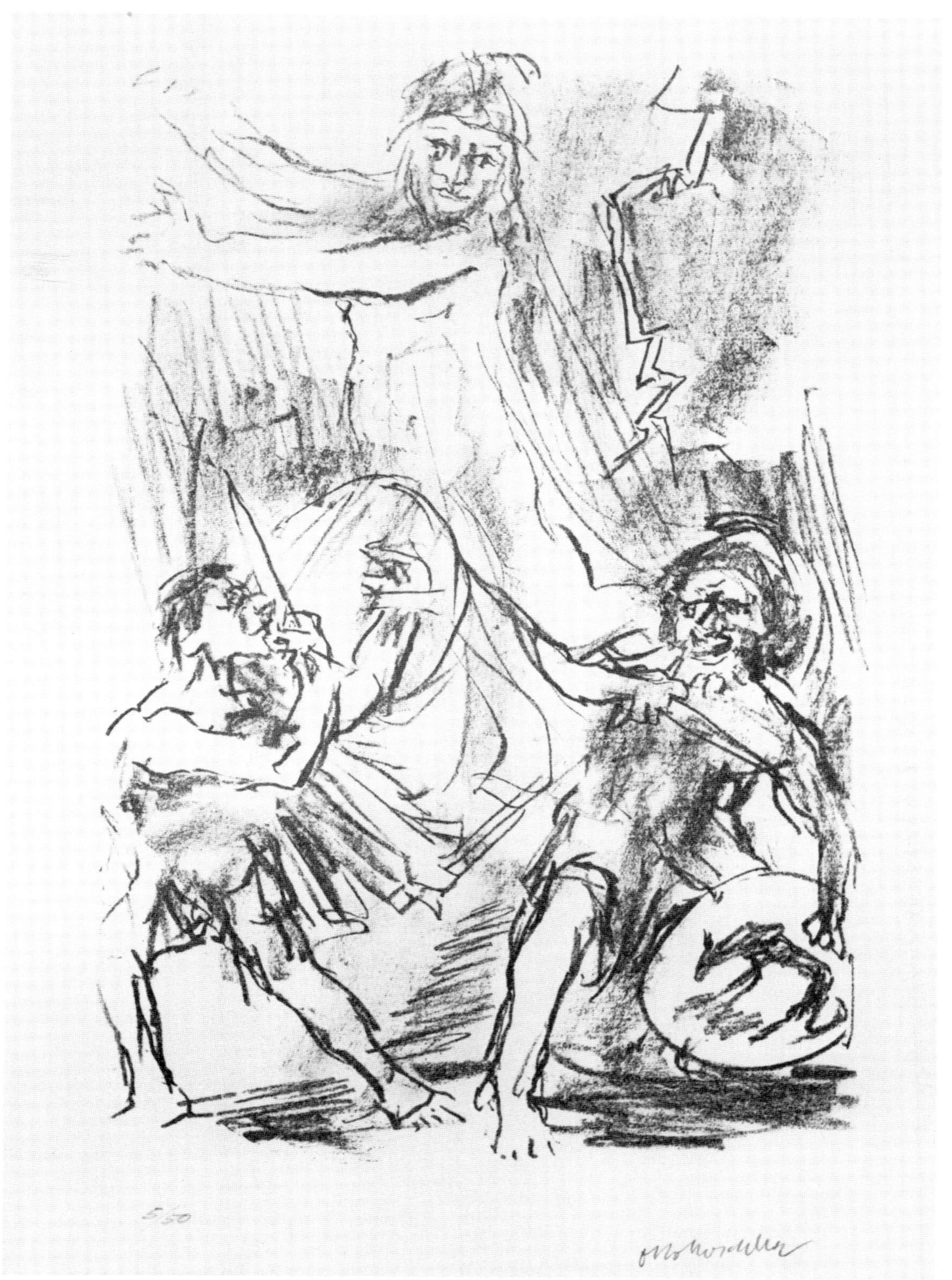

Cat. 96 *Athena Halts the Combat*, 1963–65

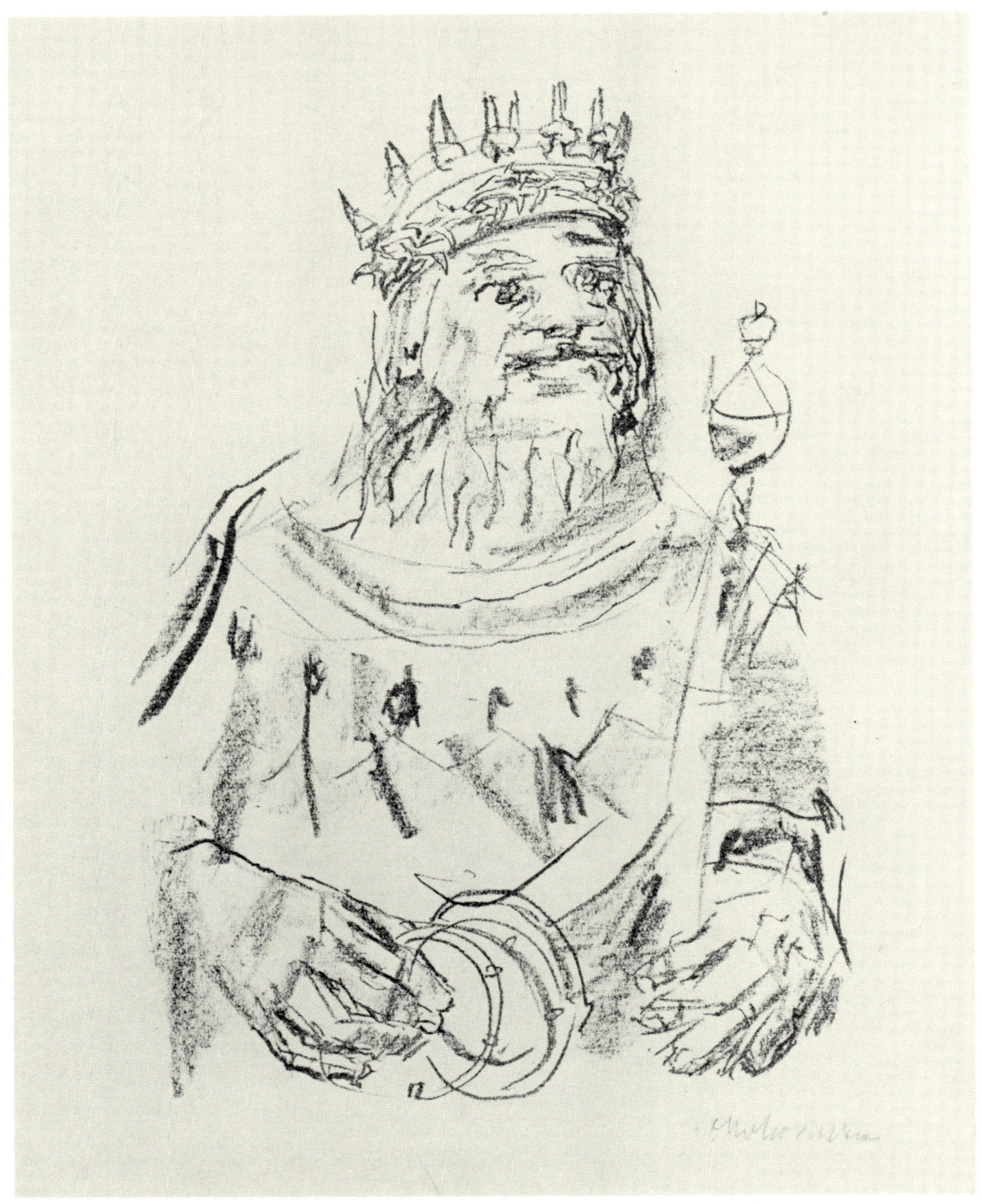

Cat. 64 *Portrait of King Lear*, 1963

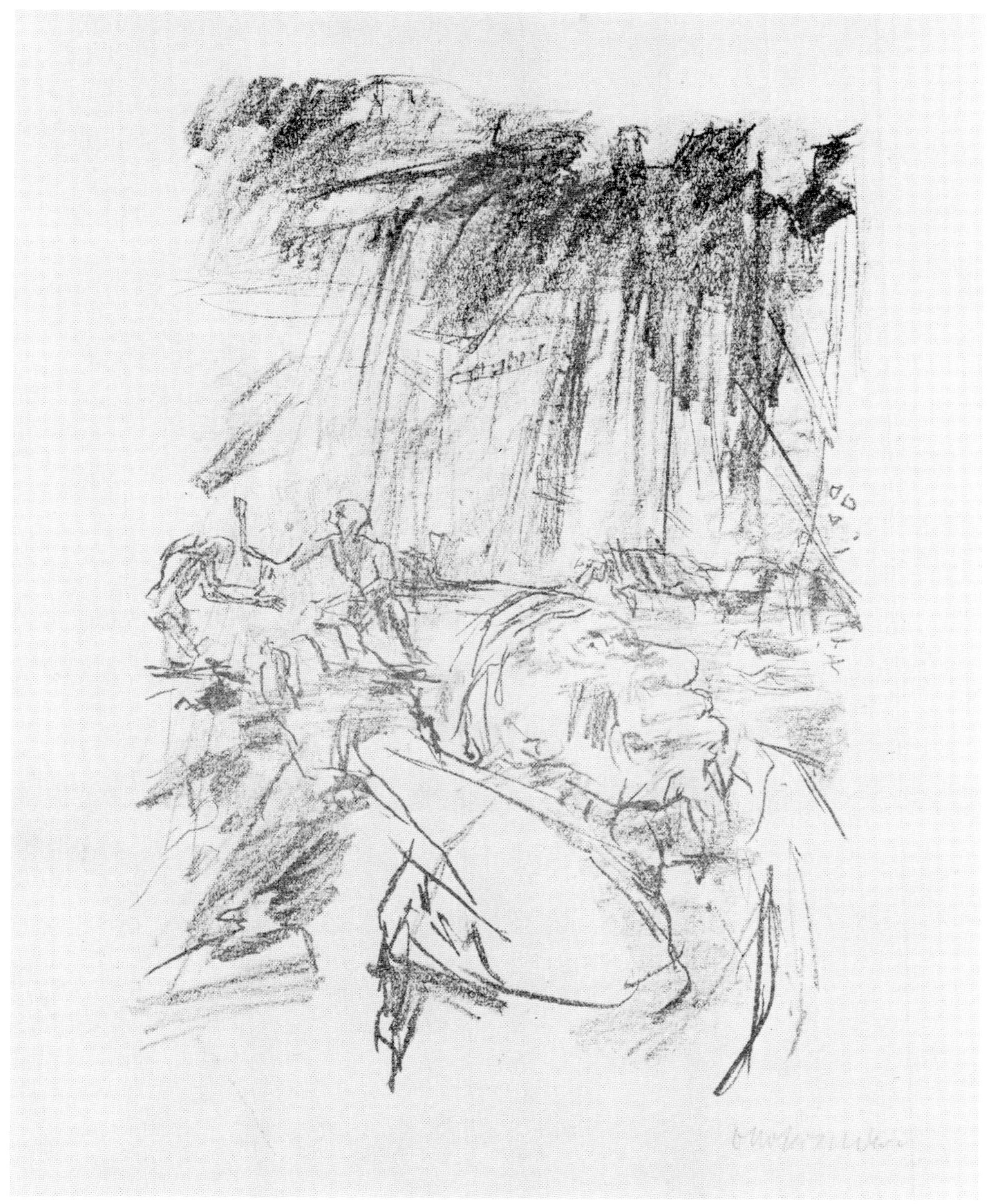

Cat. 65 *Lear: Poor naked wretches* (III, iv), 1963

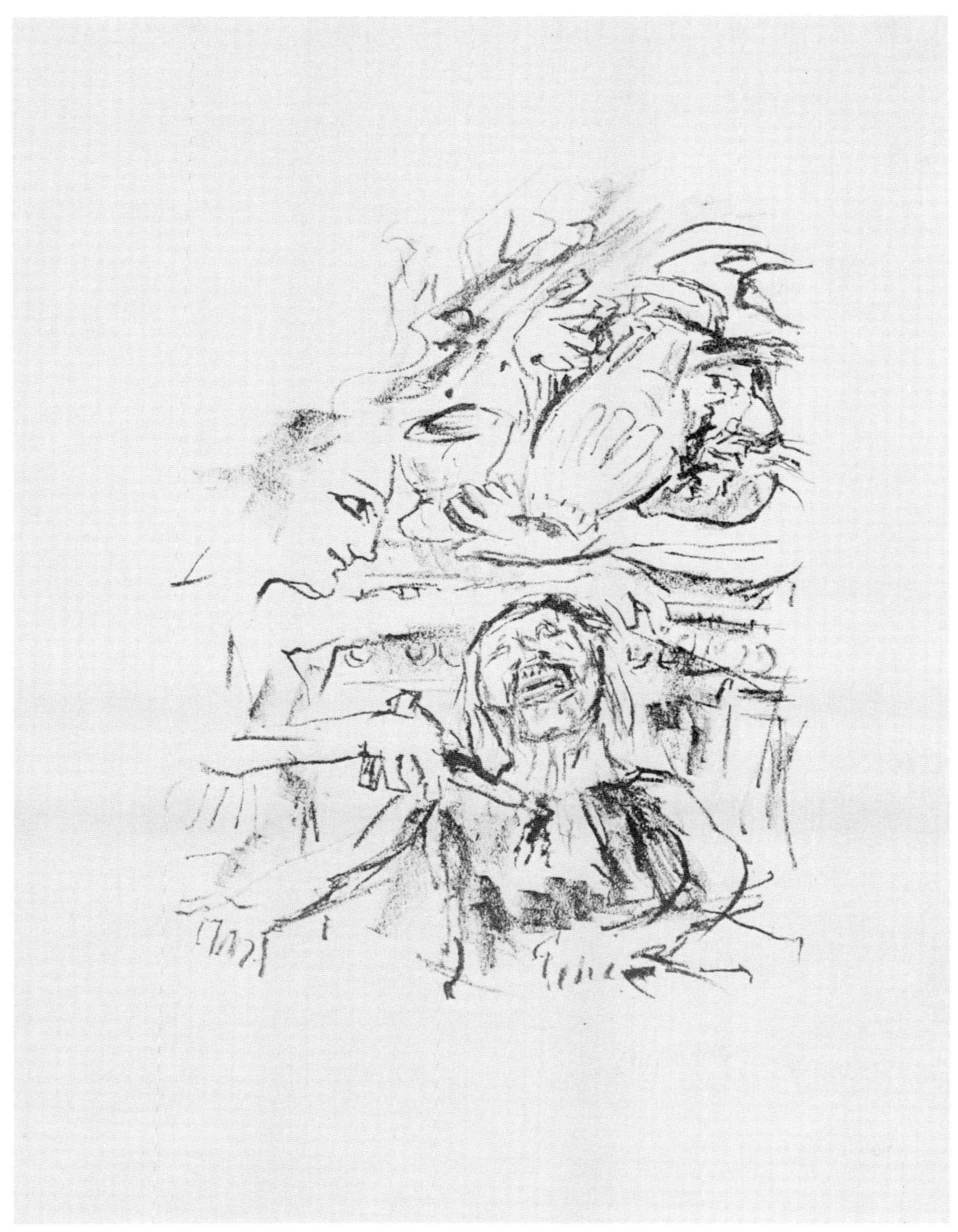

Cat. 150 *Priam is Slain at the Altar in His Palace*, 1971–72

and inventiveness of the images, which is, at least in part, aided by his willingness to reinvestigate his earlier narrative cycles.

For example, in "The Shipwreck of Ulysses" (WW 300), Kokoschka addresses a familiar motif which he resolved most brilliantly in *The Tempest* of 1914. Yet the image of Ulysses alone, suspended in a threatening environment, surrounded by water and clinging to the remains of a wrecked ship, evokes scenes which Kokoschka probed most successfully in *The Fettered Columbus* in such images as "Man with Upraised Arm and Death" (WW 50).

Kokoschka would turn to this cycle at least two more times in developing his imagery for the *Odyssey.* In "Ulysses Meets Nausikaa" (WW 301), the artist places the two nude figures in a landscape environment. As Ulysses begins to sink to his knees before Nausikaa, the two are arrested by the artist in poses which evoke an exotic, dance-like ritual analogous to the one in which Kokoschka and Alma Mahler engage in the print, "The Meeting" of 1913. In another scene, "Ulysses Awakes at the Landing in Ithaca" (Cat. 88), Ulysses holds a brightly lit torch in his right hand, a motif Kokoschka used often and especially in the earlier works, perhaps most dramatically in a scene entitled "At the Crossroads (WW 49), also from the earlier cycle.

It is not insignificant that a number of the *Odyssey* scenes echo those in *The Fettered Columbus* whose hero was yet another adventurer with whom Kokoschka identified. Soon after having completed his *Odyssey* cycle, the artist was asked in an interview to comment on the earlier work. His reply, as quoted previously, was, "Columbus, of course, is me again . . ."

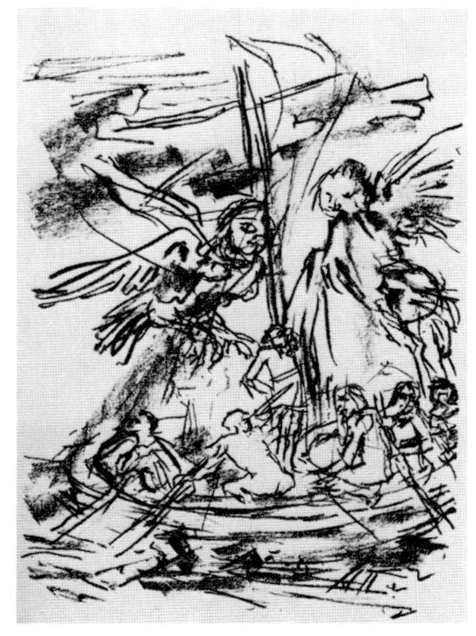

Fig. 29 *The Sirens,* 1963–65 (WW 310)

There are also other early cycles to which Kokoschka makes oblique reference in his *Odyssey.* In the scene, "The Sirens" (Figure 29), he depicts the winged sirens hovering provocatively above the ship. As discussed earlier, the artist introduced such winged prototypes in an illustration, "Sun over a Birdlike Pair," for his poem, *Allos Makar* of 1915, which was in turn inspired by Francisco Goya's etching, "Todos Caerán" (All Will Fall) from *Los Caprichos* of 1799, an image which in its provocative sexual interplay of the winged creatures is also close to Kokoschka's "The Sirens" scene. This affinity with a work by Goya, who had inspired Kokoschka often in the past, brings up an important issue of the influence of other artists on the *Odyssey* cycle.

A more unexpected source is to be found in the last scene of the series, "Athena Quiets the Battle" (Cat. 96). In it Kokoschka places Athena in the middle between two shielded figures poised for battle. In this configuration he distills the essential figures of J. L. David's *Sabine Women* of 1799, in which the central female figure serves as an instrument of reconciliation between the Roman and Sabine warriors. An important principle of Kokoschka's art is illustrated here, namely, that when he turns to a source for inspiration, he is often attracted not only by a compelling compositional resolution, or a striking detail, but also by the iconographic affinity with his own intention.

Kokoschka's illustration of the *Odyssey* saga is one of three major cycles of his late years. The other two are *Saul and David*, illustrating the Old Testament text, and his scenes for Shakespeare's *King Lear*. They are the most ambitious and even in their number echo the three major cycles of his early career, *The Chinese Wall*, *The Fettered Columbus* and the *Bach Cantata*. There are compelling continuities which reverberate between the early and late works as the above consideration of the *Odyssey* cycle demonstrates. Yet more than fifty years separate the cycles and, quite understandably, there are significant differences between them, both stylistic and iconographic. Generally, Kokoschka's late works are articulated by a broken, animated line which moves restlessly across the surface suggesting, never defining, his varied imagery—its intensity always asserts itself and is never subsumed by the subject represented.

Kokoschka's early works sustain an exquisite tension and separateness between the written word and his imagery. Karl Schorsky's observation about *The Dreaming Youths* and *Murderer, Hope of Women* holds equally true for the three cycles from his early period: "Kokoschka remains indifferent to the literal correspondance between picture and text. Only reciprocal intensification is the dramatist's aim, and that he achieves in abundance."[41]

In the late works this equation is lessened. Kokoschka's imagery aligns itself more closely with the text. Yet this is a question of degree because his late works sustain an individuality of vision. He never becomes an illustrator of the text but rather its interpreter. Part of this closer affinity between text and scene is necessitated by the fact that the artist is addressing in the later works some of the most renowned texts of western literature.

He never becomes an illustrator of the text but rather its interpreter.

Kokoschka's illustration of Shakespeare's *King Lear* initiates the evolution of his three major late cycles. The circumstances of its creation are related by Bernard Baer, who established initial contact with the artist for it after having seen the *Bach Cantata* in the Kokoschka exhibition at the Tate Gallery in 1962—a fact which in a very concrete way demonstrates the continuity between the artist's early and late works. Baer grasped the significance of Kokoschka's deeply personal narrative style when he wrote to the artist in the negotiations for the *King Lear* cycle: "Obviously we do not think of any literal form of illustration, but rather of evocations of the feeling, tensions and passions of this great tragedy."[42] Rather than setting preconditions, Baer is instead stating the only condition he knew Kokoschka would accept. What the artist was being asked to create was a visual analogue to one of literature's masterpieces. He produced in a relatively short period a series of fourteen lithographs which, while they allude to specific passages in the play, could, at the same time, stand on their own as documents of the exploration of the human spirit.

Kokoschka opens the cycle with a half-length "Portrait of King Lear" (Cat. 64), who stares quizzically out to the side. The crown atop his head, rather than being a symbol of power, becomes a cause of his anguish. Lear's immediate antecedent in Kokoschka's oeuvre is, in fact, an image of a half-length figure of *Christ with Crown of Thorns* (Cat. 59), of 1956. In the above allusion, Kokoschka is evoking, as well, his own

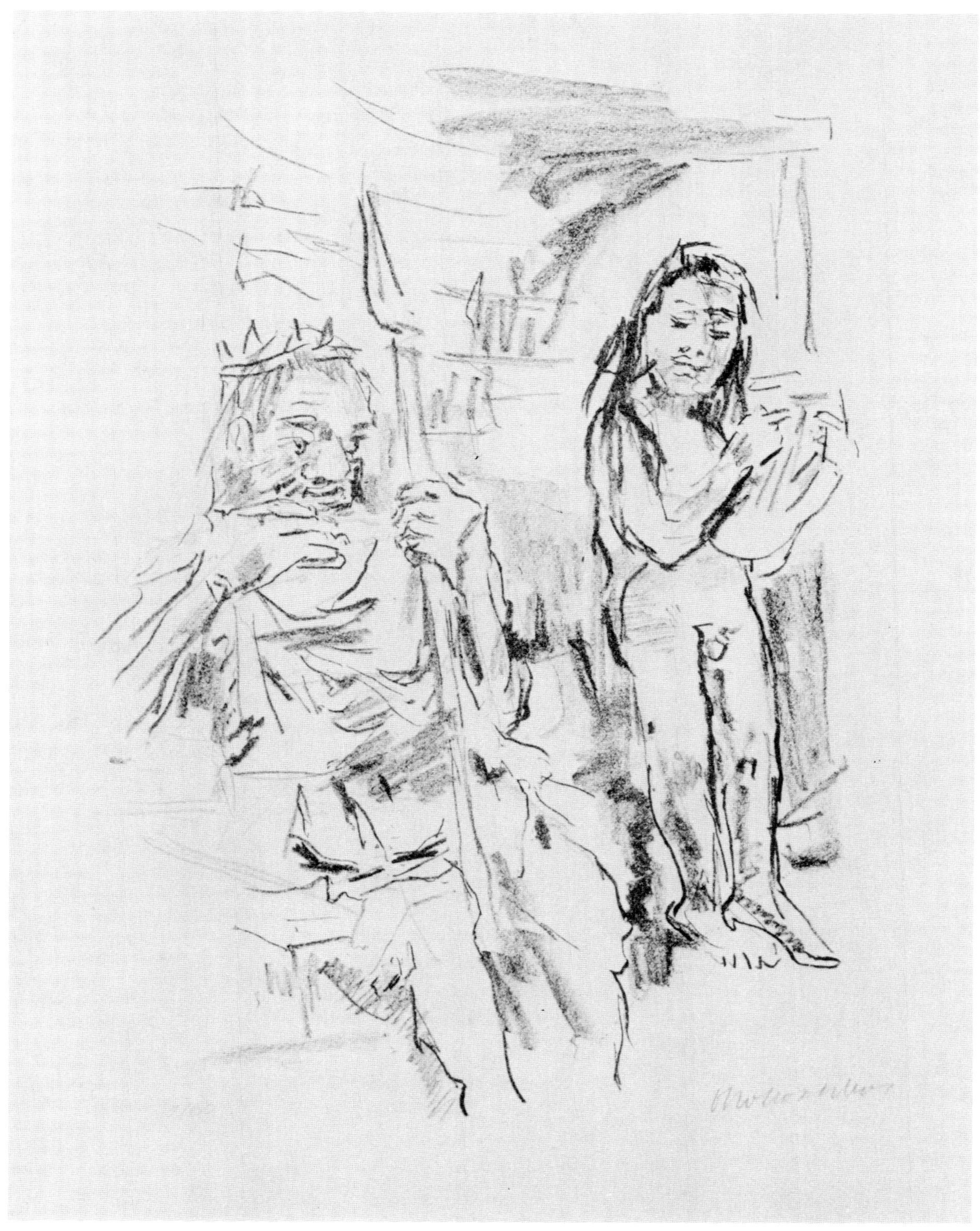

Cat. 116 *David Playing the Harp to Saul*, 1966–68

frequent association with the suffering Christ and, by extension, with Lear, one of literature's most complex and compelling elder statesmen.

The penultimate print of the *King Lear* cycle, "Lear: Poor naked wretches" (Cat. 65), portrays Lear's prayer in the storm. According to Baer, who followed the development of the cycle closely, the above scene was the last to be completed and was the most meaningful for the artist. Kokoschka's expressive translation of the critical moment in Shakespeare's play displays the artist's talent at its height. He imbues the scene with near hallucinatory power by intensifying the explosive energy of the storm in the upper portion of the work and by thrusting the image of Lear into dramatically close proximity to the viewer. The king's upper torso, culminating in a powerful, expressive head, dominates the lower portion of the print. By focusing so strongly on the head, Kokoschka insists that we, as viewers, come to grips with the intense psychological predicament of Lear. The head is tilted heavenward, his eyes staring wide open are pained by inner torment; and the storm becomes the outward manifestation of this state. The raised right hand, close to the head, accentuates the state of vulnerability and anguish.

In conflating psychological anguish with a physically threatening environment, Kokoschka reiterates a condition which occurs often in his art, especially in his works just prior to World War I. For example, it is precisely this equation which gives *The Tempest* of 1914 and *Knight Errant* of 1915 their expressive power.

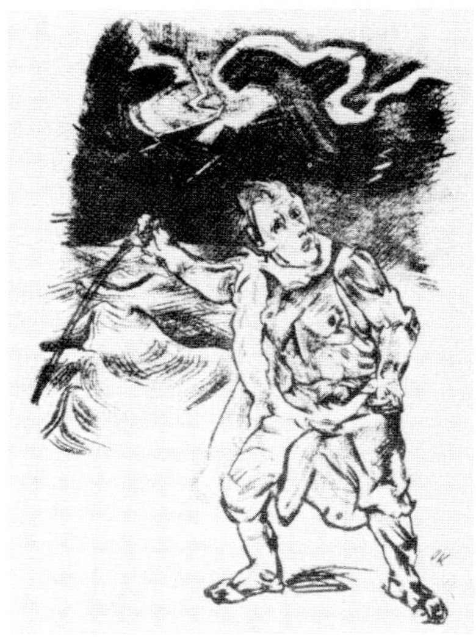

Fig. 30 *Wanderer in the Storm*, 1914 (WW 60)

Equally compelling for the *Lear* print is the image of "Wanderer in the Storm" (Figure 30), the third scene from the *Bach Cantata* cycle. The isolated figure of the wanderer in a threatening, stormy landscape at water's edge, is the artist himself. The strongly defined figure placed in the foreground dominates the scene. Above, the dark sky is animated by a ribbon of light which streaks across the top, adding a sense of nervous urgency to the whole scene. The wanderer holds a staff in the right hand, his head is tilted upward, and he stares out quizzically and anxiously. The two protagonists in the *Bach Cantata* are Fear and Hope and in the "Wanderer" Kokoschka associates himself with Fear, as the image was inspired by the following words of the cantata:

Eternity, thou fearful word
O sword that pierces my soul!
O intimation of death!
O Eternity, time without end!

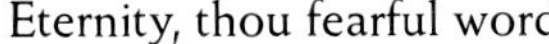

Lear could have uttered these words.

The third of the cycles, forty-one lithographic scenes for *Saul and David* illustrating the Old Testament, was undertaken by the artist in 1966, completed two years later and published in 1969. We encounter here once more not only a link with the other two cycles, but, by extension, with his earlier works. Here, too, the personal involvement with the subject is a critical factor. Thinking of the scene depicting "David Playing the Harp to Saul" (Cat. 116), Kokoschka states: "Saul is furious at being eighty,

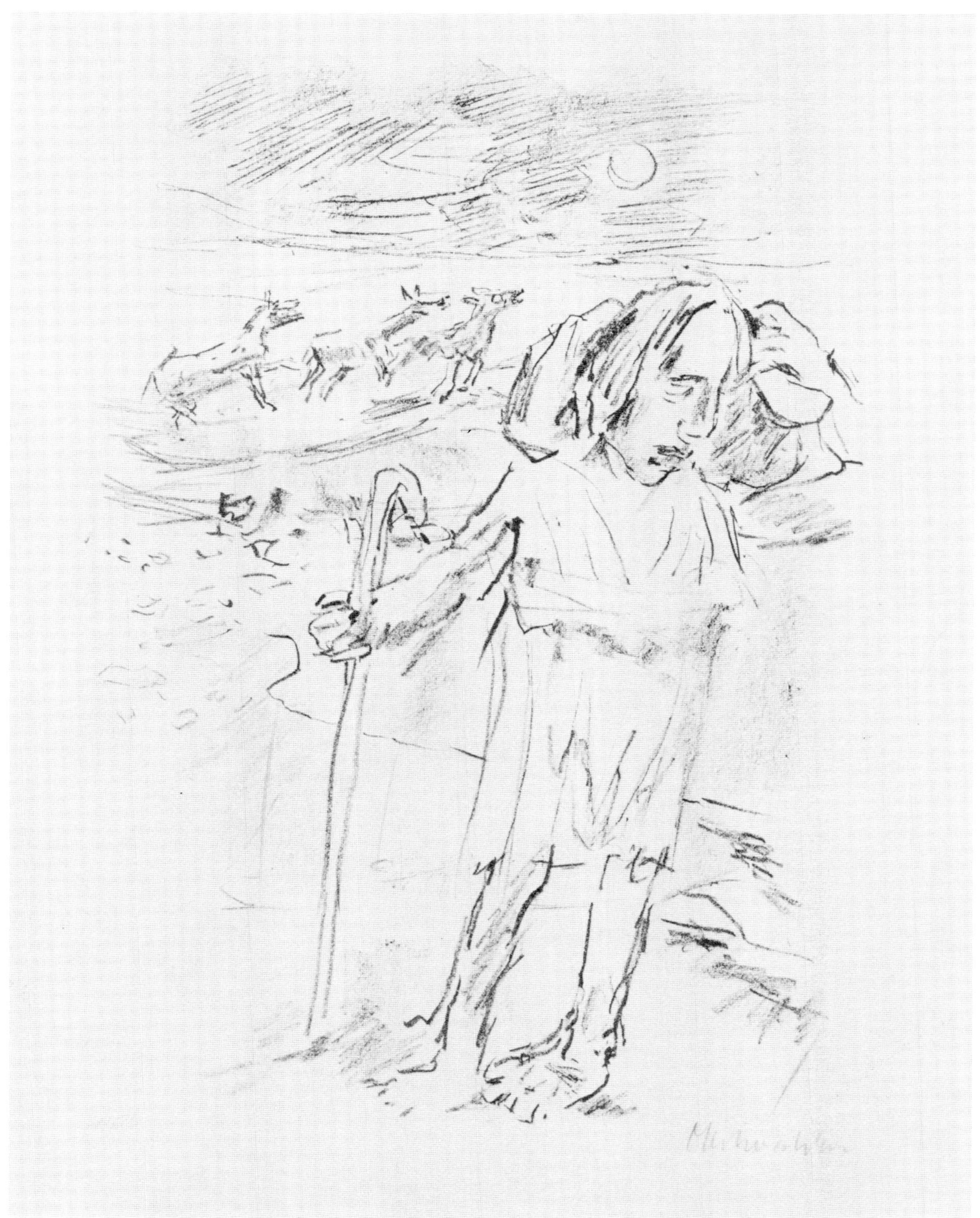

Cat. 118 *David Hiding Himself*, 1966–68

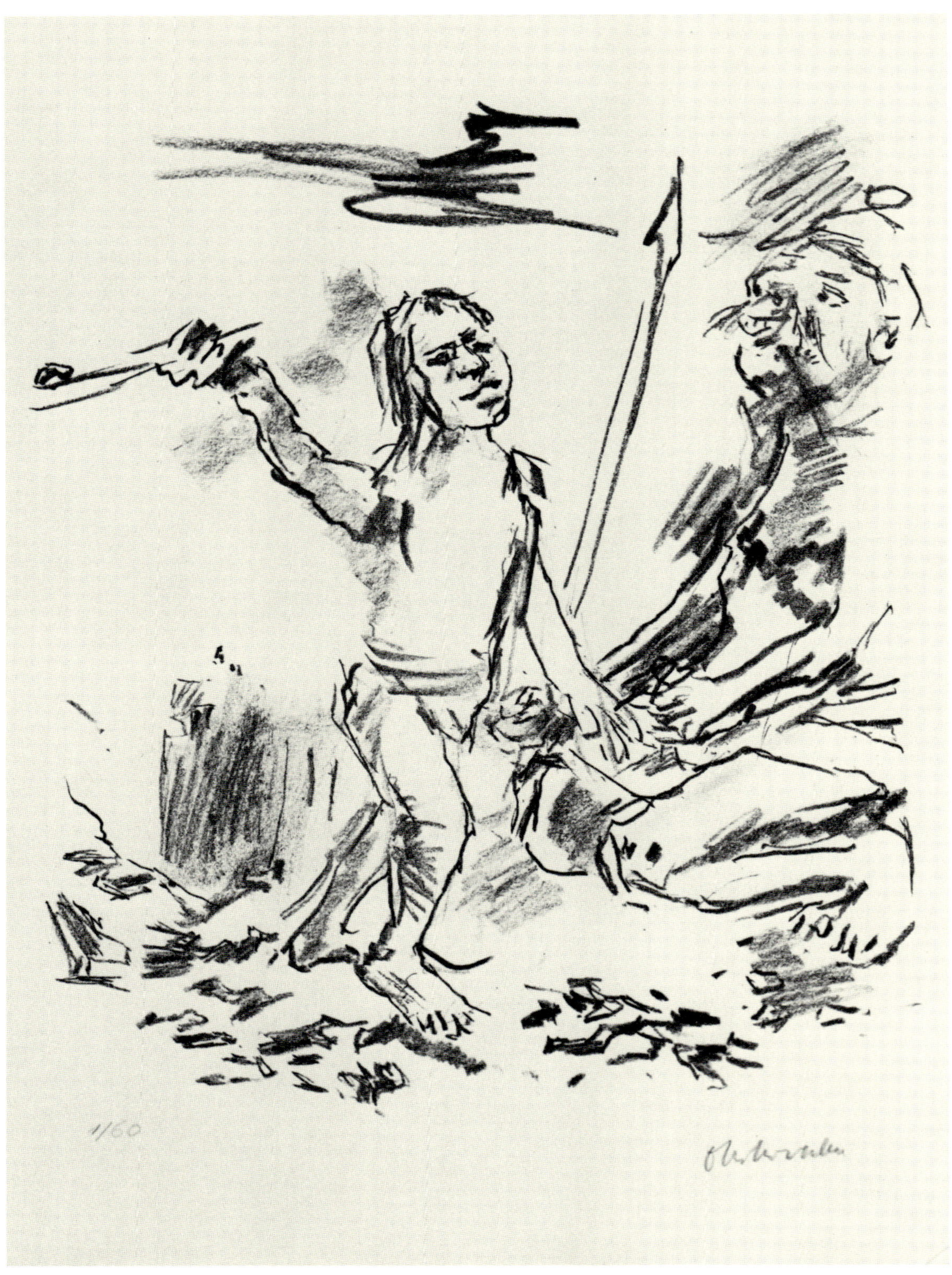

Cat. 117 *David Slayeth Goliath*, 1966–68

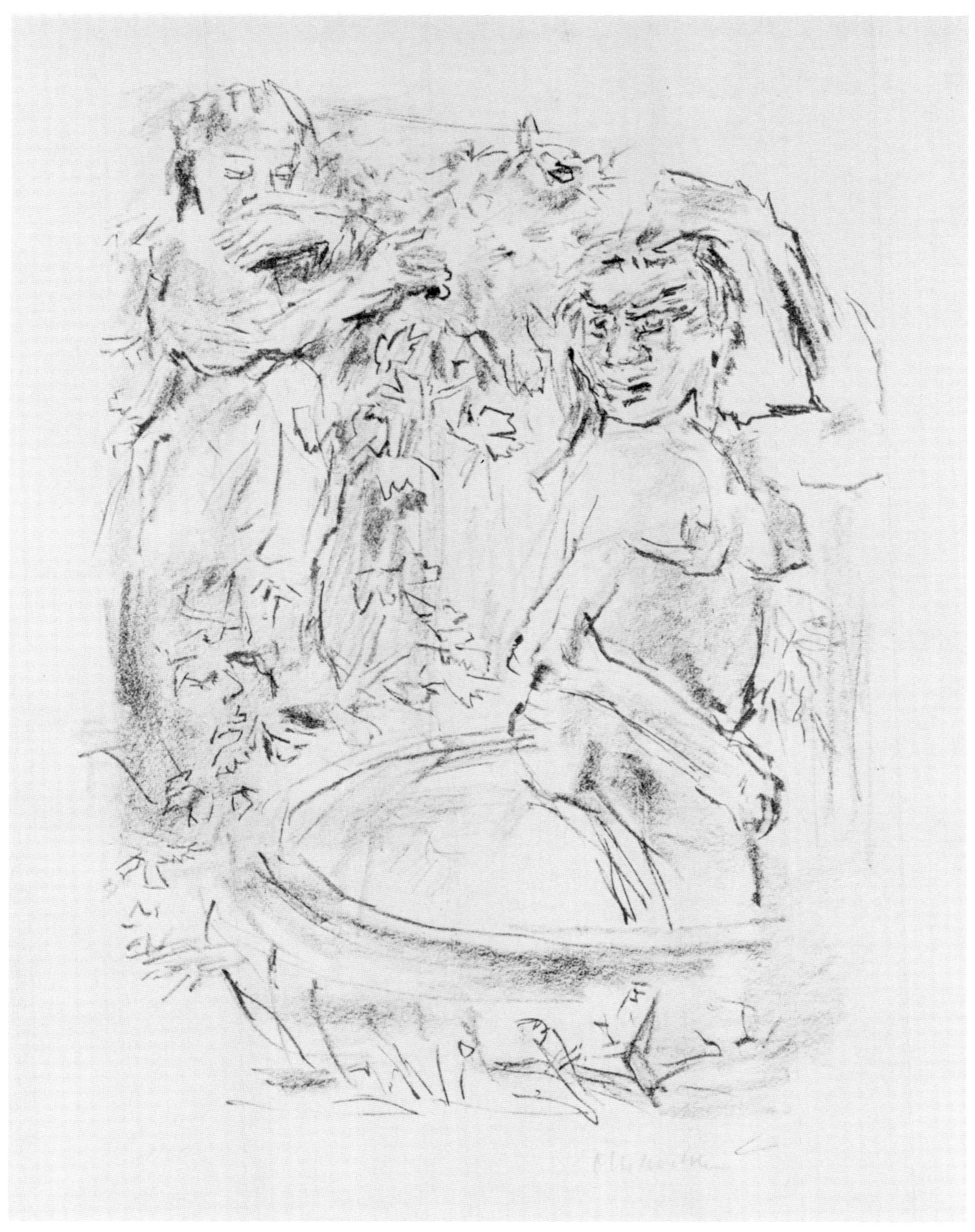

Cat. 123 *David and Bathsheba*, 1966–68

as I am. He cannot grasp the fact that he is now eighty as yesterday he was only eighteen—like David who is standing behind him—it seems only yesterday I was eighteen."[43]

A moving description of one of the major scenes in the cycle, "David Hiding Himself" (Cat. 118), comes from Count Bethusy-Huc:

> Night. The moon and the howling dogs increase for me the feeling of man being utterly exposed in this world (a feeling we find so often in the poetry of Georg Trakl), a feeling of *Angst* or some fear aroused by the inexplicable. The lithograph is strictly autobiographical as is every one of Kokoschka's creations; it is in fact a self-portrait. He creates an image here of his own great loneliness. It is an experience which has pervaded his whole life and which was essential to him. Without it he could not have said what he is going to bequeath to us . . .[44]

The aptness of these words are not only for the above scene but for "Lear" from the *King Lear* cycle, "The Wanderer" from the *Bach Cantata*, and numerous others of the artist's works. This condition was an imperative for Kokoschka—"It is not for him a cause of suffering, he sought it, and from it alone he has drawn his great visionary work."[45]

The fact that Kokoschka chooses to emphasize this scene—one which has such direct bearing on his own world view—underscores the extent to which the artist imposes on the story of Saul and David his own imprimatur. Conversely, for example, the conflict of "David Slayeth Goliath" (Cat. 117), a source of numerous masterpieces in the history of art, is interpreted by Kokoschka rather summarily—as if simply to include an important moment in the story.

When turning to scenes with issues which have sustained him throughout his career, as in "David and Bathsheba" (Cat. 123), where Bathsheba is shown in her bath, the artist gives them an intensity and focus which makes this scene, for instance, among the more dramatic images in the cycle. Bathsheba stands naked in the foreground, turned right while David is shown in the left background. Her moment of awareness that she is being watched is brilliantly captured by the abrupt twist of her head and the intense eyes reflecting both anxiety and anger. It is not her beauty that we are asked to respond to but her predicament and psychological state. Her forceful presence as a strong character in this drama bears a haunting resemblance to the images of Alma Mahler in his early works.

One of the last scenes of the series is titled "David in his Old Age" (Cat. 127). Rather than focusing on a moment in David's life, Kokoschka here addresses the condition of old age. David places his head on the womb of a nude young woman. She smiles and gently places her right hand on his slumping back. His moment in life is pointedly underscored by the skeletal head in the lower right. David's face, partly turned toward us, is, if not happy, then at least at peace. In this scene, Kokoschka seems to reach out in his old age toward a reconciliation and resolution of the dialogue

Kokoschka seems to reach out in his old age toward a reconciliation and resolution of the dialogue between man and woman . . .

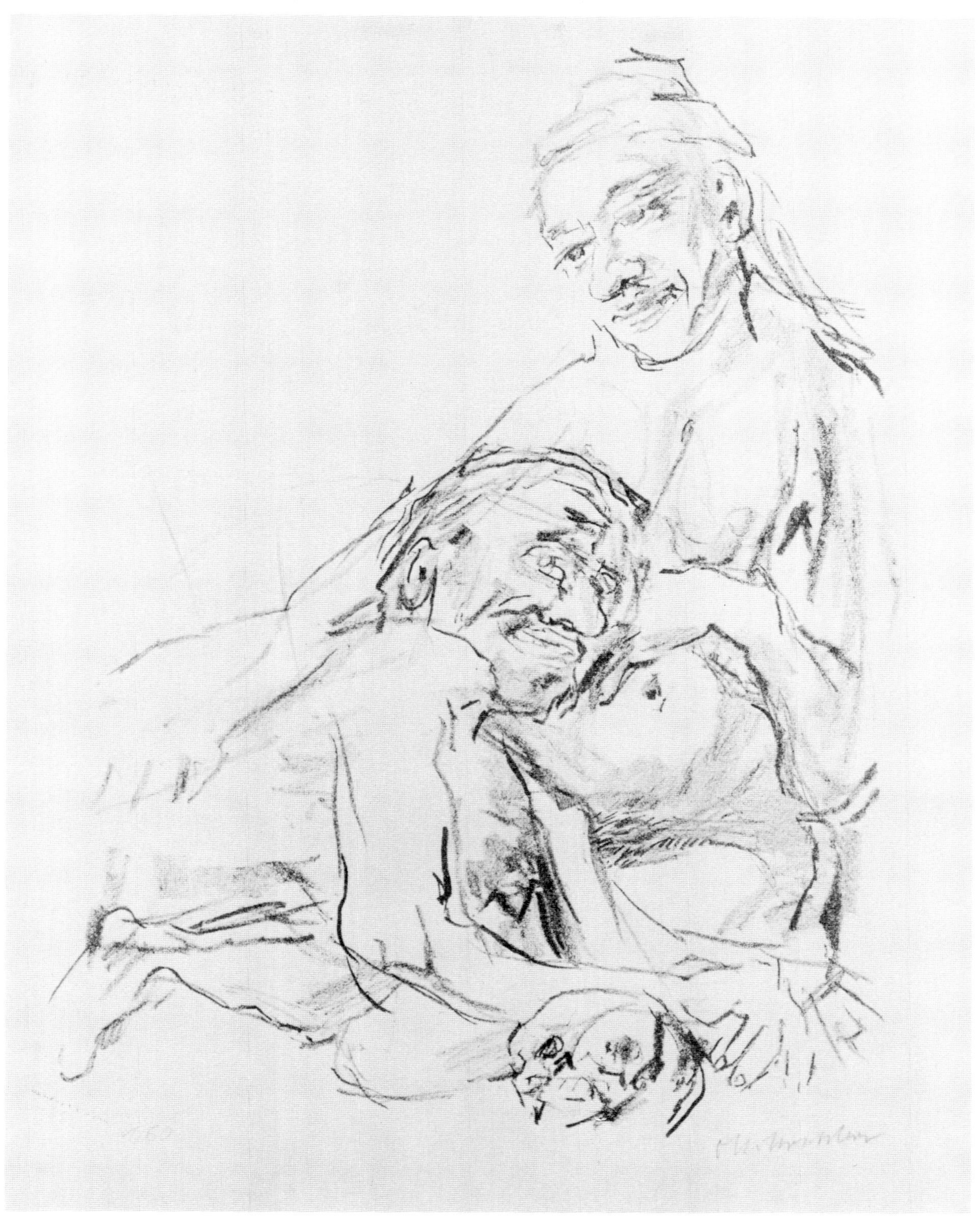

Cat. 127 *David in His Old Age*, 1966–68

between man and woman which with such brutal starkness initiated his career.

Conclusion

In a 1912 public lecture, Kokoschka decided to put into words his ideas about art. On January 27, the hall of the Academic Society for Literature and Music in Vienna was used for the purpose; for the occasion the artist made a poster which was a variant of his *Der Sturm* poster of 1910, *Self-Portrait Pointing to Breast.* Kokoschka's gesture was not intended to rival the spellbinding lecture performances of Adolf Loos or Karl Kraus—two men who could fill a hall with enthralled audiences that hung on their every challenging, finely crafted argument. The artist may have been aware of the string of strongly worded manifestos of the Futurists whom Herwarth Walden especially championed or thoughtful essays by artists like Wassily Kandinsky and others.

Ultimately, however, the need to express himself welled up from within; and by all accounts, the lecture, entitled "On the Consciousness of Vision," was a sequence of deeply felt, at times compelling, often confusing thoughts uttered haltingly from notes which were lost soon thereafter. Somewhat later, Kokoschka reconstructed the lecture in an essay titled "On the Nature of Vision," where he attempted to define the process through which his imagination distilled into visual form impulses that were stimulated both from without and from within: "The life of consciousness is boundless. It interpenetrates the world and is woven through all its imagery . . . Of the forms that come into consciousness some are chosen while others are excluded . . . Consciousness is the source of all things and of all conceptions. It is a sea ringed with visions."[46]

". . . Consciousness is the source of all things and of all conceptions. It is a sea ringed with visions."

In language which evokes the image of the artist in the tomb scene from the *Bach Cantata,* he states: "My mind is the tomb of all those things which have ceased to be . . . So that each thing as it communicates itself to me, loses its substance and passes into the Hereafter, which is my mind."[47] For nearly three-quarters of a century a stream of images had reemerged from Kokoschka's mind, manifest especially vividly in his graphic oeuvre, staggering in their number and variety, and compelling in their uncompromising vision of the world. Comenius would have approved.

NOTES

1. Oskar Kokoschka, *My Life,* London, 1974, p. 11.
2. Frank Whitford, *Oskar Kokoschka,* New York, 1986, pp. 29–30.
3. Kokoschka's poster design, done in tempera, for the Kaiser Jubilaemus Huldigungsfestzug of 1908 is executed in a rough, spontaneous, gestural manner and may approximate the lost panels. On the back of a photograph of this image, the artist referred to the reason why it was not made into a poster: "It was not readily accepted by the committee of K. J. Festunzugs because at the time mere ornamentation, meander, schemes, etc., were more accepted by the Kunstgewerbeschule which was the leader of the official taste of the time." Ernest Rathenau, *Oskar Kokoschka Drawings, 1906–1965,* University of Miami Press, Coral Gables, Florida, 1970, pp. 50– 51.
4. An assessment of the two works appears in Ivan Fenjö's *OK Die Frühe Graphic,* Vienna, 1976, pp. 11– 16. Reinhold, Count Bethusy-Huc was instrumental in the publication of the above volume, which must rank among the most beautiful books on the artist.
5. Peter Vergo, *Art In Vienna 1899–1918,* London, 1975, p. 190.
6. Edith Hoffmann, *Kokoschka, Life and Work,* London, 1947, p. 39.

7. Alessandra Comini, *Egon Schiele's Portraits,* University of California Press, 1974, p. 34.
8. Wolfgang Fischer, "Kokoschka's early works: a conversation between the artist and Wolfgang Fischer at Villeneuve on 30 January 1966," *Kokoschka Lithographs,* Arts Council of Great Britain, London, 1966, p. 10.
9. E. Hoffmann, "The Symbolist Legacy in the Work of Oskar Kokoschka," *Homage to Kokoschka,* Victoria and Albert Museum, London, 1976, p. 19.
10. Walter H. Sokel, *An Anthology of German Expressionist Drama,* New York, 1963, p. xiv.
11. W. Fischer, *op. cit.,* p. 8.
12. O. Kokoschka, *op. cit.,* p. 20.
13. E. Hoffmann, "The Symbolist Legacy in the Work of Oskar Kokoschka," *op. cit.,* p. 21.
14. W. Fischer, *op. cit.,* p. 12.
15. *Ibid.*
16. Bernard Baer, "Kokoschka's late graphic work: A publisher's view," *Homage to Kokoschka,* Victoria and Albert Museum, London, 1976, p. 39.
17. Frances Carey and Anthony Griffiths, *The Print in Germany 1880–1933,* The British Museum, London, 1984, p. 18.
18. Karl Kraus, *Die Chinesische Mauer,* Frankfurt-am-Main, 1967, p. 279.
19. Jaroslaw Leshko, "Oskar Kokoschka's The Tempest," *Arts Magazine,* January 1978, pp. 95–105.
20. W. Fischer, *op. cit.,* p. 12.
21. Jaroslaw Leshko, "Oskar Kokoschka's Still-Life with Cat, Rabbit and Child," *Arts Magazine,* January 1980, pp. 84–88.
22. E. Hoffmann, *Kokoschka, Life and Work, op. cit.,* p. 126.
23. O. Kokoschka, *op. cit.,* p. 78.
24. Victor H. Miesel, *Voices of German Expressionism,* Englewood Cliffs, New Jersey, 1970, p. 146.
25. E. Hoffmann, *Kokoschka, Life and Work, op. cit.,* pp. 167–168.
26. W. Fischer, *op. cit.,* p. 14.
27. F. Carey and A. Griffiths, *op. cit.,* p. 25.
28. *Ibid.,* p. 26.
29. E. Hoffmann, *Kokoschka, Life and Work, op. cit.,* p. 169.
30. *Ibid.,* p. 170.
31. *Ibid.,* p. 169.
32. J. P. Hodin, *Kokoschka, the Artist and His Time,* London, 1966, p. 167.
33. *Ibid.*
34. E. Hoffmann, *Kokoschka, Life and Work, op. cit.,* p. 114.
35. Herbert Read, Foreword, E. Hoffmann, *Kokoschka, Life and Work, op. cit.,* p. 8.
36. Fritz Schmalenbach, *Oskar Kokoschka,* Greenwich, Connecticut, 1967, p. 28.
37. H. M. Wingler, *Introduction to Kokoschka,* London, 1958, p. 38.
38. Robert Hughes, "In London: A Visionary Maestro," *Time Magazine,* July 21, 1986. p. 69.
39. Karl Schorsky, *Fin-De-Siècle Vienna,* New York, 1980, p. 335.
40. B. Baer, *op. cit.,* p. 39.
41. K. Schorsky, *op. cit.,* pp. 337–338.
42. B. Baer, *op. cit.,* p. 37.
43. *Ibid.,* p. 40.
44. E. L. Gombrich, Introduction, *Homage to Kokoschka, op. cit.,* p. 9.
45. *Ibid.*
46. E. Hoffmann, *Kokoschka, Life and Work, op. cit.,* pp. 285, 287.
47. *Ibid.,* p. 287.

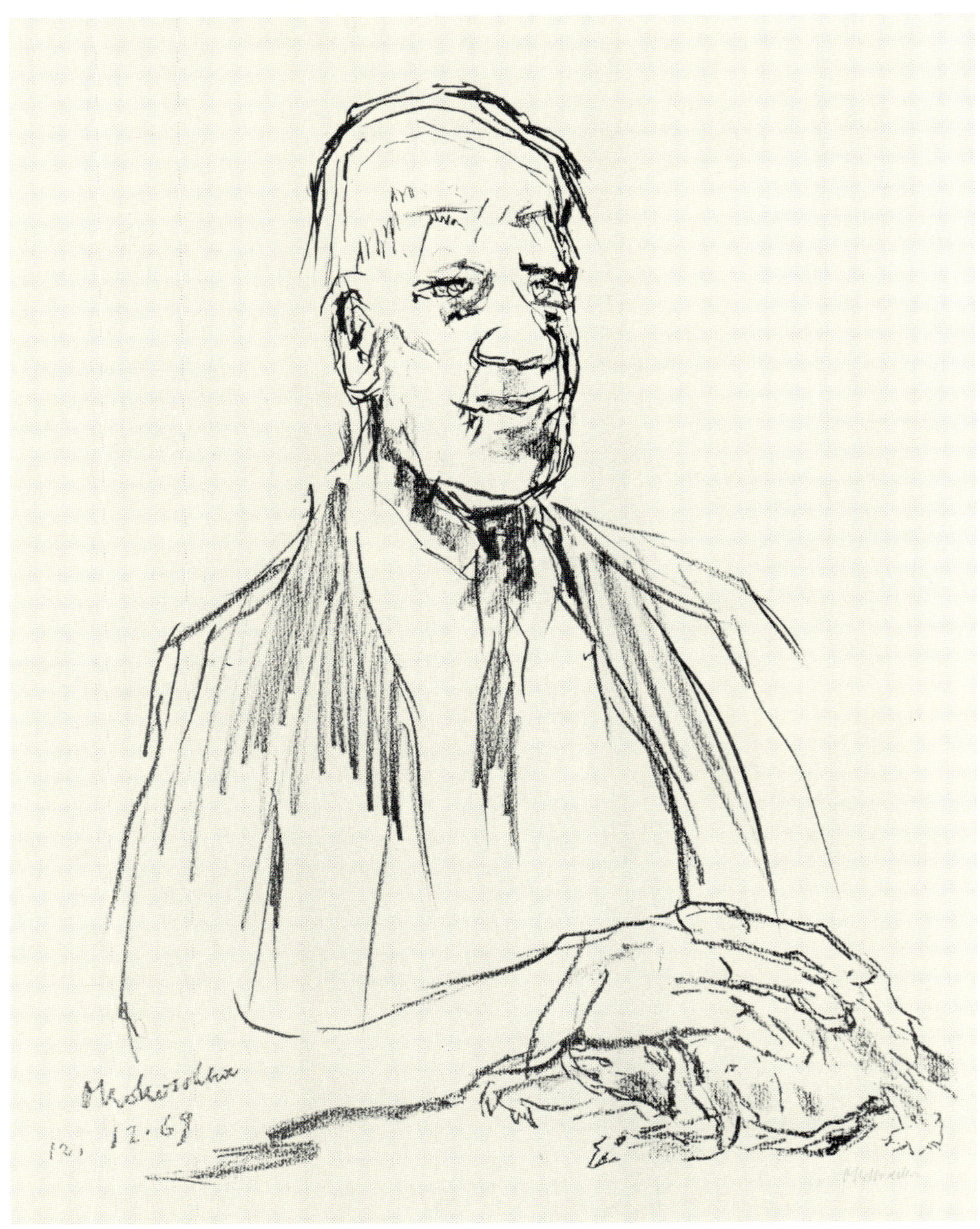

Cat. 141 *Self-Portrait with Tortoise*, 1969

Catalogue

All works in this exhibition have been or are currently in the Bethusy-Huc collection. Unless otherwise indicated, all works are on paper in black ink. Dimensions are given in millimeters, then in inches with height preceding width. Page numbers refer to illustration locations.

WW = Wingler/Welz. *Kokoschka, Das druckgraphische Werk.* Salzburg, Galerie Welz. Vol. I, 1975; Vol. II, 1981.

LL = lower left	CR = center right
LR = lower right	UL = upper left
CL = center left	UR = upper right

PRINTS

1. *Ex Libris Lorenz Kellner*, 1906
   Woodcut, WW 1
   120 x 80 (4 3/4 x 3 1/8)
   Text: Und das Wort ist Fleisch geworden/ Ex Libris Dr. Lorenz Kellner

2. *Ex Libris Frau Emma Bacher*, 1907
   Lithograph
   75 x 60 (3 x 2 3/8)
   Signed in stone CL: OK

3. *Three Angels Over a Wheat Field (Bookplate Study ?)*, c1907
   Lithograph
   73 x 71 (2 7/8 x 2 3/4)
   Signed in stone CL: OK

Wiener Werkstätte Postcards, 1906–08
14 from series of 15
Collection Victoria and Albert Museum, London

4. *Rider and Sailing Ship* (Front Cover)
   Color lithograph on cardboard, WW 3
   123 x 81 (4 7/8 x 3 1/4)
   Signed in stone on saddle blanket: OK
5. *Flower Garden*
   Color lithograph on cardboard, WW 4
   110 x 76 (4 3/8 x 3)
   Signed in stone LR: OK
   Text: Herzlichen Grüss
6. *Hunter and Animals*
   Color lithograph on cardboard, WW 5
   124 x 84 (4 7/8 x 3 3/8)
   Signed in stone LR: OK
7. *Flute Player and Bats*
   Color lithograph on cardboard, WW 6
   130 x 80 (5 1/8 x 3 1/8)
   Signed in stone LL above cage: OK
8. *Biedermeier Era Woman in a Meadow*
   Color lithograph on cardboard, WW 7
   122 x 84 (4 7/8 x 3 3/8)
   Signed in stone LR: OK
9. *Maiden with a Lamb, Threatened by Robbers*
   Color lithograph on cardboard, WW 8
   130 x 80 (5 1/8 x 3 1/8)
   Signed in stone LR: OK
10. *Musicians*
    Color lithograph on cardboard, WW 9
    134 x 87 (5 1/4 x 3 3/8)
    Signed in stone CR: OK
11. *Maiden with Sheep in the Mountains*
    Color lithograph on cardboard, WW 10
    132 x 82 (5 1/4 x 3 1/4)
    Signed in stone LR: OK
12. *Alpine Farm Woman and Cow*
    Color lithograph on cardboard, WW 11
    132 x 85 (5 1/4 x 3 3/8)
    Signed in stone CL: OK
13. *Three Shepherds, Dog and Sheep*
    Color lithograph on cardboard, WW 12
    134 x 85 (5 1/4 x 3 3/8)
    Signed in stone in foremost shepherd's robe: OK
14. *Mother with Three Children*
    Color lithograph on cardboard, WW 13
    131 x 78 (5 1/8 x 3 1/8)
    Signed in stone CL: OK
15. *Three Maidens, Lamb and Birds of Paradise*
    Color lithograph on cardboard, WW 14
    125 x 81 (5 x 3 1/4)
    Signed in stone LR: OK
    Text: Fröhliches Osterfest
16. *Maiden by a Window*
    Color lithograph on cardboard, WW 15
    134 x 87 (5 1/4 x 3 3/8)
    Signed in stone LL: OK
17. *Maiden in a Meadow by a Village*
    Color lithograph on cardboard, WW 17
    128 x 79 (5 x 3 1/8)
    Signed in stone CL: OK

18. *Ex Libris Mitzi and Dr. Josef Binder*, 1911
    Lithograph
    102 x 64 (4 x 2 1/2)
    Signed in stone CL: OK

19. *Ex Libris Lotte Franzos*, 1911
    Lithograph
    59 x 68 (2 3/8 x 2 3/4)
    Signed in stone LL: OK

20. *Ex Libris Robert Freund*, 1911
    Lithograph
    80 x 57 (3 1/8 x 2 1/4)
    Signed in stone LL: OK

21. *Ex Libris Lily and Arthur Fürst*, 1911
    Lithograph
    45 x 34 (1 3/4 x 1 3/8)
    Signed in stone LL: OK; below design: OKokoschka Fecit

Allos Makar, 1914 (published 1915)
Series of 5

22. *Seated Male and Female Nude*
    Lithograph, WW 69
    173 x 116 (6 7/8 x 4 5/8)
    Signed in stone LR: OK
23. *Man Lying in a Woman's Lap*
    Lithograph, WW 70
    153 x 148 (6 x 5 7/8)
    Signed in stone CR: OK
24. *Man in a Boat*
    Lithograph, WW 71
    144 x 191 (5 5/8 x 7 1/2)
    Signed in stone LR: OK
25. *Sun Over a Birdlike Pair* (p. 44)
    Lithograph, WW 72
    180 x 151 (7 1/8 x 6)
    Signed in stone LR: OK
26. *Man and Woman with a Snake*
    Lithograph, WW 73
    155 x 122 (6 1/8 x 4 7/8)
    Signed in stone LR: OK
    Text: Allos makar (in Greek letters)

The Passion, 1916
4 from series of 6

27. *Christ on the Mount of Olives* (p. 30)
    Lithograph, WW 78
    272 x 315 (10 3/4 x 12 3/8)
    Signed in stone LL: OK; in margin: Kokoschka verkeundigung
28. *The Crowning with Thorns*
    Lithograph, WW 79
    256 x 309 (10 1/8 x 12 1/8)
    Signed in stone LL: Kokoschka; LR: Christi Dornenkrönung OK
29. *The Last Supper*
    Lithograph, WW 83
    210 x 270 (8 1/4 x 10 5/8)
    Signed in stone LR: OK
    Text: "Der Bildermann" Masthead

30. *The Resurrection*
Lithograph, WW 81
252 x 300 (10 x 11⅞)
Signed in stone LR: OK

31. *Rest on the Flight into Egypt*, 1916
Lithograph, WW 84
224 x 289 (8⅞ x 11⅜)
Signed in stone LL: OK

32. *The Dream (Shakespeare Vision)*, 1916–17 (p. 4)
(published 1918)
Lithograph, WW 86
265 x 238 (10½ x 9⅜)
Inscribed in stone LL: We are such stuff as dreams are made on [sic], and our little life is rounded with a sleep . . .
Signed in pencil LR: OKokoschka

33. *Romana Kokoschka*, 1917 (p. 25)
Lithograph, WW 110
294 x 210 (11⅝ x 8¼)
Signed in pencil LR: Oskar Kokoschka

34. *Dr. Fritz Neuberger*, 1916 (published 1917)
Lithograph, WW 111
385 x 275 (15¼ x 10⅞)
Signed in pencil LR: OKokoschka

35. *Walter Hasenclever*, 1917 (p. 54)
Lithograph, WW 114, 18/110
331 x 219 (13 x 8⅝)
Signed in stone LR: OK
Signed in pencil LR: OKokoschka

36. *Corona* I, 1918 (published 1919)
Lithograph, WW 126
557 x 403 (22 x 15⅞)
Signed in pencil LR: Oskar Kokoschka 1918

37. *Katia (Käthe Richter)*, 1918 (published 1919)
Lithograph, blue ink, WW 133
693 x 499 (27⅜ x 19¾)
Signed in stone LL: Katia OK
Signed in pencil LR: OKokoschka

38. *Max Reinhardt*, 1919
Lithograph, WW 136
625 x 473 (24⅝ x 18⅝)
Signed in pencil LR: OKokoschka
Collection Victoria and Albert Museum, London

39. *Hermine Körner*, 1920 (p. 57)
Lithograph, blue ink, WW 138, proof
677 x 475 (26¾ x 18¾)
Signed in pencil LR: Litho Probe druck OKokoschka

40. *Tilla Durieux*, 1920
Lithograph, dark brown ink, WW 139, 22/150
627 x 469 (24¾ x 18½)
Signed in stone LR: OK
Signed in pencil LR: OKokoschka
Collection Victoria and Albert Museum, London

The Concert, 1920 (published 1921)
4 from series of 5

41. *The Concert* I *(Naomi)* (p. 47)
Lithograph, sanguine ink, WW 140, 14/50
698 x 467 (27½ x 18⅜)
Signed in pencil LR: OKokoschka

42. *The Concert* II *(Hagar)* (p. 48)
Lithograph, WW 141, 48/100
667 x 485 (26¼ x 19⅛)
Signed in pencil LR: OKokoschka

43. *The Concert* IV *(Miriam)* (p. 51)
Lithograph, WW 143, 41/100
693 x 491 (27¼ x 19⅜)
Signed in pencil LR: OKokoschka

44. *The Concert* V *(Deborah)* (p. 52)
Lithograph, WW 144
684 x 523 (27 x 20⅝)
Signed in pencil LR: OKokoschka with inscription

45. *Ruth* II *(Ruth Landshoff)*, 1922
Lithograph, WW 153, 100/176
459 x 374 (18⅛ x 14¾)
Signed in pencil LR: OKokoschka

45. *Maria Orska*, 1922
Lithograph, WW 158, 16/247
559 x 399 (22 x 15¾)
Signed in pencil LR: OKokoschka

47. *Self-Portrait from Two Sides as Painter*, 1923 (p. 58)
Color lithographic poster, WW 164
1252 x 882 (49¼ x 34¾)
Inscribed in stone above: OKokoschka Sept./Okt./23; below: Geöffnet 9–12 und 2–6 sonntags 10–12 uhr/Kunstsalon Wolfsberg/109 Bederstr. Zürich 2
Signed in pencil LR: Oskar Kokoschka 1923
Collection Victoria and Albert Museum, London

48. *Trudl with Straw Hat*, 1931
Lithograph, WW 173
352 x 433 (13⅞ x 17)
Signed in pencil LR: OKokoschka

49. *Christ Helping the Starving Children*, 1945–46 (p. 39)
Lithograph WW 180
610 x 485 (24 x 19⅛)
Inscribed in stone on cross: INRI/in Memory of the Children of Europe/who have to die of cold and hunger this/Xmas
Signed in stone LR: OK
Signed in ink LR: Original litho Oskar Kokoschka London 45
Collection Victoria and Albert Museum, London

50. *Olda Kokoschka*, 1949
Drypoint, WW 183, 22/55
208 x 146 (8⅛ x 5¾)
Signed in pencil LR: Oskar Kokoschka

51. *Magical Form (The Magician)*, 1951 (p. 62)
Lithograph, WW 185, 6/15
505 x 370 (19⅞ x 14½)
Signed in pencil LR: OKokoschka
Collection Victoria and Albert Museum, London

52. *The Fox and the Sour Grapes*, 1952
Color lithograph, WW 186
409 x 553 (16⅛ x 21¾)
Signed in pencil LR: OKokoschka

53. *Greyhound*, 1952
Color lithograph, WW 187
373 x 630 (14⅝ x 24¾)
Signed in pencil LR: OKokoschka

54. *Gitta*, 1953
Lithograph, WW 199
418 x 570 (16½ x 22½)
Signed in stone LR: OK
Signed in pencil LR: OKokoschka

55. *Amor and Psyche*, 1955
Color lithograph, WW 205, proof
585 x 513 (23 x 20¼)
Signed in pencil LR: Probeandruck OKokoschka Xmas, Villeneuve 73

56. *Self-Portrait*, 1956 (p. 68)
Color lithograph, WW 206, 6/90
582 x 420 (22⅞ x 16½)
Signed in pencil LR: OKokoschka 1956

57. *Two Girls with a Dove*, 1956
Color lithograph, WW 208, 23/70
605 x 469 (23 7/8 x 18 1/2)
Signed in pencil LR: OKokoschka

58. *L'Enfant de Bethléem (Madonna in a Street Battle)*, 1956 (p. 43)
Color lithograph, WW 209, proof
505 x 427 (19 7/8 x 16 3/4)
Inscribed in stone LC: L'Enfant de Bethléem; CR: OKokoschka
Inscribed and dated in pencil LR: Pr. Dr. Litho OK 56

59. *Christ Crowned with Thorns*, 1956 (p. 41)
Lithograph, WW 210, 61/65
539 x 388 (21 1/4 x 15 1/4)
Signed in pencil LR: Pr. Dr. Litho OKokoschka

60. *The Action Painter*, 1959
Lithograph, WW 212, proof
437 x 400 (17 1/4 x 15 3/4)
Signed in stone LR: OK 1959
Signed in pencil LR: Pr. Dr. OKokoschka

61. *Episode in Naples*, 1960
Color lithograph, WW 214, proof
390 x 275 (15 3/8 x 10 7/8)
Signed in pencil: Probedruck Litho 1961 Oskar Kokoschka

62. *Harbor at Hamburg*, 1961
Lithograph, WW 216, proof
460 x 610 (18 1/8 x 24)
Signed in stone LL: OK 61
Signed in pencil LC: Probedruck OKokoschka 61

63. *The Ancestor of All Fish*, 1961
Color lithograph, WW 217
418 x 601 (16 1/2 x 23 5/8)
Inscribed in stone LL: Urvater der Fische; LR: OK 61
Signed in pencil LR: OKokoschka

King Lear, 1963
5 from series of 16

64. *Portrait of King Lear* (p. 82)
Lithograph, WW 223
379 x 261 (14 7/8 x 10 1/2)
Signed in pencil LR: OKokoschka

65. *Lear: Poor naked wretches* (III, iv) (p. 83)
Lithograph, WW 229
373 x 267 (14 5/8 x 10 1/2)
Signed in pencil LR: OKokoschka

66. *Lear and the Fool: Arraign her first 'tis Goneril* (III, vi)
Lithograph, WW 230
377 x 263 (14 7/8 x 10 3/8)
Signed in pencil LR: OKokoschka

67. *Goneril and Edmund: Decline your head* (IV, ii)
Lithograph, WW 232
381 x 264 (15 x 10 3/8)
Signed in pencil LR: OKokoschka

68. *Cordelia: O, you kind gods, cure this great breach in his abused nature* (IV, vii)
Lithograph, WW 235
359 x 255 (14 1/8 x 10)
Signed in pencil LR: OKokoschka

69. *King Lear and the Fool*, 1963
Lithograph, WW 239, proof
370 x 282 (14 5/8 x 11 1/8)

70. *Friedrich Welz*, 1963
Lithograph, WW 241
564 x 445 (22 1/4 x 17 1/2)
Signed in stone LR: Mein lieber Welzius OKokoschka, 1963
Signed in pencil LR: Litho, 1963, OKokoschka
Inscription and date (27.vi 70) in ink LL

Homage to Hellas, 1961 (published 1964)
7 from series of 26

71. *Acropolis* I (p. 77)
Lithograph, WW 247, 61/65
475 x 595 (18 3/4 x 23 3/8)
Signed in pencil LR: OKokoschka

72. *Sheep Dog*
Lithograph, WW 252, 61/65
304 x 477 (12 x 18 3/4)
Signed in pencil LR: OKokoschka

73. *Dionysos Riding an Ass* (p. 10)
Lithograph, WW 254
359 x 334 (14 1/8 x 13 1/8)
Signed in pencil LL: OKokoschka

74. *Olympia*
Lithograph, WW 257
497 x 600 (19 5/8 x 23 5/8)
Signed in pencil LL: OKokoschka

75. *Aegina* II
Lithograph, WW 258
495 x 605 (19 1/2 x 23 7/8)
Signed in pencil LR: Proof OKokoschka

76. *Mistra*
Lithograph, WW 261, 55/65
495 x 654 (19 1/2 x 25 3/4)
Signed in pencil LC: OKokoschka

77. *The Blond Ephebe*
Lithograph, WW 267, proof
325 x 260 (12 3/4 x 10 1/4)
Signed in stone LR: OK 61
Signed in pencil LR: Probedruck Lithographie 1962 OKokoschka

Apulia, 1963 (published 1964)
2 from series of 20
Collection Mr. and Mrs. Andrew Macnab

78. *Three Hogs*
Lithograph, WW 276, proof
350 x 468 (13 3/4 x 18 3/8)
Signed in pencil LR: Proof OKokoschka

79. *Olive Grove*
Lithograph, WW 278, 25/50
397 x 537 (15 5/8 x 21 1/8)
Signed in pencil LR: OKokoschka

Apulian Journey, 1963
2 from series of 5
Collection Mr. and Mrs. Andrew Macnab

80. *Fish and Lobster*
Lithograph, WW 290, proof
355 x 480 (14 x 18 7/8)
Signed in pencil LR: Proof OKokoschka

81. *Woman of Apulia*
Lithograph, WW 292, 2/50
476 x 375 (18 3/4 x 14 3/4)
Signed in pencil LR: OKokoschka

82. *Ezra Pound*, 1964 (published 1965) (p. 65)
Lithograph, WW 293
460 x 370 (18 1/8 x 14 5/8)
Signed in stone LL: XII 64
Signed in pencil LL: OKokoschka

The Odyssey, 1963–65 (published 1965)
14 from series of 44

83. *Plants with Grasshopper and Lizard (Title Page)*
Lithograph, WW 294
257 x 248 (10 1/8 x 9 3/4)
Text: The Odyssey (in Greek) in ochre ink

84. *Pallas Athena*
Lithograph, WW 295, 5/50
355 x 280 (14 x 11)
Signed in pencil LR: OKokoschka

85. *Council of the Gods*
Lithograph, WW 296, 5/50
377 x 259 (14 7/8 x 10 1/4)
Signed in pencil LR: OKokoschka

86. *Polyphemos*
Lithograph, WW 305, 5/50
349 x 265 (13 3/4 x 10 3/8)
Signed in pencil LR: OKokoschka

87. *Sacrificial Offering in Hades*
Lithograph, WW 308, 5/50
383 x 265 (15 1/8 x 10 3/8)
Signed in pencil LR: OKokoschka

88. *Ulysses Awakes after Landing on Ithaca* (p. 78)
Lithograph, WW 313, 5/50
372 x 260 (14 5/8 x 10 1/4)
Signed in pencil LR: OKokoschka

89. *Athena Disperses the Fog and Reveals Ithaca*
Lithograph, WW 315, 5/50
385 x 267 (15 1/8 x 10 1/2)
Signed in pencil LR: OKokoschka

90. *Athena Commands Telemachos to Return*
Lithograph, WW 317, 5/50
375 x 257 (14 3/4 x 10 1/8)
Signed in pencil LR: OKokoschka

91. *Telemachos Receives a Sign*
Lithograph, WW 318, 5/50
385 x 269 (15 1/8 x 10 5/8)
Signed in pencil LR: OKokoschka

92. *Ulysses and Telemachos in Eumaios' Hut*
Lithograph, WW 319, 5/50
342 x 279 (13 1/2 x 11)
Signed in pencil LR: OKokoschka

93. *The Suitors Hurrying into the Harbor*
Lithograph, WW 320, 5/50
380 x 262 (15 x 10 3/8)
Signed in pencil LR: OKokoschka

94. *Ulysses Pulls the Bow*
Lithograph, WW 331, 5/50
345 x 256 (13 5/8 x 10 1/8)
Signed in pencil LR: OKokoschka

95. *The Reunion of Ulysses and Penelope*
Lithograph, WW 335, 5/50
371 x 259 (14 5/8 x 10 1/4)
Signed in pencil LR: OKokoschka

96. *Athena Halts the Combat* (p. 81)
Lithograph, WW 338, 5/50
374 x 253 (14 5/8 x 10)
Signed in pencil LR: OKokoschka

Marrakesh, 1965 (published 1966)
3 from series of 18

97. *In the Palm Forest*
Lithograph, WW 340, 44/60
259 x 374 (10 1/4 x 14 3/4)
Signed in pencil LR: OKokoschka

98. *The City Gate, Marrakesh*
Lithograph, WW 350, 44/60
257 x 380 (10 1/8 x 15)
Signed in pencil LR: OKokoschka

99. *Camel Market* II
Lithograph, WW 356, 44/60
262 x 365 (10 3/8 x 14 3/8)
Signed in pencil LR: OKokoschka

100. *Konrad Adenauer,* 1966
Lithograph, WW 359, III/XXXV
405 x 345 (16 x 13 5/8)
Signed in stone LR: OK 16.IV.66
Signed in pencil LR: OKokoschka

101. *Pegasus,* 1966
Lithograph, WW 360
930 x 640 (36 5/8 x 25 1/4)
Signed in stone LR: OK
Inscribed, signed and dated in pencil LR:
Oskar Kokoschka/OK

102. *Berlin, A Glimpse Over the Wall,* 1966
Lithograph, WW 363
674 x 998 (26 1/2 x 39 1/4)
Signed in stone LR: Berlin, OK, 25.8.66
Inscribed and signed in pencil LR:
OKokoschka

103. *Self-Portrait with Statuette,* 1966 (p. 69)
Lithograph, WW 364, XX/XXXV
620 x 506 (24 3/8 x 19 7/8)
Signed in stone LR: OK 66
Signed in pencil LR: OKokoschka

104. *The Power of Music (Morning and Evening),*
1966
Lithograph, WW 366
461 x 578 (18 1/8 x 22 3/4)
Signed in stone LR: OKokoschka 66
Inscribed, dated and signed in pencil LR:
OKokoschka

Le Bal Masqué, 1965-67 (published 1967)
5 from series of 7

105. *Le Cerf, le Cygne sont des Masques....*
Color lithograph, WW 367
310 x 580 (12 1/4 x 22 7/8)
Signed in pencil LR: OK

106. *Pour moi, notre physionomie réelle....*
Color lithograph, WW 369
275 x 545 (10 7/8 x 21 1/2)
Signed in pencil LR: OK

107. *L'Enlèvement est un symbole....*
Color lithograph, WW 370
448 x 585 (17 5/8 x 23)
Signed in pencil LR: OK

108. *Amélia est bien heureuse....*
Color lithograph, WW 371
468 x 630 (18 3/8 x 24 3/4)
Signed in pencil LR: OK

109. *Les Perspectives de la Mort....*
Color lithograph, WW 372
438 x 643 (17 1/4 x 25 3/8)
Signed in pencil LR: OK

110. *Manhattan* I, 1966 (published 1967)
Lithograph, WW 375, 74/75
577 x 637 (22 3/4 x 25 1/8)
Signed in stone LL: OK
Signed in pencil LR: OKokoschka

111. *El Djem,* 1967 (published 1971)
Lithograph, WW 379, 1/50
477 x 664 (18 3/4 x 26 1/8)
Signed in pencil LR: OKokoschka

London From the River Thames, 1967
2 from series of 9

112. *Houses of Parliament* III
Lithograph, WW 382, 65/75
558 x 765 (22 x 30 1/8)
Signed in pencil LR: OKokoschka

113. *Tower Bridge* II (p. 9)
Lithograph, brown ink. WW 386, 51/75
515 x 772 (20 1/4 x 30 3/8)
Signed in pencil LR: OKokoschka

114. *Mercury,* 1967 (published 1969)
Lithograph, WW 389
263 x 209 (10 3/8 x 8 1/4)
Signed in stone LR: OK
Signed in pencil LR: OKokoschka

Saul and David, 1966–68 (published 1969)
14 from series of 41

115. *Saul Delivereth Jabesh Gilead*
Lithograph, WW 396, 1/60
384 x 293 (15 1/8 x 11 1/2)
Signed in pencil LR: OKokoschka

116. *David Playing the Harp to Saul* (p. 87)
Lithograph, WW 389, 1/60
381 x 269 (15 x 10 5/8)
Signed in pencil LR: OKokoschka

117. *David Slayeth Goliath* (p. 90)
Lithograph, WW 401, 1/60
350 x 301 (13 3/4 x 11 7/8)
Signed in pencil LR: OKokoschka

118. *David Hiding Himself* (p. 89)
Lithograph, WW 404, 1/60
395 x 275 (15 1/2 x 10 7/8)
Signed in pencil LR: OKokoschka

119. *David and Abigail*
Lithograph, WW 410, 1/60
357 x 300 (14 x 11 3/4)
Signed in pencil LR: OKokoschka

120. *Saul and the Witch at Endor*
Lithograph, WW 412, 1/60
371 x 291 (14 5/8 x 11 1/2)
Signed in pencil LR: OKokoschka

121. *David's Lament*
Lithograph, WW 416, 1/60
414 x 290 (16 1/4 x 11 3/8)
Signed in pencil LR: OKokoschka

122. *Nathan's Vision*
Lithograph, WW 419, 1/60
375 x 279 (14 3/4 x 11)
Signed in pencil LR: OKokoschka

123. *David and Bathsheba* (p. 91)
Lithograph, WW 420, 1/60
387 x 287 (15 1/4 x 11 1/4)
Signed in pencil LR: OKokoschka

124. *Nathan's Parable of the Ewe Lamb*
Lithograph, WW 422, 1/60
377 x 269 (14 3/4 x 10 5/8)
Signed in pencil LR: OKokoschka

125. *David Cursed by Shimei*
Lithograph, WW 426, 1/60
381 x 299 (15 x 11 3/4)
Signed in pencil LR: OKokoschka

126. *Absalom's Death*
Lithograph, WW 427, 1/60
406 x 240 (16 x 9 1/2)
Signed in pencil LR: OKokoschka

127. *David in His Old Age* (p. 93)
Lithograph, WW 430, 1/60
394 x 301 (15 1/2 x 11 7/8)
Signed in pencil LR: OKokoschka

128. *David's Charge to Solomon*
Lithograph, WW 432, 1/60
389 x 288 (15 3/8 x 11 3/8)
Signed in pencil LR: OKokoschka

129. *Uriah's Letter (Ver Sacrum)*, 1968 (published 1969)
Lithograph, WW 435, 34/70
337 x 278 (13 1/4 x 11)
Signed in pencil LR: OK

"The Frogs" of Aristophanes, 1967–68 (published 1969)
5 from series of 12

130. *Imaginary Portrait of Aristophanes*
Drypoint, WW 437
260 x 200 (10 1/4 x 7 7/8)
Inscribed (in Greek in reverse) in plate: Aristophanes
Signed in pencil LR: OKokoschka

131. *Dionysos Dressed as Herakles with Xanthias Carrying an Ass on his Back*
Drypoint, WW 438
260 x 200 (10 1/4 x 7 7/8)
Signed in pencil LR: OKokoschka

132. *The Frogs*
Drypoint, WW 440
260 x 200 (10 1/4 x 7 7/8)
Signed in pencil LR: OKokoschka

133. *Pluto Invites Dionysos to Decide the Contest*
Drypoint, WW 446
260 x 200 (10 1/4 x 7 7/8)
Signed in pencil LR: OKokoschka

134. *Exodus*
Drypoint, WW 448
261 x 202 (10 1/4 x 8)
Signed in pencil LR: OKokoschka

135. *Kouros* I, 1968 (published 1970) (Back Cover)
Offset lithograph after drawing, WW 449
941 x 605 (37 x 23 7/8)
Signed in stone LR: OKokoschka

136. *Kouros* II, 1968 (published 1970)
Lithograph, sanguine ink, WW 450
890 x 503 (35 x 19 3/4)
Signed in stone LL: OKokoschka
Signed in pencil LR: OKokoschka

137. *Achilles Falls from his Chariot*, 1969
Lithograph, WW 453
227 x 384 (8 7/8 x 15 1/8)
Signed in stone LL: OK
Inscribed, signed and dated in pencil LR: OKokoschka

Penthesilea, 1969 (published 1970)
2 from series of 10

138. *Penthesilea Tries to Eat the Dead Achilles* (p. 71)
Drypoint, WW 461, 37/100
197 x 292 (7 3/4 x 11 1/2)
Signed in pencil LR: OKokoschka

139. *Penthesilea Kills Herself* (p. 73)
Drypoint, WW 463, 37/100
198 x 292 (7 3/4 x 11 1/2)
Signed in pencil LR: OKokoschka

140. *Tiger*, 1969 (published 1970)
Lithograph, WW 464
Signed in stone LR: OKokoschka 11.12.69
Inscribed and signed in pencil LR: OKokoschka

141. *Self-Portrait with Tortoise*, 1969 (published 1970) (p. 96)
Lithograph, WW 465, IV/X
660 x 520 (26 x 20 1/2)
Signed in stone LL: OKokoschka 12.12.69
Signed in pencil LR: OKokoschka

142. *The Observer ("My Critics and I")*, 1970
Drypoint, WW 467, proof
235 x 177 (9 1/4 x 7)
Signed in pencil LR: Probedruck OKokoschka 1970

143. *Self-Portrait*, 1970
Drypoint, WW 468, 1/40
153 x 92 (6 x 3 5/8)
Signed in pencil LR: OKokoschka

144. *Self-Portrait with Etching Needle*, 1970 (published 1971)
Drypoint, WW 469, 40/100
293 x 200 (11 1/2 x 7 7/8)
Signed in plate CR: OK 70
Signed in pencil LR: OKokoschka

145. *River God*, 1957 (published 1972)
Color lithograph, WW 471, XIV/75
291 x 205 (11 1/2 x 8 1/8)
Signed in pencil LL: OKokoschka

146. *Leda and the Swan*, 1972 (published 1975)
Drypoint, WW 474, proof
195 x 155 (7 5/8 x 6 1/8)
Signed in pencil LR: OKokoschka 1972

The Women of Troy, 1971–72 (published 1973)
8 from series of 15

147. *Hector's Helmet*
Lithograph, WW 476, 1/50
341 x 304 (13 3/8 x 12)
Signed in pencil LR: OKokoschka

148. *Hector's Body Dragged by Achilles' Chariot*
Lithograph, WW 477, 1/50
286 x 232 (11 1/4 x 9 1/8)
Signed in pencil LR: OKokoschka

149. *Andromache Mourning Over Hector's Body*
Lithograph, WW 478, 1/50
337 x 380 (13 1/4 x 11)
Signed in pencil LR: OKokoschka

150. *Priam is Slain at the Altar in his Palace* (p. 84)
Lithograph, WW 481, 1/50
340 x 252 (13 3/8 x 10)
Signed in pencil LR: OKokoschka

151. *Cassandra Prophesies Disaster for the Victors*
Lithograph, WW 484, 1/50
340 x 265 (13 3/8 x 10 3/8)
Signed in pencil LR: OKokoschka

152. *Cassandra is Led Away to Agamemnon's Ship*
Lithograph, WW 485, 1/50
327 x 253 (12 7/8 x 10)
Signed in pencil LR: OKokoschka

153. *Andromache with Astyanax in her Arms....*
Lithograph, WW 487, 1/50
335 x 260 (13 1/8 x 10 1/4)
Signed in pencil LR: OKokoschka

154. *The Body of Astyanax is Brought on Hector's Shield*
Lithograph, WW 489, 1/50
273 x 238 (10 3/4 x 5 3/8)
Signed in pencil LR: OKokoschka

155. *Olda*, 1972 (published 1974)
Drypoint, WW 491, 1/40
158 x 98 (6 1/4 x 3 7/8)
Signed in pencil LR: OKokoschka

156. *Self-Portrait*, 1972 (published 1975)
Drypoint, WW 492, 1/40
152 x 91 (6 x 3 5/8)
Signed in pencil LR: OKokoschka

Jerusalem Faces, 1973 (published 1973–74)
1 from series of 6

157. *His Beatitude Benedictos I, Greek Orthodox Patriarch of Jerusalem* (p. 66)
Lithograph, WW 495
620 x 500 (24 3/8 x 19 3/4)
Signed in stone by sitter LR: Patriarch Benedictos

158. *Golda Meir* (II), 1973 (published 1974)
Lithograph, WW 499
413 x 315 (16 1/4 x 12 3/8)

Comenius, 1975 (published 1976)
2 from series of 6

159. *Comenius and Christl*
Lithograph, WW 505
464 x 350 (18 1/4 x 13 3/4)
Signed in pencil LR: OKokoschka

160. *Emperor Ferdinand*
Lithograph, WW 506
314 x 238 (12 3/8 x 9 3/8)
Signed in stone LR: OK
Signed in pencil LR: OKokoschka

161. *The Woodpecker*, 1971 (published 1972)
Color lithograph after watercolor, WW 510
458 x 389 (18 x 15 3/8)
Stamped on reverse LR: OKokoschka 72

162. *Blooming Appleblossoms*, 1959 (published 1974)
Color lithograph after watercolor, WW 514, IX/XX
469 x 627 (18 1/2 x 24 5/8)
Signed in pencil LR: OKokoschka

163. *Lilies and Larkspur*, 1967 (published 1977)
Color lithograph after watercolor, WW 526, XIII/XV
565 x 473 (22 1/4 x 18 5/8)
Signed in pencil LR: OKokoschka

164. *Monique* II, 1966 (published 1977)
Lithograph, dark brown ink, WW 531, 7/50
515 x 375 (20 1/4 x 14 3/4)
Signed in pencil LL: OKokoschka

165. *Orchids*, 1969 (published 1978)
Lithograph after brush drawing, WW 532, 36/50
450 x 370 (17 3/4 x 14 5/8)
Signed in pencil LR: OKokoschka

"Comenius" Portfolio, 1973 (published 1976)
3 from series of 7

166. *The Flight of Comenius and his Company*
Serigraph, WW 537, 120/350
460 x 555 (18 1/8 x 21 7/8)
Inscribed in silkscreen LL: OKokoschka Gut zum Druck; LR: Comenius auf der Flucht/ originalgetreu OKokoschka 1976

167. *Rembrandt in Front of his Studio*
Serigraph, WW 538, 120/350
395 x 565 (15 1/2 x 22 1/4)
Inscribed in silkscreen LR: Gut zum Druck OKokoschka; (Comenius) Rembrandt vor seinem Atelier; originalgetreu OKokoschka 1976

168. *Comenius and Rembrandt in Conversation*
Serigraph, WW 539, 120/350
275 x 405 (10 7/8 x 16)
Inscribed in silkscreen LL: Gut zum Druck OKokoschka; LC: Bühnenentwurf für "Comenius" von OK 1957; LR: originalgetreu OKokoschka 1976

169. *The Goat*, 1975 (published 1977)
Lithograph, WW 542
155 x 205 (6 1/8 x 8 1/8)
Signed in stone LL: OK
Inscribed and signed in pencil LR: OKokoschka

Pan, 1975–76 (published 1978)
4 from series of 18

170. *Pan (Title Page)*
Lithograph, WW 543
222 x 175 (8 3/4 x 6 7/8)
Inscribed in stone UL: Knut HAMSUM/PAN
Signed in pencil LR: OKokoschka

171. *Aesop the Dog with Lieutenant Glahn*
Lithograph, WW 544
305 x 285 (12 x 11 1/4)
Signed in stone LL: OK
Signed in pencil LL: OKokoschka

172. *The Death of Lieutenant Glahn*
Lithograph, WW 559
265 x 280 (10 3/8 x 11)
Signed in stone LR: OK
Signed in pencil LR: OKokoschka

173. *Lieutenant Glahn*, 1946–77 (published 1978)
Color serigraph, WW 560
240 x 307 (9 1/2 x 12 1/8)
Signed in pencil LL: OKokoschka 78

174. *Tiger*, 1976
Lithograph, dark brown ink, WW 565
365 x 465 (14 3/8 x 8 1/4)
Signed in stone LR: OK 22.2.76

175. *Pan Playing the Pipes*, 1976 (published 1977)
Lithograph, WW 566, 27/100
260 x 198 (10 1/4 x 7 3/4)
Signed in pencil LR: OKokoschka

DRAWINGS AND REPRODUCTIONS

176. *Madonna (Bookplate Study)*, c1906 (p. 19)
Graphite and ink
125 x 100 (4 7/8 x 4 3/8)
Text: Frau Emma Bacher

177. *Lovers (Bacher Bookplate Study)*, c1906 (p. 19)
Graphite and ink
110 x 84 (4 3/8 x 3 3/8)
Text: Frau Emma Bacher

178. *Bookplate Study*, 1911
Pen and ink
67 x 79 (2 5/8 x 3 1/8)

179. *Karl Kraus*, 1912
Lithographic reproduction after drawing
303 x 220 (12 x 8 5/8)
Signed in plate LR: OK

180. *The Agony in the Garden*, 1916 (p. 35)
Graphite
360 x 298 (14 1/8 x 11 3/4)
Later inscription and signature

181. *Michael Swoboda*, 1920 (p. 61)
Charcoal
520 x 390 (20 1/2 x 15 3/8)
Signed in charcoal LR: OK

182. *Sketch for King David*, n.d.
Graphite
205 x 255 (8 1/8 x 10)
Inscribed and signed in pencil LR: OK

183. *Gattamelata*, 1948 (p. 75)
Colored chalk
185 x 270 (7 1/4 x 10 5/8)

184. *Exhibition Poster*, 1951
Offset lithograph after drawing
678 x 490 (26 3/4 x 19 1/4)
Inscribed in stone LR: OK; above: Oskar Kokoschka/Neue Galerie Der Stadt Linz; below: Gründer u. Leiter: Wolfgang Gurlitt June-August 1951
Signed in pencil LR: OKokoschka

185. *Roses at Villeneuve*, 1961
Offset reproduction after watercolor
420 x 550 (16 1/2 x 21 5/8)
Signed in pencil LL: OKokoschka 61

Museum Staff

(partial list)

Administration

Richard V. West
Director
Thomas R. Mathews, Jr.
Assistant Director for Administration
Shelley S. Ruston
Assistant Director,
Publications and Programs

Curatorial

Robert Henning, Jr.
Chief Curator
Nancy M. Doll
Curator of Modern Art
Barry M. Heisler
Curator of Collections
Merrily Peebles
Curator of Exhibitions
Susan Shin-tsu Tai
Curator of Oriental Art
Timothy Hearsum
Curator of Photography
Terry Atkinson
Designer

Barbara Luton
Director of Development
Deborah Tufts
Curator of Education
Elaine Poulos Dietsch
Registrar
Ron Crozier
Librarian
Virginia Cochran
Director of Grants and Public Relations
Wilbur Cox
Director of Planned Giving
Gale Poyorena
Controller
Penny Mast
Bookstore Manager
Dean Dawson
Building Superintendent
Larry Larson
Chief of Security